Resolving Conflicts at Work

Kenneth Cloke
Joan Goldsmith

Resolving Conflicts at Work

A Complete Guide for Everyone on the Job

Jossey-Bass Publishers • San Francisco

Copyright © 2000 by Jossey-Bass Inc., Publishers, 350 Sansome Street,
San Francisco, California 94104.

All rights reserved. No part of this publication may be reproduced,
stored in a retrieval system, or transmitted, in any form or by any means,
electronic, mechanical, photocopying, recording, or otherwise, without
the prior written permission of the publisher.

Jossey-Bass books and products are available through most
bookstores. To contact Jossey-Bass directly, call (888) 378-2537,
fax to (800) 605-2665, or visit our website at www.josseybass.com.

Substantial discounts on bulk quantities of Jossey-Bass books are
available to corporations, professional associations, and other
organizations. For details and discount information, contact the special
sales department at Jossey-Bass.

Credits are on p. 251.

Manufactured in the United States of America on Lyons Falls
Turin Book. This paper is acid-free and 100 percent totally
chlorine-free.

Library of Congress Cataloging-in-Publication Data

Cloke, Ken, 1941–
    Resolving conflicts at work: a complete guide for everyone on the job
/ Kenneth Cloke, Joan Goldsmith.
        p.   cm.
    ISBN 0-7879-5059-9 (hd: alk. paper)
    1. Conflict management.   2. Interpersonal relations.   3. Personnel
management—Psychological aspects.   4. Industrial psychology.
I. Goldsmith, Joan.   II. Title.
    HD42 .C56 2000
    650.1'3—dc21

                                                                99-050522

FIRST EDITION
HB Printing   10 9 8 7 6 5 4 3 2 1

Contents

Preface   xi

Introduction: 8 Paths from Impasse to Transformation   1

Path 1. Understand the Culture and Context of
         the Conflict   19

Path 2. Listen with Your Heart   47

Path 3. Embrace and Acknowledge Emotions   79

Path 4. Search Beneath the Surface for Hidden Meaning   112

Path 5. Separate What Matters from What's in the Way   135

Path 6. Learn from Difficult Behaviors   167

Path 7. Solve Problems Creatively and Negotiate
         Collaboratively   198

Path 8. Explore Resistance and Mediate Before
         You Litigate   226

Index   243

This book is dedicated to our families,
from whom we have learned both
the pain of conflict and the joy of resolution:
To Dick, Shirley, Bill, Angie, Elka, Nick, Kristen, and Glen;
Leonard, Miriam, Steve, Sam, Shetu, Tinku, and Soraya.

We have thought of peace as passive
and war as the active way of living.
The opposite is true.
War is not the most strenuous life.
It is a kind of rest cure compared
to the task of reconciling our differences.
From War to Peace is not from the strenuous
to the easy existence.
It is from the futile to the effective,
from the stagnant to the active,
from the destructive to the creative way of life. . . .
The world will be regenerated by the people
who rise above these passive ways
and heroically seek by whatever hardship,
by whatever toil
the methods by which people can agree.

—*Mary Parker Follett*

Preface

Philosophers have written that a universe can be found in a grain of sand. This book is our effort to describe the universe we have found in the sands of conflict, which we have studied, sifted, and reshaped professionally, helping thousands of people in workplaces resolve their disputes over the last twenty years.

We have observed firsthand the pain, loss, and irretrievable damage that have been suffered by individuals, organizations, and relationships as a result of conflict. We have also seen miracles of transformation, people moved to forgiveness and reconciliation, creative solutions revealed, and hundreds of lives, relationships, and organizations reclaimed. These are the two faces of conflict, the destructive and the creative, the impasse and the transformation.

Everyone sees both faces of conflict, though most of us find ourselves focusing more on the first than the second. We have all learned how to fight and how to surrender, how to run away and how to stand up for what we believe in, how to hide what we think and how to say what we really mean, how to resist change and how to embrace it, how to live as though nothing matters, and how to challenge ourselves and improve our lives.

Each of us has learned destructive and creative ways of responding to conflict. To move from the destructive to the creative, from impasse to transformation, we need to draw from within ourselves what we already know, become more aware of our deeper patterns, learn from our conflicts, reinforce the positive knowledge and skills we already possess, and reduce our tendency to slip into negative or destructive responses.

Very few of us have received training in how to work collaboratively to resolve our conflicts. Few schools teach it. Few corporations, nonprofits, or government agencies orient their employees to
constructive approaches to conflict, in spite of the fact that nearly
all their employees will confront serious conflict during the course
of their working lives.

While some organizations train their leaders or managers in conflict resolution, classes are usually brief and oriented to making the
conflict go away. Yet most of these leaders and managers face conflicts
on a daily basis, spending as much as 80 or 90 percent of their time
trying to resolve or contain them. When we make conflicts go away,
we cheat ourselves and others out learning from them, correcting
what led to them in the first place, and transcending them.

We have written this book to assist everyone who works: employees, leaders, managers, teachers, principals, union representatives, workers in corporations, nonprofits, schools, or government
agencies. Everyone can increase the level of their skills, not just in
making conflicts go away but in discovering their deeper underlying
truths, resolving the underlying reasons that gave rise to them, and
using them to drive personal and organizational transformation.

To assist you in discovering these truths for yourself, we present
you with a number of alternative paths, each leading to the center
of the conflict. We offer you a new set of tools to resolve it—not just
hammers and wrenches but mirrors and scalpels. The mirrors are to
help you reflect on what you may be doing to encourage the conflict
and see how you can use that information to trigger a personal or
organizational transformation. The scalpels are to assist you in eliminating unproductive, destructive, unwanted behavior patterns, and
free you to approach your conflicts in a more constructive way. Our
object is not to tell you what to do when you are in conflict, but to
lead you to your own truth, as we have been led to ours.

No single tool or technique will work in every situation or at all
times. If there is any set principle in conflict resolution, it is that
there are no set principles. Success proceeds from a synergistic combination of intellect and emotion, honesty and empathy, reason and
intuition, head and heart, allowing each to guide the other. We can

continually improve our subjective and objective conflict resolution skills, and learn better ways of expressing our feelings as well as our ideas.

We hope you will follow the paths we describe and create an organizational environment in which conflict is integrated and accepted, celebrated and honored, an environment in which settlement is not settled for, and resolution provides a beginning for organizational transformation and personal mastery.

The paths we describe are about the magic of listening, collaboration, and forgiveness. Our basic message is to follow your intuition, be guided by your heart, expand your empathy, and be willing to risk deep and compassionate honesty about whatever you see. While there are times and places where being deeply honest can get us into trouble, for the most part we overcensor ourselves and in the process cheat ourselves and others out of learning and growth.

If you are willing to take the risk of being deeply empathic and honest, we can promise that both the conflict and the process of resolution will open to you—and the organization in which you work— extraordinary opportunities for improvement, including personal growth, reduced costs, deeper and more satisfying relationships, and improved morale. Since the places we get stuck or find ourselves at impasse, both personally or organizationally, express themselves as conflicts, the release, resolution, or transformation we seek leads directly through our conflicts.

Finally, everyone can improve their skills and become more effective at communicating and resolving conflict, but we each need to discover our own best approach. In this book, we have identified eight separate paths to help you create your approach to conflict and assemble your toolbox from the many alternative techniques we cite. Your challenge will be to discover your own path, by looking inside yourself and recognizing the direction the conflict is taking you.

We encourage you to learn from the people with whom you are in conflict, without whom it will be impossible to fully recognize what the conflict is trying to teach you. We know we cannot teach you anything you do not want to learn. We invite you to open yourself and those with whom you work to these lessons. We are pleased you have chosen to learn with us.

Acknowledgments

Everyone faces their conflicts alone, yet no one resolves them alone. The process requires collaboration, support, safe havens, and understanding from those who have been there and are willing to reach out for peace and reconciliation. As we have provided this, at one time or another, for one another, the two of us are deeply grateful to our friends and mediation associates who have traveled this road with us.

We want to thank our friends, who have taught us many lessons about transformation and been deeply committed to transforming their own lives and the lives of others: Betty and Monte Factor, Warren Bennis and Grace Gabe, Sidney and Yulin Rittenberg, Blenda Wilson and Louis Fair, Karen King, Elaine Brown, Marvin and Cathy Treiger, Nancy Hollander and Steve Portuges, Peggy Dulany, Roberto Mizrahi, Mario Savio (deceased), Helen Bernstein (deceased), Eileen Brown, Joan Dunlop, Marcia Schiff and Ron O'Connor, Enrique Oltuski, Mariela Columbié, Arturo Rodriguez, Loly Fernandez, Alexis Codina, Eduardo Cruz, Angel Luis Portuondo, Manuel Monett, Ariel Ricardo, Oneida Alvarez.

We also want to thank the many courageous organizational leaders with whom we have worked, who have allowed us to try out many of the ideas presented here: Edgar Hayes, Elahe Hessamfar, Peter Schneider, Tom Schumacher, Alice Dewey, Tom Hayden, Jerry Cooper, Jerry Scro, Angie Stockwell, Sylvester Mendoza, Greg Wallace, Jimmy Loyce, Cindy Rigney.

A special thanks goes to Warren Bennis, for believing in us and in our book. Finally, we want to thank our editor, Leslie Berriman, our agent, Mike Cohn, our indexer and friend, Carolyn Thibault, and our supportive staff, Sam Goldsmith, Matt Kramer, Solange Raro, Anne Roswell, and Grace Silva.

Center for Dispute Resolution
Santa Monica, California   KENNETH CLOKE
October 1999   JOAN GOLDSMITH

Introduction:
8 Paths from Impasse
to Transformation

The rules of the game: learn everything, read
everything, inquire into everything. . . . When two
texts, or two assertions, or perhaps two ideas, are in
contradiction, be ready to reconcile them rather
than cancel one by the other; regard them as two
different facets, or two successive stages of the same
reality, a reality convincingly human just because it
is complex.

—*Marguerite Yourcenar*

Each of us experiences innumerable miscommunications and conflicts in the course of our lives that affect us deeply and daily. It is
impossible to grow up in a family, live in a neighborhood, attend
school, work at a job, have an intimate relationship, raise children,
or actively participate in the world without experiencing frequent
conflicts.

Much of our childhood is spent in conflict with our parents, siblings, and playmates, who teach us the first and most difficult lessons
of life. Our families continue to generate conflicts throughout our
lives. As we proceed through school, we learn hard lessons about rejection and compromise, about how to succeed and fail in disputes
with teachers and peers, and about shame, rage, and fear.

In our adult lives, our workplaces are profoundly influenced by
conflicts between workers and supervisors, competing departments,
and coworkers. Our competitive economy, status-conscious society,
and politicized government generate chronic disputes between

haves and have-nots, ins and outs, us and them, powerful and pow-erless, all battling over the distribution of scarce resources.

Our most intimate relationships are often embroiled in conflicts, and either deepen or dissolve with them. Our society and cultures are saturated with conflicts that scream at us from headlines, ads, and movies and subtly shape our psyches. Our neighborhoods and eth-nic communities are deeply divided by racial prejudice, hatred of those who are different, and conflicts over needs and expectations.

We pay a heavy price for these conflicts, in litigation, strikes, re-duced productivity, poor morale, wasted time and resources, loss of important relationships, divided organizations, and reduced oppor-tunities for learning and change.

Yet many of these conflicts are either avoidable or completely unnecessary. Most arise from simple miscommunications, mis-understandings, seemingly irrelevant differences, poor choices of language, ineffective management styles, unclear roles and respon-sibilities, and false expectations. The causes of our conflicts often have *nothing at all* to do with the issues we are fighting over, and can be corrected through learning and dialogue.

More important, each and every conflict we experience in life contains two truths—the truth of impasse, that we are stuck in a problem from which we would like to escape; and the truth of trans-formation, that it is possible to become unstuck and move on to a higher order of conflict by understanding at a deep level what got us stuck in the first place.

Every organization in which we work generates conflicts—every corporation, school, nonprofit, and government agency. Each of these conflicts reflects in some way a challenge the organization has yet to face or is not facing well. Each reveals a paradigm that has begun to shift, a problem that has not been solved, an opportunity for improvement.

You can make a significant contribution to the effectiveness of your organization, and impact the lives of your coworkers, the sat-isfaction of your customers, and the morale of your staff by leading them from impasse to transformation. To do so, it will be necessary for you to understand how and why we get stuck in conflict and engage in behaviors we know are inappropriate.

The Dark Side of Conflict

When we are in conflict, we all say things we don't mean and mean things we don't say. Only rarely do we communicate at a deep level what we really, honestly feel. We seldom speak from our hearts or expose our most vulnerable levels of being, or do so in ways the other person can hear. Why do we fall into this trap? Why is it so hard to do what we know is right?

Our conflicts have the capacity to confuse and hypnotize us, and we come to believe there is no way out other than battle. Conflict possesses a dark, hypnotic, destructive power: the power of attachment when it is time to leave, the power of demonization when it is time to forgive, the power of articulate speech when it is time to be silent or to listen. Conflict alternately strokes and crushes our egos, fuels and exhausts our will, energizes us and freezes us in fear. It speaks to a deep, ancient part of our soul that thirsts for power and delights in revenge.

When we are engaged in conflict, our emotions become enormously powerful and overwhelming. When we experience strong emotions, they feel limitless and unstoppable, irresistible and all-defining. Part of the seduction of strong emotion is that it encourages us to define ourselves and what we want in absolute terms, to identify with the seemingly infinite power of our feelings, to surrender control to something larger than ourselves.

We have all experienced times in our lives when we lacked the skills we needed to communicate honestly and empathically with others. We have all been aggressive, judgmental, and hypercritical, or passive, apathetic, and defensive. Our efforts at honesty have been interpreted as attack, and our empathy as weakness. We have not known how to temper our anger with compassion, how to listen to the other person's pain when we were being attacked, how to discover what caused the other person to act as they did, how to take responsibility for our own miscommunications and conflicts. We have failed to find ways of working with our opponents to find solutions. As a result, we have felt trapped in our conflicts, that there was no exit, no way out.

At the same time, we have resisted apologizing for our behavior, acknowledging that we have miscommunicated, or recognizing that our feelings originated with us and often have nothing to do with the other person. We have become trapped in self-denial, simply by focusing exclusively on what the other person did. Yet we may have been in conflict because we felt unhappy with our lives, or because we needed attention, or felt rejected, or did not stand up for ourselves, or felt insecure or upset by criticism, or were ashamed of our own cowardice, or did not have the skill to respond effectively to other people's behavior.

Instead of facing our own internal reasons for being upset, we become angry with others, claiming our cause as noble and right. We describe our conflicts in terms of injustice, unfairness, harassment, aggression, dishonesty, evil, rejection, and inequality, as opposed to being about petty incidents. We are seduced by the apparent importance of our conflicts and hypnotized by the adversarial process. We feel cleansed when we transform our narrow, petty concerns into strong feelings.

In the process, we miss the truth: that these petty concerns can be transcended by increasing our awareness of the deeper reasons that caused them. We can rise above them by being honest with others about what is really bothering us, by genuinely listening to people with whom we disagree and learning from them. We can let go of our emotional investment in the continuation of the fighting and discover solutions.

The Secret, Transformative Power of Conflict

When we are willing to face the dark side of our own participation in conflict, we are able to recognize its extraordinary capacity to transform our lives by shifting the way we act and understand ourselves, how we experience others and conduct our relationships, and how we learn and grow. It turns out that the resolution of conflict and the discovery of a better way of being, working, and living in the world occur simultaneously.

If this proposition seems shocking to you, think about a time when your life shifted dramatically and your relationship to the world around you was transformed. Did your transformation present itself to you in the form of a conflict? Did you achieve a flash of realization while in the midst of a dispute? Were you changed as a result of confrontation or criticism, divorce or discipline? Before you achieved clarity, did you feel torn between alternatives? If so, you are not alone.

The ancient Chinese Buddhist philosopher Hui-Wu wrote: "The whole world is a door of liberation, but people are unwilling to enter it." Conflict is one of these doors. We invite you to begin your own transformation by consciously and skillfully engaging your conflicts, experiencing them completely, and reaching genuine closure.

By the term *transformation*, we refer to dramatic, all-encompassing, lasting change. Transformation is not minor, incremental, small scale, linear, or transitory. It leaves us different from the way we were before, and alters our sense of reality. Transformation means allowing what is stuck in the past to die so our present and future can live.

By using the processes we describe in this book, you can create a new sense of yourself and your organization, a new direction in your life, a new understanding of your adversaries, and a new approach to resolving future conflicts, miscommunications, and misunderstandings. The energy, focus, and personal investment that are part of all conflicts can drive your personal and organizational growth, learning, and transformation. These opportunities are open to each of us in every one of our conflicts.

Surprisingly, large-scale transformations require simple actions. We ask you to make two commitments. First, to change the way you *are* when you are in conflict, to listen and learn—internally to your own voice and sense of truth, and externally to the voice of your adversary. Second, to change the way you *act*, to explore options without bias, to separate problems from people, to explore reasons for resistance, and to act with commitment.

Within these twin spheres of being and action, there are innumerable techniques, methods, approaches, questions, and processes that can give birth to transformation, yet these will be different for each person and situation. Not every method will work for everyone or every conflict at all times. What matters is your search for what works for you, right now, with this person, in this conflict. We offer a toolbox, not a magic wand.

8 Paths from Impasse to Transformation

In the chapters ahead, we identify eight paths leading from impasse to personal and organizational transformation. Each will improve your ability to take a do-it-yourself approach, so you can confront, embrace, struggle with, and resolve your conflicts. We investigate each path and offer detailed directions on how to follow and practice it, and transform yourself as you go.

While some may seek a step-by-step guide guaranteed to help you navigate life's difficulties, we have found the recipe approach to conflict resolution frequently fails. It cannot anticipate the unexpected or account for individual uniqueness. It cannot appreciate the wholeness of conflict, which is not resolvable by slicing it into smaller pieces. Instead, we offer a series of somewhat circular, iterative, intersecting paths leading to the center of your conflict.

By calling them paths, we want to shift from the usual approach to conflict resolution, which consists of a series of linear steps leading closer and closer to resolution. In our experience, transformation does not take place in steps, and resolution is rarely a linear process. Rather, it is a state of mind or intention that you cannot locate on any map, but must find for yourself. There is no guaranteed technique that will lead you there, yet *every* conflict resolution technique has the potential to open your eyes to the truth—which is that you have been there all along.

The word *path* implies a journey to a place unimaginable and indescribable before you arrive, and for this reason, we ask you to come from a space of openness, possibility, and curiosity, bringing a desire for resolution and commitment to the process. We know from our experience that if you pursue any of these paths, opportunities for transformation may open for you. We invite you to take this journey with us. Here are the paths explored in each chapter:

1. *Understand the culture and the context of conflict.* Discovering the meaning of the conflict, both for yourself and your adversary, leads not simply to settlement but increased awareness, acceptance, and resolution of the underlying reasons for the conflict.

2. *Listen with your heart.* Listening actively, openly, empathically, and with your heart can take you to the center of your conflict, where all paths to resolution and transformation converge.

3. *Embrace and acknowledge emotions.* When intense emotions are brought to the surface and communicated openly and directly to the person to whom they are connected, invisible barriers are lifted to resolution and transformation.

4. *Search beneath the surface for hidden meaning.* Beneath the issues in conflict lie hidden fears, desires, interests, emotions, histories, and intentions that tell us what is really wrong. These can become a source of liberation and transformation.

5. *Separate what matters from what's in the way.* The road to resolution and transformation lies not in debate over who is right but in dialogue, not in competition over positions but collaboration to satisfy mutual needs.

6. *Learn from difficult behaviors.* In every conflict we confront difficult behaviors that provide us with opportunities to improve

our skills and develop our capacity for empathy, patience, and perseverance.

7. *Solve problems creatively and negotiate collaboratively.* Creative problem solving helps resolve conflicts. Transformation requires the energy, uncertainty, and duality of enigma, paradox, and contradiction, which are part of every conflict. Solving problems means committing to action.

8. *Explore resistance, and mediate before you litigate.* All resistance reflects an unmet need, and can be seen as a request for authentic communication. Exploring resistance helps us unlock our conflicts and overcome impasse. Mediation encourages collaboration, dialogue, and solutions that meet mutual needs without the pain and expense of litigation.

To discover a path from impasse to transformation, you need to begin with the following seemingly contradictory propositions:

- There are no paths.
- Paths are hard to find.
- It is easy to get lost.

- No one travels the same path.
- The path is the destination.

- Paths are everywhere.
- The path is where you are.
- There is no such thing as being lost.

- We all travel the same path.
- The path is irrelevant.

To make these conflicting ideas clearer, answer two questions: First, how far apart are people when they are in conflict? There are two answers—one is an infinite distance, since they cannot communicate at all; the other is no distance, since the conflict makes them inseparable. Second, where are their conflicts located? Again there are two answers—one is between them, since conflict is a relationship; the other is inside themselves, because their attitudes, ideas, emotions, and intentions are indispensable to the continuation of the dispute.

Because each person is different, and different at every moment, there can be no single tried-and-true approach to conflict resolution that will work for everyone every time. There can be no simple step-by-step method for dropping a paradigm or becoming a different person than you were before, other than through nonlinear methods of honesty and empathy, analysis and intuition, reflection and curiosity, precision and kindness, awareness and equanimity.

The Path of Organizational Transformation

Conflicts can be destructive not only interpersonally, but organizationally as well. All our organizations, from corporations to nonprofits, schools, and government agencies, can be revitalized and achieve remarkable transformations by embracing and learning from their conflicts.

Breaking the downward spiral of unresolved organizational conflicts, whether they result in paralyzing impasses, petty personal disputes, or large-scale systemic dysfunctions, requires leadership and courage. The true organizational warriors, as Mary Parker Follett recognized in the quotation that opens this book, are those who refuse to visit personal harm on others and promote honest and empathic communication, traveling paths that promise transformation.

Moments of insight and transformation in organizations are rare and often frightening. The idea that conflict can be enriching may seem illogical or confusing because most of our experiences with conflict have taught us the opposite. While we often behave badly in our conflicts and rarely reach moments of resolution or transformation, it is nonetheless true that the possibility of profound personal and organizational transformation is always present in *every* conflict we encounter.

To discover this possibility, we need to dramatically shift the way we approach organizational conflicts, and the way we behave and participate when we are in them. We need to change how we think about our organizations, ourselves, and the people with whom we are in conflict. It is often difficult for us to do so because we are so preoccupied with what it will cost us to resolve our disputes that we fail to consider the cost of *not* resolving them.

The Costs of Unresolved Conflicts

While it takes time to resolve disputes, it also takes time *not* to resolve them. If we count up the time and money we spend on unresolved conflicts, it is nearly always far in excess of the time and money it would take to sit down and work out solutions. This is particularly true in organizational conflicts, as the two of us have observed in the thousands of conflicts we have resolved over the last twenty years. Here are some examples drawn from conflicts we helped resolve:

• *"I'm so furious! Why can't he understand what I'm trying to tell him!"* We heard this from a supervisor trying to comprehend why a manager reporting to him did not reorganize the department as he suggested. We discovered the supervisor had not actually *told* his manager what he wanted because he liked the man, assumed he understood what was needed, and didn't want to cause him trouble or seem like he was micromanaging. Instead, he communicated poorly, became angry when he had not been understood, almost fired the manager, and cost the organization considerable time and money to fix the problem.

• *"I made it very clear to him that I didn't want him to touch me or flirt with me, but I couldn't say so directly because I didn't want to be rude."* A woman who filed a sexual harassment lawsuit against her boss told us in mediation why she had been unable to say "no" or ask him to stop. When we spoke with her boss, he said he thought she enjoyed his shoulder massages and flirtatious comments, and added, "If she had just told me, I would have stopped immediately." The price they and the organization paid for her lack of communication and his failure to read her signals ran well over a million dollars, without counting emotional costs and damaged careers.

• *"I'm leaving because there are too many people in this organization who won't carry their weight or do their fair share of the work, and no one will call them on it.*" This statement was made by the director of a company leading a year-long effort to introduce self-managing teams. She was frustrated to the point of resigning because she could not surface the group's unspoken agreement: "I won't call you on your shortcomings if you don't call me on mine." If we had not helped her find a constructive way to surface and discuss the problem she would have left, costing the company a highly valued director and the expense of finding and training a qualified replacement.

In each of these cases, people became involved in serious, life-altering conflicts because they were unable to communicate what they really wanted or were afraid of the conflict that would result if they did! Yet each of these individuals, their colleagues, and organizations paid an enormous price for their fear of conflict, unwillingness to tell each other the truth, and lack of skill in listening. In retrospect, nothing they could have said would have been as powerful or destructive as what they thought and did not say.

If we could calculate the total amount of time, energy, money, and resources we waste on unresolved conflicts—the intimacies we lose in families; the relationships we destroy; the decreased productivity at work from gossip, absenteeism, illness, and poor morale; the disruptions and lawsuits; the accidents and workers' compensation cases—the total would be staggering. We have squandered our potential for growth and learning and missed possibilities for improved relationships and personal transformations. These are the real reasons for conflict resolution.

Settlement Versus Resolution

In organizations, people often sweep conflicts under the rug in hopes they will go away. They do not fully communicate what they want, and settle for partial solutions or no solution at all. This cheats them out of learning from the conflict and discovering ways of improving. Denying the existence of conflicts does not make them disappear, it gives them greater covert power. Organizations often encourage managers to suppress disagreements and be seen as "good soldiers," sacrificing honesty, creativity, and peace of mind.

In most workplaces, people routinely accept humiliation and abuse in order to keep their jobs. How much humiliation and abuse have you accepted? Who has played the role of pacifier, accommodater, avoider, or settler in your conflicts? What price have they paid for doing so? What price have others paid by being unable to resolve their conflicts fully, by having to dissemble or pretend, or by carrying the conflict within themselves?

There is an enormous difference between communicating superficially to *settle* conflicts, and communicating deeply to *resolve* them. We focus our energies on settling conflicts when we are uncomfortable with them or are frightened by them or wish to avoid or suppress them, or think we need to pacify our opponents. We try to make conflicts go away because we experience them as stressful, uncontrollable, violent, frightening, and irrational. We lack the skill to handle our own intense emotions, or because we do not know how to respond safely to the intense emotions of others. We see our conflicts as failures or expressions of irresponsibility. We do not think them important or useful. We are afraid of hurting the other person's feelings.

But if we suppress the conflict, the dispute may disappear before we have had a chance to discover its underlying causes, correct the problem, learn from it, or break through to the other side. If this is our approach, we will tend to seek settlement for settlement's sake and cheat ourselves and others out of opportunities for transformation.

It may come as a shock to read that we do not advocate peace for its own sake, or settlement as always better than battle. As we see it, peace without justice quickly becomes oppressive. Surface settlements often lead to silence, anger, and sullen acceptance. By contrast, resolution leads to learning, change, partnership, community, and forgiveness. We all know the terrible price paid for the settlement of disputes with Adolf Hitler at Munich prior to World War II, and advocacy of "peace at any price."

In the Eye of the Storm

When we seek resolution, we are guided by a desire to get to the center of our conflicts. We then come to a place where we are closer both to our adversaries and to ourselves, to our problems and to their solutions. We arrive at a place where we can strengthen our capacity for revitalized and productive relationships. This is "the eye of the storm," a peaceful place at the heart of every conflict where learning, dialogue, and insight occur. Journeying to the eye of the storm is the path to resolution and transformation.

At the center of our conflicts we discover that listening respectfully to our adversaries, jointly fixing the problem, creating dialogue over issues that divide us, working through our differences, and acknowledging what we have in common are more effective than running away or surrendering or fighting.

Working for resolution requires a shift in how we think about conflict and behave in its presence. We reach resolution when we do not run away from confrontation, and no longer see people with whom we disagree as enemies. Then we see conflicts as essential to change, growth, learning, awareness, intimacy, effectiveness, and relationships, as voices of a new paradigm and indicators of a readiness for change, as guides to what is not working and requests to make life better.

Paradoxically, we often fight because we do not believe it is possible to resolve our disputes, so we become aggressive to avoid defeat. Sometimes we fight because we need to express strong feelings or beliefs about an issue—when we are trying to remedy an injustice, or when the other side refuses to listen, or when conflict offers an antidote to stagnation and apathy.

Being aggressive is sometimes the only way to spark genuine communication and honest dialogue—not because it is *right*, but because it is the only way to get those in power to listen. Yet hidden in the allure of principled opposition is the price we pay for having an enemy. This price is explored more fully in each of the eight paths to resolution that follow.

Lasting change takes place by moving through conflict to deeper resolution, through divergence to convergence, through antagonism to unity, through opposition to transcendence. In this way, conflict resolution is an expression of the highest personal, social, and political responsibility, an antidote to unfairness and injustice, an effective way of bringing about social change, and sometimes the only way of expressing opposition to policies and practices we don't like.

Conflict as a Teacher and Source of Transformation

Our greatest sources of inspiration and personal satisfaction come from love rather than hate, from moments of connection with others rather than times of aggression and opposition. Yet even while we are searching for insight and transformation or trying to rise above the fray, we find ourselves mired in petty squabbles and disputes that make our efforts to rise above them almost laughable.

Every conflict we face in life is rich with positive and negative potential. It can be a source of inspiration, enlightenment, learning, transformation, and growth—or of rage, fear, shame, entrapment, and resistance. The choice is not up to our opponents, but to *us*, and our willingness to face and work through them.

The German philosopher Nietzsche wrote: "When you look into the abyss, the abyss also looks into you." Looking into conflict means giving up your illusions, no longer seeing yourself as a victim or other people as enemies. It requires giving up your fear of engaging in honest communication with someone you distrust. By skillfully confronting your problems, entering into them and passing through to the other side, you can develop, grow, learn, and become more available to the people you value in your life.

Locating Opportunities for Transformation

If you would like to pursue the approach we have identified, where and how do you begin? The starting place for traveling any of these

eight paths is your willingness to be open to learning and commitment to finding a resolution.

You can position yourself to approach and engage in conflicts
constructively through the following actions. As you review them,
notice shifts in the ways you think about yourself, your opponent,
and your conflict.

- *Set the stage for dialogue.* Move out of your office and into a
neutral environment, even one that is warm and open, such as a
garden or park. Consider asking your opponent to join you for a
walk, or for lunch. Be open and friendly rather than hostile and ac-
cusative. Invite honesty and model it in return.

- *Disengage your fight-or-flight response, clear your mind of every-*
thing you think you already know about the conflict, and listen empathi-
cally to your opponent. The best way to learn from your conflicts is
by listening to them. Responsive, active, and empathic listening
techniques are based on your recognizing that all conflict is fundamentally a *request for communication.* To listen, you need to understand others and control your emotional responses, to realize that
angry people need to vent. Refuse to take whatever is said or done
personally. When your own fragility makes you angry and defensive,
you may forget that you always have a choice about how to respond
to others. The largest part of your own anger often has nothing to
do with the person to whom you are directing it, but everything to do
with their actions and behaviors.

- *State, clearly and without anger, your emotional needs and self-*
interests, and listen carefully to those expressed by others. Giving in to
anger only encourages the conflict, cheapens the victory, and makes
the other side look good, or permits them to dismiss your integrity
and willingness to listen. Asking for what you want or need is essential if you are going to give up your anger and negotiate as equals.

- *Look below the surface of what is being said to resolve the un-*
derlying reasons for the dispute. Your conflict is probably not about the
issues over which you are busy arguing. There are always issues that
lie beneath the surface and need to be brought into the open for
conflicts to be resolved. Rather than starting with your opponent,

start with yourself, and think what you might be able to do to respond more powerfully to their actions.

- *Separate the person from the problem, the future from the past, and positions from interests.* Most people in conflict begin and end with the idea that the other person *is* the problem, that they are right about what happened, and there is only one solution, which is theirs. Conflict becomes an opportunity when you treat the problem as an *it* rather than as a *you*. Resolutions become possible when you stop debating over positions (what you want) and start dialoging over interests (why you want it). Interests can usually be satisfied in multiple ways, whereas positions are nearly always opposed and represent only a small range of possible outcomes. Positions are traps that narrow your thinking, perceptions, and imagination. By contrast, interests are rarely mutually exclusive. They broaden your choices and help you look to the future, which is the only part of the conflict you can do anything about.

- *Brainstorm all potential solutions to your conflict, listing as many as possible, and ask the other person to work with you to develop criteria to resolve it.* When you are in conflict, you probably spend most of your energy trying to get the other person to accept your solution, or poking holes in theirs, rather than searching for alternatives that benefit both of you. Brainstorming is one useful technique for expanding the range of possible solutions and not assuming the only alternatives are victory or defeat. Another method is agreeing on appropriate criteria for a satisfactory resolution.

- *Negotiate collaboratively rather than aggressively, and look for values, standards, or rules that will help resolve the dispute fairly, to your mutual satisfaction.* Using a collaborative process and agreeing on a set of shared values, standards, or mutually acceptable ground rules shifts anger into problem solving. It is useful to search for what will satisfy the other parties' interests as well as your own. A dissatisfied opponent has a strong interest in continuing the dispute.

- *Use informal problem solving, mediation, and other conflict resolution techniques to overcome impasse, clarify areas of agreement, and reach closure.* It is possible to enormously expand the degree of opportunity you will be able to find in your conflicts through informal problem solving. If you are stuck, try to find an experienced third party to help mediate the conflict rather than litigate it.

• *Let go of your judgments about your opponent and focus instead on improving your own skills at handling their difficult behaviors. Then let go, forgive yourself and the other person, and move on with your life.* Your judgments about people are often distractions, ways of admitting you don't know how to respond skillfully to their behaviors. As you confront your judgment that you are right and they are wrong, you will discover how locked-in you are to fighting, and how far you are from forgiveness. It is important to learn how to let go of your conflicts and release yourself in the future from what has been done to you in the past. At the same time, do not lose sight of the lessons you have learned that affect your ability to avoid future conflicts. Find a way to forgive yourself and others, while *not* forgetting what happened. It is not "forgive and forget" but "remember and forgive." This is something you do not for your opponent, but to release yourself from the conflict and get on with your life.

• *Don't surrender just so the conflict will go away. The point is not to avoid conflict but to turn it into a collaboration and an opportunity.* Conflict resolution does not mean giving in to your opponents. When you surrender you cheat yourself and your opponents out of opportunities for learning and transformation which you can only achieve by confronting what the conflict is trying to teach you.

• *Recognize the larger organizational and social issues that express themselves through conflict, and discover how your committed actions and acceptance of responsibility contribute to a more peaceful world.* You are not an island unto yourself. As organizations and society become more complex, problematic, and riddled with conflict, examine your conflicts more closely to see how they reflect these larger problems, yet are experienced by you as interpersonal. Examine your own role in contributing to change, organizational collaboration, and social justice, and engage in committed actions that allow you to grow and feel connected to others.

• *Search for completion.* Your conflicts may go on and on because you have not completely communicated what you think or feel, or because you do not believe you have been heard. Summarizing what the other person said, asking them to feed back to you what they think you said, and making sure nothing is held back are useful strategies in allowing you to end the conversation and walk away feeling something has been transformed.

Many of these steps will doubtless appear counterintuitive to you. We know that embarking on these steps requires support and guidance as well as self-knowledge and strength. We also know we can't be there to help you when you are on the spot, when you haven't the foggiest notion what to do or say. In that moment, our only advice is to speak from your heart, let your spirit shine, reach out to those on the other side, and trust your intuition. The rest will seem easy.

Understand the Culture and Context of the Conflict

Only someone who is ready for everything, who
doesn't exclude any experience, even the most
incomprehensible, will live the relationship with
another person as something alive and will himself
sound the depths of his own being. For if we
imagine this being of the individual as a larger or
smaller room, it is obvious that most people come
to know only one corner of their room, one spot
near the window, one narrow strip on which they
keep walking back and forth. In this way they have
a certain security. And yet how much more human
is the dangerous insecurity that drives those
prisoners in Poe's stories to feel out the shapes of
their horrible dungeons and not be strangers to the
unspeakable terror of their cells. We, however, are
not prisoners.

—*Rainer Maria Rilke*

Every society and every organization produces a culture of conflict,
a complex set of words, ideas, values, behaviors, attitudes, arche-
types, customs, and rules that powerfully influence how its members
think about and respond to conflict. Cultures of conflict are shaped
in and by our social experiences. They set parameters for what we
think is possible when we are in conflict and define what we can
reasonably expect, both from ourselves and from others. They shape
our capacity to ask risky questions, alter how we see our opponents

and ourselves, and tell us what is acceptable behavior and what is not.

Every workplace and organization, school and neighborhood, family and relationship generates spoken and unspoken rules about what we should and should not say or do when we are in conflict. Each of these entities produces a separate and distinct culture, which exerts enormous pressure on us to respond to conflict in expected ways.

These organizational cultures place a premium on conflict avoidance, while others reward accommodation or compromise. A number of highly competitive corporate cultures give high marks for aggression in conflict. Most have a clear set of rules regarding who can behave aggressively with whom over what.

When we scan our organizational cultures, we search in vain for signs of support for genuine collaboration with opponents, open dialogue about problems, persistence in reaching for resolution, and self-critical honesty. Instead, we find a set of dismissive attitudes that regard these efforts as "touchy-feely" and covert rules for retribution or reprisal for speaking the truth. Novelist Albert Camus, observing a similar phenomenon, wrote: "Through a curious transposition peculiar to our times, it is innocence that is called upon to justify itself." Sadly, it is rarely aggression, avoidance, or accommodation that require explanation, but collaboration, honesty, peacemaking, and forgiveness that seem to demand justification.

Conflict Messages in Popular Culture

The seductive, hypnotic power of aggression is enhanced by powerful images communicated through popular media, to which we are continually subjected. Newspapers are sold with it through the injunction "if it bleeds, it leads." Television programs alternately accentuate or trivialize it. Sporting events bristle with it. Soap operas play with it. Advertising captures its images, or creates an artificial world where it doesn't exist. Look carefully at the messages that are broadcast every day through movies, television, newspapers, magazines, radio, and advertising, and ask what ideas are being communicated about conflict.

As we experience this assault, our threshold of acceptance for violence is lowered, our capacity for making peace is undermined, and we become more and more addicted to the adrenaline rush of aggression, or more fearful and avoidant.

Like addicts, we are alternately numbed and "shot up" with conflict. Pacifism is equated with passivity, thoughtfulness with stupidity, aggression with intensity, and cruelty with seriousness of character. These distorted images are brought to us through a titillating array of commercial products that encourage our addiction. We are presented with visual images that generate tensions, and conflicts that can only be resolved through the purchase of tranquilizing, painkilling, disgrace-averting, druglike products.

Some of the effects of this continuous immersion in conflict are immediate, clear, and pervasive. They include a brutalization of the soul, a loss of empathy for the suffering of others, a gripping fear of violence, an anxiety about social acceptance, a numbing capitulation to unacceptable behaviors, a cynicism about human worth, an avoidance of intimacy, a political paranoia, a retreat into compliant behavior, and a "bread and circuses" atmosphere that diverts attention from problems that seem unsolvable because no one is capable of paying attention to the issues, or overcoming the fear of opposition.

We have created a cultural ecosystem based on miscommunication and conflict, where we spend an extraordinary amount of time trapped in disputes with others, confused over unclear messages and trying unsuccessfully to make our needs and feelings understood. Yet we spend little time learning what our conflicts are actually about—what caused them, what really upsets us, why we have such a hard time saying what we really think or feel directly, openly, and honestly. We fail to learn how we can respond more skillfully to our own strong emotions and those of others.

Our challenge is to release ourselves from these relentless cultural messages and encourage a culture that values peacemaking, dialogue, resolution, and transformation. Each of us is capable of changing our responses to conflict, and as we do, we gradually shift the subcultures we create around us, in our homes, families, organizations, schools, and communities. As we achieve a critical mass, our larger culture and society will begin to change as well.

As solitary individuals engulfed in a global culture of conflict that promotes violence and aggression, making small changes in our micro-environments at work may appear meager and unimportant. Yet making small changes helps us see that larger changes are possible. We can all make an effort to improve the organizational cultures where we work, reveal the destructive effects of individual behavior, and reduce the level of acceptance of hostility and aggression, including caustic verbal insults and vitriolic e-mail attacks. We can surface covert behaviors, encourage honest communications, and invite our opponents to engage in collaborative dialogue. In the process, we will increase our awareness of some of the more subtle forms of violence we practice, as expressed in the metaphors and language we use when we are in conflict.

The Language of Conflict

The words we use to describe our conflicts reflect a set of hidden assumptions about ourselves and others and the meaning of our conflicts. These words shape our expectations and experiences and limit our choices. The language we use when we are in conflict reveals a great deal about our secret biases and attitudes, our limitations and incapacities, our deepest needs and fears, and even what we are able to imagine as solutions.

As we unravel the language of conflict and search for hidden meanings, we begin by deepening our understanding of how language creates meaning. The ancient wisdom of an anonymous Eskimo carver tells us to look closely at the language we use, and see it as an act of creation: "Words do not label things already there. Words are like the knife of the carver. They free the idea, the thing, from the general formlessness of the outside. As a man speaks, not only is his language in a state of birth, but also the very thing about which he is talking."

Each of us has a choice about how to describe the conflicts in our lives. We can describe them as experiences that imprison us or lead us on a journey, as a battle that embitters us or an opportunity for learning. Our choice between these contrasting attitudes and approaches will shape the way the conflict unfolds. By changing our language, we change what is possible.

Your language choices tell you more about yourself than they do about the people you are describing. Consider the words you would use to describe your adversary in a conflict. If, for example, you describe this person as "arrogant," stop for a moment and see if you can think of anything positive you might say about someone who is arrogant. If you wanted to describe them favorably, you might say they were "self-confident" or "determined."

If you chose the word *arrogant* over the word *self-confident*, you did so for reasons that reveal more about your own issues of self-confidence than they do about the other person's arrogance. Think of it this way: if you were completely clear and unambiguous in your self-confidence, why would someone else's arrogance bother you? Is it possible your comment represents overcompensation for your own lack of self-confidence? Might their arrogance appear to others as self-confidence?

In this way, every insult you hurl at your opponents can be followed like a thread running backward to our own psyche. From the anger of the speaker, you learn something about what has upset them, and can make reasonable guesses as to why. The same point can be made no matter what insult you choose. For every insult there is a more or less positive way of saying the same thing. Every use of a negative term indicates a sensitivity or weakness on your part. And every insult about someone else's behavior can be turned to promote your own learning and transformation.

The same point can be made regarding descriptions of conflict. When the two of us teach courses on conflict resolution, we often ask, "What is one word that expresses what you feel or do when you're in conflict?" The initial responses include words like *anger, frustration, shame, rage, stress, avoidance, repression,* and similar negative expressions. We then ask whether there is anything positive that can be gained from conflict, and hear words like *change, intimacy, growth, opportunity, release, resolution, listening, learning, trust, communication,* and *completion.*

Try this yourself. Describe a recent conflict or miscommunication you experienced listing the first words that come to mind, both negative and positive, and see what feelings and ideas emerge from your subconscious. Then ask yourself what led you to the negatives, how you could implement the positives, and how you might become better at resolving your conflicts as a result.

What accounts for this shift in how you view conflict, from negative to positive? The positive words express an understanding that conflicts hold secrets that can help relationships improve. Yet it is only by confronting and working through the negative words that the positive words can become accurate. The ability to use positive words indicates an awareness that a transformational potential exists in your conflict.

The positive words represent what you *want* in the conflict, while the negative words represent what you are *doing* to get it. But if you try to use negative means to achieve positive ends, you will quickly discover that it is impossible to get there from here; that anger does not easily translate into intimacy, any more than shame results in trust.

Metaphors and the Meaning of Conflict

Although the reasons we cite for our conflicts are grounded in facts and logic, our experience of conflict is emotional. But rather than participate in direct emotional communication with people we do not trust, we transmit our feelings indirectly through the language we use to describe facts or reveal logic. For this reason, the language of conflict is highly charged and full of allusion, metaphor, and symbolism.

Poets, novelists, and lyricists have invented a rich cultural language that allows us to express in any tongue the complex and convoluted emotional truth of our conflicts. Listen to your own words when you are in conflict. What metaphors, symbols, and allusions do you use to make your feelings known? What words do you wrap around your emotions? How do these words differ when you describe your opponent and yourself?

Consider, for example, three common conflict metaphors, together with common phrases that expose an underlying belief about the nature and meaning of conflict. These metaphors are drawn from our culture, and employ phrases whose meaning may or may not be intended. By scrutinizing the language you use in conflict, you can discover how simple words and phrases shape what you feel and how you respond. Listen to the symbolism and hidden meanings contained in the phrases listed in the following sections.

Conflict as War

Common Phrases:

"Your position is indefensible."

"We shot down that idea."

"We've got a battle on our hands."

"He dropped a bomb on me."

"I won."

Our use of warlike metaphors to describe conflict reveals an underlying belief that the other person is out to get us, and nothing can be done to resolve the dispute short of total victory. Yet it is often the case that victory turns into defeat, and defeat is transformed into victory. Even victory can be a kind of defeat, because crushing the other side reduces the winner's capacity for compassion, peace, forgiveness, and reconciliation.

Aggressive, hostile attitudes and willingness to do battle against the competition are richly rewarded in many competitive corporate cultures. Unfortunately, warlike attitudes toward our external opponents are often turned inward to generate fiercely competitive attitudes within an organizational culture, reducing collaboration and shared values and increasing distrust among coworkers.

Reassessing our language, checking the assumptions hidden in combative metaphors, and adapting more collaborative terminology encourages us to find and adopt new metaphors. One example of a corporate leader who found new options to an aggressive approach to conflict is Jeffrey Katzenberg, CEO of Dreamworks. In an interview describing his new company, Dreamworks, Katzenberg, who was well known for his hyperaggressive conflict style as head of Disney Studios, spoke as follows to a *New York Times* reporter:

> I am aware that for a long period of time I operated like a mercenary soldier. Someone else wrote the music, and I marched to their tune. And if someone poked me in the chest, I would hit them with a baseball bat. And if they hit me with a bat, I would blast them with a bazooka. And I would escalate this until I reached nuclear-bomb time. This was the way I was taught. . . . And it's a very angry place to come from in life. It's a hostile, angry and predatory way to live life. The truth is, if you asked me to look back and say, because I behaved that way, that's why I was successful, I would now say: No. If I had been more conciliatory, I would have been more successful.

The use of warlike metaphors is grounded in the assumption that our opponents are evil, which justifies the evil we do to them. Demonizing them disarms our compassion and gives us permission to hurt them as we feel they have hurt us. In doing so, we fail to understand why the other person hurt us. The reason may be that we unknowingly caused them pain. Someone else may have hurt them in the past, in a similar way. They may have decided to pass the pain on rather than experience it themselves, or take a preemptive strike and protect themselves from future harm.

By explaining this dynamic, we are not excusing their behavior. Rather we are questioning demonizing assumptions and the belief that by injuring others we do not also injure ourselves. Demonizing and retaliation make us more brutal, insensitive, and uncaring than we were before. It is not necessary that we make the person who hurt us into an enemy in order to communicate our displeasure with what they have done.

Metaphors of war generate hatred, which does not disappear once our opponent leaves. It hurts them and damages us as well, filling us with hostility, tension, stress, and the seeds of physical illness. Warlike metaphors fill us with rage. As a result, we may aggressively express our anger or pain to the other person so we can let go of it—not appreciating their need to respond in kind and continue the conflict.

The good news is that while warfare and hatred are internalized through metaphors, so are love and forgiveness. To see how, contrast the military approach to conflict with a different metaphor and set of phrases that see conflict as an opportunity for learning, personal transformation, improved relationships, improved resolutions, and organizational change.

Conflict as Opportunity

Common Phrases:

"This difficulty presents us with a real challenge."

"Your feedback has given me some ways to improve."

"We now have a chance to make things better."

"What are all the possibilities for solving this problem?"

"Let's work together to find a solution."

This simple shift in language reflects a profound transformation in the way we think about conflict. Metaphors that describe conflicts as opportunities for improvement signal a transition from assuming our opponents are hostile to assuming they are allies and can help us solve our problems. They move us from assuming a negative outcome to expecting a positive one. In doing so, they promise us possibilities of learning, growing, and improving our relationships.

Warlike metaphors keep us locked in a closed system leading to a dead end. War has a single fixed terminus, a defined yet inherently unpredictable stopping place, which is a battle that can only result in victory for one and defeat for the other. Shifting to metaphors of opportunity allows us to engage in open-ended exploration of common problems and to pursue a broad range of outcomes that go beyond victory and defeat. When conflict is seen as opportunity, anything becomes possible. More important, we become the shapers of our own conflict experiences, in charge of where and how they end, and responsible for their outcomes.

If you come from a metaphor of opportunity, every conflict can be seen to contain multiple possibilities, not merely for learning and improvement but for deeper levels of personal intimacy, improved understanding of yourself and others, better and more lasting resolutions, clearer communications, and more trusting relationships. Seen in this light, your conflicts open the way to personal and organizational transformation. These possibilities cannot be mandated. They occur only when you discover the information your conflict has hidden from you, or is waiting for you to discover.

These hidden opportunities do not reveal themselves easily, but they can be helped to come into the open. We were recently asked to assist a small but highly successful company in resolving a conflict between its two top officers. They were battling for control of the company, although their ostensible fight was over who would get the best office, the plushest furniture, the largest head count, and the biggest expense account.

Our way of shifting from metaphors of war to those of opportunity consisted of asking them if they would be willing to transfer their competition to something that mattered to the company, such as who could create the greatest customer satisfaction, who could inspire their direct reports to produce the best results, and who could reduce costs and streamline operations the most. They laughed, admitted they had been acting like children, and agreed to use their conflict to help drive organizational improvement.

As you confront problems and conflicts throughout your life, instead of fighting against them and exhausting yourself and others, consider whether it would not be more interesting and enjoyable to find out why they happened the way they did. You may discover what you can do to resolve them better or faster and move them to a higher level. In this way, it is possible to see opportunities in every conflict.

One rationale for continuing to use warlike metaphors is that shifting your language and thinking to metaphors of opportunity will force you to take responsibility for what you have contributed to the conflict. The more you own the impact of your participation in the conflict, the greater the opportunity that will emerge. In the process, you will be brought face to face with your own inner nature. You will hear your own authentic voice as you listen for the authenticity of others.

Metaphors of war focus attention on your opponent, while metaphors of opportunity focus on you. There is a third kind of metaphor that focuses on the relationship between you and your opponent, and shifts attention from the goal or destination of the conflict to seeing it as a process or journey.

Conflict as Journey

Common Phrases:

"Your idea points to a solution."

"This isn't getting us anywhere."

"Where do you want to go with that?"

"Let's do it together."

"I think we've arrived at an agreement!"

"Let's search for common ground."

When we approach our conflicts as journeys rather than as wars or opportunities, as travels that can take us somewhere new, we are able to transcend the idea that we are trapped or stuck in our conflicts. This allows us to move beyond the idea that we can learn from our conflicts to the actual journey itself. In doing so, we increase our capacity to move with rather than against others, and to see anything new as interesting rather than frightening. We may even learn to anticipate with pleasure our next opportunity to travel the path of conflict in search of mutual growth and discovery.

Seeing conflict as a journey will encourage you to explore your relationships with your enemies, discover your hot buttons and the reasons you allow them to be pushed, and take pleasure in finding better solutions in partnership with your opponents. Journeys create expectations and anticipations of growth, self-improvement, awareness and forgiveness. They offer release from the stress of feeling trapped, and making enemies out of people you have not taken time to know or understand.

At a recent conflict resolution seminar the two of us conducted for Los Angeles school principals, one of the participants told a story about transforming his school by shifting his attitude toward conflict and seeing it as a journey. His school was run-down and needed a face-lift. Several teachers suggested he paint over a faded, peeling mural that had been at the school for many years. He did, and other faculty protested that they had liked the mural, which respected their ethnic diversity.

Instead of becoming defensive or counterattacking, he implemented an alternative strategy. He met with the entire faculty and asked them to join him in a journey of discovery to see what they could learn from this experience. He invited all sides to express their arguments and defenses and examine their mutual responsibility for the misunderstanding and conflict. He began by admitting his own error, something he would not have done if he were describing the conflict as a war. This led to a consensus decision-making process that resulted in an improved educational program for students, an agreement to replace the mural with new ones designed by the entire school community, and a renewed sense of partnership and trust.

Our conflicts can all become external journeys in search of the other person, and internal quests in search of our authentic selves. Our ability to hear our own inner voice is reflected externally in our ability to listen to others with empathy, just as our ability to accept ourselves is based on our capacity to feel compassion for others.

There are many other metaphors we can apply to our conflicts. Try to discover them in your shouting matches, arguments, insults, and conversations. As you investigate these hidden messages, see whether you can use the information contained in metaphors to move more skillfully toward resolution. As you gradually become more skillful, you can begin intentionally shifting and reframing the metaphors your opponent is using, and introducing metaphors of solution to counter metaphors of entrapment or despair.

Discovering Opportunities in the Context of Conflict

Conflict gives you an opportunity to deepen your capacity for empathy and intimacy with your opponent. Your anger transforms the "Other" into a stereotyped demon or villain. Similarly, defensiveness will prevent you from communicating openly with your opponents, or listening carefully to what they are saying. On the other hand, once you engage in dialogue with that person, you will resurrect the human side of their personality—and express your own as well.

Moreover, when you process your conflicts with integrity, they lead to growth, increased awareness, and self-improvement. Uncontrolled anger, defensiveness, and shame defeat these possibilities. Everyone feels better when they overcome their problems and reach resolution, and worse when they succumb and fail to resolve them. It is a bitter truth that victories won in anger lead to long-term defeat. Those defeated turn away, feeling betrayed and lost, and carry this feeling with them into their next conflict.

Conflict can be seen simply as a way of learning more about what is not working and discovering how to fix it. The usefulness of the solution depends on the depth of your understanding of the problem. This depends on your ability to listen to the issue as you would to a teacher, which depends on halting the cycle of escalation and searching for opportunities for improvement. Different, even opposing points of view will help you create a larger, more complex picture of what you may perceive as a simple, narrow issue. You are then able to discover richer, more comprehensive, and more effective solutions.

Once you have gained a deeper understanding of the other person, yourself, and the conflict, there is the relationship—the interaction and connection between these elements—to be understood. For example, two coworkers may experience a conflict over the distribution of workloads, but it may escalate as a result of how they communicate their needs to one another. This dynamic can lead to false or uncommunicated expectations. Listening to each other allows them to see how interdependent their relationship is, and to adjust their tasks so each feels fairly treated.

Increased awareness of the deeper causes and subtle nature of conflict, the intricacies of interpersonal communication and group process, of how and why we get angry and with whom, allows us to develop a more profound understanding of our chronic conflicts. As a result, we become less inclined to respond to our fight-or-flight reflex and more inclined to listen. This is the opportunity of opportunities, through which we gain insight into our feelings and actions and those of others. We then act with greater self-awareness to prevent our conflicts from escalating to the point where their opportunities become hidden.

When we alter how we see our opponent, we automatically change our definition of ourselves, which alters our understanding of the content of our dispute, our relationship, and the nature of conflict generally. Similarly, shifting the way we think about conflict has an immediate impact on how we think about our opponent.

The Impact of Context: Failing to See the Opportunities

If it is possible for us to see our conflicts as opportunities or journeys, why do we persist in engaging in them as a form of warfare? What fuels our negative attitudes toward conflict? How do we get trapped in it? Why do we respond to perceived hostility or aggression in such futile, counterproductive, self-defeating ways?

The answers to these questions can be found in the context we have created for perceiving and engaging in our conflicts. Once we define the "Other" as evil, resort to aggression and warfare is automatic. The metaphors we use and the language we apply in thinking about the problem and what we will do about it are congruent with our sense of context.

The driving force in our creation of conflict cultures and selection of symbolic language is our understanding of the context of opposition. Let us begin by diagraming our typical responses to any perceived aggression. Assume that the first move in our conflict is made by the other person, whom we will call A, and that A has engaged in some action that we, B, perceive as aggressive, hostile, and directed against us. To make this clear, we will illustrate the opening move in the conflict as follows:

$$A \longrightarrow B$$

We are not concerned here with what A actually intended, or with the subject matter of the dispute, or with whether some third party did something to trigger A's actions—we are concerned only with what B perceives. From B's perspective, A is behaving hostilely, and that is all that counts.

On the basis of this diagram, what can we predict about what B will do next? What options are available to B, based on the perceived hostility from A? The next chart illustrates the most common responses to perceived aggression. As you scan this chart, think about the responses you use most often. If you are observing any of B's typical responses in what other people are directing toward you, you can assume you have become A in their eyes.

If A attacks B (A ➤ B), B can respond in several ways:

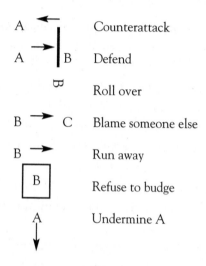

A ←	Counterattack
A → | B	Defend
ᗺ	Roll over
B → C	Blame someone else
B →	Run away
[B]	Refuse to budge
A ↓	Undermine A

Notice that in each of B's responses, A is more dominant and powerful, while B appears weaker and merely responding to A's cues. Notice also that A gets something from every one of B's responses:

- If B counterattacks, A will have succeeded in getting B's attention, and may earn support or sympathy from others by no longer appearing to be the one who initiated the problem.
- If B withdraws, A wins.
- If B becomes defensive, A can say B is not listening.
- If B blames C or refuses to budge, A can say B is refusing to accept responsibility for the problem.
- A may even look like the innocent victim of B's unprovoked attack to an outside observer who did not actually see A attack B first!

In each of these responses, B does A a favor by entering the conflict, and increases A's power by responding in the ways diagramed. Notice also that to someone who does not know A or is unaware of A's prior aggression, B may appear to be the aggressor, or at least, seem troubled, "crazy," or "a difficult personality" it would be wise to avoid.

A and B are acting out of a context in which the Other is the enemy. Their approach dictates their responses based on ancient, instinctual reactions and primitive strategies of fight-or-flight that originate in an area of the brain called the amygdala. Through higher-level thinking, we have developed more subtle undermining strategies than simply attacking things or running away—like shifting the blame onto others, or undermining our opponent's support, or gossiping to others about what A did to us.

Nonetheless, it is extremely rare that we act out of a context of opportunity or journey, in which our initial response to a perceived attack may be to ask our attacker to sit down and talk about what happened openly and honestly, or listen responsively, empathically, and constructively to their point of view, or jointly define and explore the problem. This is difficult because we have already labeled A's approach as an attack. If we label it as a response to rejection, or a request for communication, or an identification of something that is not working as well as it might and can be improved, our response will be quite different.

The problem with all the options we have outlined is that none of them have anything to do with listening, or support our understanding and coming to terms with the underlying issues in the dispute. They do not assist us in finding solutions to our problems, or contribute to improving the quality of our relationships. This is especially unfortunate if A is a coworker. Each of these options keeps us at war with one another and trapped in our conflicts.

Whether we are A or B, we will become trapped in conflict unless we shift our context or framework for understanding the Other, examine our assumption of aggression, and halt our instinctual responses. Only then can we focus our energies on finding solutions to our problems, develop a deeper understanding of our dispute, or become more skillful in responding to it.

These instinctual negative responses sap our energy and make it more difficult for us to achieve our goals. They undermine our cooperation, aggravate our differences, polarize our points of view, feed our anger, increase our suspicion and distrust, obstruct our communication, increase our tension and stress, obscure our vision, and result in the loss of our closest relationships. And they have nothing to do with what is really bothering us, so they waste our time in futile, endless disputes.

What, then, do we do if we want to reach a different set of outcomes? How can we respond differently when we perceive aggression directed against us by A? What are the practical alternatives available to us?

The Impact of Context: Creating Opportunities and Journeys

If you want to respond to your conflicts positively, treat them as opportunities and journeys, and achieve the ends you and your opponent desire, you will benefit by learning how to disarm your instinctual responses. Once you listen to your conflicts, your opponents can listen to you and together you can search for collaborative and constructive solutions.

But how *do* you overcome your initial reactions of fight-or-flight and join someone you fear, hate, or distrust who appears to be attacking you? The answers, though easy to suggest, are not at all easy to implement—particularly if you are in the grips of ancient, powerful, and hypnotizing emotions. To make this shift, you need to create a new context for understanding your opponent, yourself, the content of the dispute, your relationship, and the nature of conflict.

If, for example, you assume the other person is not attacking you but has merely confused you with the problem and probably doesn't even know enough about you to be interested in attacking who you are, you will hear what they are saying differently. You will be able to respond by focusing their attention on the problem as an "it" rather than as a "you." If you hear their attack as a request for assistance or attention or support, you will be able to say, "How can I help you?" or "How can we work together to solve this problem?" If you hear their attack as a critique of your communication skills and an invitation to learn, you may say, "I apologize for not communicating clearly enough with you. Can you give me some feedback so I can do better next time?"

None of these responses is easy, but each one leads away from warfare and toward opportunity. Each lets you take the first step on a journey in the direction of improved relationships, skills, and self-esteem. As illustrated in the next chart, there are a number of practical ways you can shift your response from one that is based on perceived aggression to one that is based on potential collaboration.

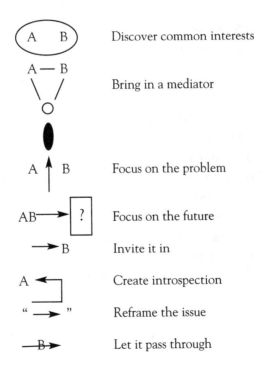

In each of the collaborative responses, the cycle of aggressive or defensive responses is halted. How does this happen? It occurs because B is no longer willing to respond as though A was aggressive, because the focus has shifted from people to problem, because B is engaged in dialogue about mutual concerns, and not arguing about the past but thinking together about the future—in other words, because B is operating out of a collaborative context.

As B, you can halt the escalation of your conflicts simply by refusing to accept the roles A has created for you. B does not have to be the victim of A's aggression or accept A's definition of the problem or A's version of B's role in their interaction. In other words, it only takes one to stop the tango.

Notice in this chart that B gains power while at the same time eliminating the reasons that prompt A's continued aggression. B's collaborative approach also deprives A of the reactions that reward aggressive behavior. This new response by B makes A appear uncooperative if he or she continues to act in an aggressive manner.

Despite the simplicity of this approach, it is extremely difficult in practice to convert your initial responses to A from negative to positive. In your effort to do so, it may help to recognize that A is being aggressive for reasons that have more to do with A's needs than your actions. It may also be that A is simply trying to communicate with you. If you can find a way to satisfy A's needs while not taking A's behavior personally or rewarding it, even by letting it pass without comment, in many cases the aggression will disappear.

Shifting your responses from aggression to collaboration is not easy, but is possible for all in every conflict. Collaborative responses begin with simple steps, each of which can be part of a strategy to create solutions rather than obstacles. In developing such a strategy, you can identify actions that move you in the direction you want to go.

The Impact of Context: Alternative Strategies for Responding to Conflict

Aggression and collaboration are only two of our most common strategies for responding to conflict. When we are in conflict, we generally adopt one or more of the following strategies, which we implement by engaging in actions designed to support it.

- Avoidance
- Accommodation
- Aggression
- Compromise
- Collaboration

The following chart, drawn from research by Thomas and Kilman, reveals the relationship between these alternative approaches by differentiating the strategies we employ when our concern for people is more important than our concern for results:

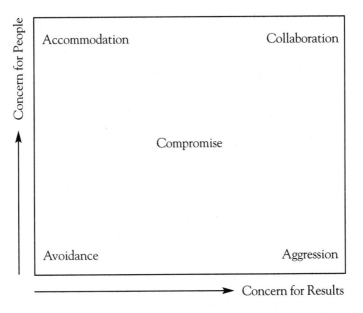

The key to choosing an effective strategy is deciding what you want to communicate. If you are primarily concerned for people as opposed to results, you will choose accommodation. And if you accommodate, you will automatically convey a concern for people as opposed to results, just as you will communicate the opposite when you become aggressive. When you are collaborative, you communicate both, and your relationships with others and what you want to achieve appear equally important.

To understand the differences between these strategies, imagine that you have just been asked to work late. If you use avoidance, you may hide in your office or duck out the back door. If you use accommodation, you will do the work, but feel resentful and probably do it poorly. If you use aggression, you will refuse to do it and trigger an argument. If you use compromise, you will agree to do it today if someone else will do it tomorrow. And if you use collaboration, you will suggest you both do it together.

None of these strategies is wrong. In fact, a skillful person is able to employ each strategy at the appropriate moment to solve a problem in the appropriate way. Each is simply a different approach or choice for responding to conflicts, and there are times when each is useful and appropriate. If the context you have for conflict is one in which you see yourself with multiple options, you will be able to choose the most appropriate strategy for the circumstance. There is no rule book for employing these strategies, there is only your analysis of the situation, your goals, and your concern or interests. Here are some of the reasons you might choose one strategy over another in responding to a given conflict:

Reasons for Avoiding or Dodging the Conflict

- You regard the issue as trivial.
- You have no power over the issue or can't change the results.
- You believe the damage due to conflict outweighs its benefits.
- You need to cool down, reduce tensions, or regain composure.
- You need time to gather information and can't make an immediate decision.
- You can leave it to others who are in a position to resolve the conflict more effectively.
- You regard the issue as tangential or symptomatic and prefer to wait to address the real problem.

Reasons for Accommodating or Giving In to the Conflict

- You realize you were wrong or want to show you can be reasonable.

- You recognize that the issue is more important to others and want to establish good will.
- You are outmatched or losing, and giving in will prevent additional damage.
- You want harmony to be preserved or disruption avoided.
- You see an opportunity to help a subordinate learn from a mistake.

Reasons for Aggression or Engaging in the Conflict

- You want to engage in quick, decisive action.
- You have to deal with an emergency.
- You are responsible for enforcing unpopular rules or discipline.
- You see the issues as vital and you know you are right.
- You need to protect yourself against people who take advantage of collaborative behavior.

Reasons for Compromise or Negotiating the Conflict

- Your goals are moderately important but can be satisfied by less than total agreement.
- Your opponents have equal power and you are strongly committed to mutually exclusive goals.
- You need to achieve a temporary settlement of complex issues.
- You need a quick solution and the exact content doesn't matter as much as the speed with which it is reached.
- Your efforts at either competition or collaboration have failed, and you need a backup.

Reasons for Collaborating or Using Teamwork to Resolve the Conflict

- You believe it is possible to reach an integrative solution even though both sides find it hard to compromise.
- Your objective is to learn.

- You believe it is preferable to merge insights that come from different perspectives.
- You need a long-range solution.
- You want to gain commitment and increase motivation and productivity by using consensus decision making.
- You want to empower one or both participants.
- You see it as a way to work through hard feelings and improve morale.
- You want to model cooperative solutions for others.
- You need to help people learn to work closely together.
- You want to end the conflict rather than paper it over.
- Your goals require a team effort.
- You need creative solutions.
- You've tried everything else without success.

(*Source:* Adapted from Thomas-Kilman Instrument.)

While each of us should be able to use all these strategies in appropriate circumstances, a strategy of collaboration generally produces the best results. On the other hand, there are times when the most effective strategy is to walk away or surrender, and there will be times when there is no alternative other than aggression.

The difficulty is that avoidance, accommodation, compromise, and aggression are all easier to use when we are in a conflict than collaboration. In part, this is because we learned avoidance when we were infants, we all grew up in families where we had to learn how to accommodate, most of us learned aggression from our siblings and peers, and we learned compromise at school, at work, and in our most intimate relationships. We do not learn collaboration nearly as early or as well.

It is difficult for us to collaborate because it takes strength to become vulnerable when we are under attack, because we do not get sympathy for collaboration, and because our culture does not support it. But there are strong reasons for adopting a general strategy of collaboration, the greatest of which is that it is the most effective way of ending the conflict completely, and starting on the path to transformation.

The Opportunity of Collaboration

If all you ever do in response to conflict is avoid it, you will sooner or later be unable to participate in it constructively. You will ultimately end up feeling apathetic and uncaring. If all you ever do is accommodate, you will eventually become frightened of conflict. You will end up feeling used and resentful. If you are always aggressive in your conflicts, you will grow angry over small things, and end up feeling hostile and embittered. If you compromise all the time, you will not stay with any conflict long enough to produce a real transformation or breakthrough, and you will end up feeling dissatisfied and perhaps compromised.

If, however, all you ever do is collaborate, you will be able to learn from your conflicts and end up feeling good about yourself and others, like a team member who contributes to the common good. While there are good reasons for each of the strategies we have discussed, collaboration is the only one that does not result in a long-term problem.

If you are interested in improving your relationship with another person, the best way of doing so is through collaboration. Each of the other strategies leaves either you or your partner feeling less than completely successful. For this reason, we emphasize the collaborative approach—not because it gets quicker results or is always the best approach, but because it goes deeper and is more lasting than the other approaches, and because it encourages learning.

A large communications company in which we worked was attempting to implement a sweeping new structure, but the change process had resulted in what the managers dubbed "public compliance and private defiance." As we probed the sources of covert resistance, we found the conflicts and disagreements triggered by the change process were being avoided and swept under the rug by leaders who hoped the problems would simply disappear.

Instead, they festered and simmered beneath a facade of compliance and behind closed doors, fueling a growing resistance to change. We interviewed employees, opened conversations about the real barriers, and drew the underlying conflicts out into the open. As we did so, we were able to see relief and renewed energy bubbling to the surface. The energy represented a desire to participate and collaborate in the change effort, from which employees had been excluded. Opening the process to allow their input on how it could work better transformed their defiance into collaborative problem solving. The transformation was so complete that the executive council, which included executives who had been most resistant to the change, volunteered to make their annual bonuses contingent on its success.

In our day-to-day lives, we are faced with an unending array of choices about what to say or do and how to behave. When we step back from the pressures and demands of the moment to develop strategies for guiding our behavior, we feel more empowered and proactive, more open to experience and better able to find the transformative potential that is hidden in our conflicts. The shift from feeling victimized, powerless, reactive, overwhelmed, destructive, or passive in our conflicts to feeling powerful, proactive, constructive, and collaborative is based on the context on which we operate and on our ability to choose strategies that support our intentions and commitments. Consciously choosing strategies and sticking to them makes us less driven by the choices of others, the emotional whims of the moment, or the dictates of circumstance.

Learning from Conflict

As we have indicated, it is relatively easy for most of us to avoid, accommodate, behave aggressively, or compromise our conflicts, but we do not find it nearly so easy to join our opponents in a mutual search for collaborative solutions. Yet collaboration yields the greatest opportunities, and the most exciting journeys.

Once you choose to come from a context of collaboration, you will need to learn how to respond to your opponents in ways that bring them closer rather than push them further away. Instead of papering over your conflicts or giving in to them or sweeping them under the rug or escalating them through rage, or even compromising them, you will need to engage them directly if you are going to learn from them. How exactly do you do that?

We propose the following specific actions for you to take in reaching out and establishing a more collaborative relationship with your opponent. As you review these actions, bring to mind a conflict in which you are presently engaged, and answer the questions that follow each action. Here are some of the main ways to start collaborating and learning from your conflicts:

• *Begin by recognizing and affirming that the conflict you are experiencing can become a positive learning experience, pointing the way to opportunities for growth or change, or indicating the need to break a system or shift a paradigm.* Can you think of any ways the conflict you are presently experiencing can be looked at positively? Is there some way it can be seen as a learning experience, or as an opportunity for growth or change? How?

• *Use empathy to place yourself in the other person's shoes, while at the same time recognizing that there is a difference between understanding their behavior and condoning it, between forgiving them and forgiving what they did.* Try to see things from the other person's point of view. Why do you think they acted as they did? How do they see your actions? What could you learn about their motivation or interests that could help you understand what they want? How could you respond to them more skillfully as a result?

• *Shift your focus from holding on to power and supporting your position to sharing responsibility and supporting the satisfaction of interests on both sides.* If you let go of the desire to hold on to your power or position, what might you learn as a result? What changes would you be willing to make? What would happen if the other person in the dispute did the same? What are your interests? What are theirs? What interests do you share? How might both be satisfied?

- *Focus your efforts beyond settlement to full resolution of all the underlying issues in your dispute.* What would accommodation, or settlement for settlement's sake, leave out of the equation? What are the deeper, underlying issues in your dispute? What would it take to resolve them? How can you bring these issues up so they can be resolved?

- *Be deeply honest, both with yourself and the other person, and give truthful and timely feedback.* What feedback can you give the other person in the conflict that is truthful and at the same time moves the conflict toward resolution? How long has it taken from the time of the incident for you to give it? Why so long? How can you shorten that time period? What feedback might the other person give you? What feedback can you give yourself?

- *Speak and act with impeccable integrity and clarity, without judgment, from your heart and spirit and not just from your head.* Have your actions and communications been crystal clear and of the highest integrity? If not, why not? What can you say to the other person that comes straight from your heart and your spirit, and at the same time is clear and lacks personal judgments?

- *Search for collaborative alternatives that increase cooperation, create common ground, and focus on shared interests.* Either alone or with the other person, brainstorm some of the things you could do together to increase your cooperation and partnership. Identify what you might both do to find or create common ground.

We want to reemphasize the practicality and importance of collaboration, resolution, and transformation. These are real possibilities, not illusions. They become immediately available to us when we search for opportunities and commit to a journey of joint responsibility and action.

Listen with Your Heart

I want to write about the great and powerful thing that listening is. And how we forget it. And how we don't listen to our children, or those we love. And least of all—which is so important too—to those we do not love. But we should. Because listening is a magnetic and strange thing, a creative force. . . . This is the reason: When we are listened to, it creates us, makes us unfold and expand. Ideas actually begin to grow within us and come to life. . . . Who are the people, for example, to whom you go for advice? Not to the hard, practical ones who can tell you exactly what to do, but to the listeners; that is, the kindest, least censorious, least bossy people you know. It is because by pouring out your problem to them you then know what to do about it yourself. . . . So try listening. Listen to your wife, your children, your friends; to those who love you and those who don't; to those who bore you; to your enemies. It will work a small miracle—and perhaps a great one.

—*Brenda Ueland*

Most of us take for granted that the people who hear us understand whatever we say. We assume they agree or approve if they do not directly and clearly indicate their disagreement. We operate under the mistaken assumption that successful communication is based on *what we say* rather than on *what they understand*.

For example, what do we do when we travel to another country and speak to someone who does not understand our language? We speak louder, or become frustrated and angry, or talk as though the listener were a child, or wave our arms vigorously, or repeat ourselves over and over. We assume one of these methods will help us be understood. We ignore the fact that the person with whom we are trying to communicate does not understand the meaning of our words.

Many of the conflicts and miscommunications we experience in life result from this approach to communication, which reflects an assumption that we communicate merely by speaking. In conflict, we feel that if we can only make the other person hear our point of view, they will automatically understand and agree with it. Speaking the same language reinforces this assumption without making it any safer. Even with a common language our listener may interpret our words from a different context or frame of reference. They may attribute a different meaning from the one we intended due to cultural assumptions, biases, or needs that reshape our message.

Each of us operates out of an unspoken context for understanding the events and communications that fill our lives. We all give a personal shape to reality. We interpret it according to our own experiences, needs, and expectations that have a powerful impact on our interpretation of any communication we receive and the choices we make as a result. A successful communicator is one who listens for and understands that contextual framework, and sends messages that stand a better chance of being understood because they fit into it.

For example, women and men often have difficulty communicating with one another, as Deborah Tannen recognized in her book, *You Just Don't Understand*. As an illustration, many women interpret expressions of sympathy as a sign of support, whereas many men interpret them as an affirmation of weakness. For many women, making joint decisions is a sign of intimacy; for many men it is a sign of dependence. Many women interpret a request by their boss for a status report as an invitation to communicate, but many men interpret it as an effort to find something wrong with their work. For many women, it is important to have their most painful feelings recognized and validated; for many men talking about their pain means giving in to it.

Effective communication starts with the speaker taking responsibility for understanding the language, perspectives, and experiences of the listener, and framing their message in terms that make sense within the framework of the listener's experience. The "language" of the listener may include a different perspective or point of view, a different set of needs or interests, or a different frame of reference for understanding the issue. It may be a difference in the style or etiquette or culture of communication. It may be that the communication raises collateral issues that make listening difficult for the receiver.

If we do not pay attention to the context that shapes understanding in our listeners, we may communicate accurately by accident, but we will not have communicated well, fully, or strategically, and may end up in conflict as a result. How, then, can we learn to be more strategic in our communications and encourage the other person to listen to us?

We start when the speaker becomes a listener actively searching for clues on how to communicate more effectively with the listener, taps into their context and frame of reference, learning how to read their contextual framework and how to speak their language, and saying what needs to be said in ways that can be easily understood.

The Cost of Poor Communication

We have all observed and participated in ineffective, even destructive communication in our family, work, and public life. And we have all experienced the results of poor communication by others. Yet in spite of our wealth of experience, we do not often fully appreciate the price we pay for poor communication.

Three members of the executive staff of a large public service agency described the lack of listening by their colleagues in their workplace, and the price the organization paid for it as follows:

> Executive Staff meetings are not a place where we have true dialogue or air problems or where there is an effort to understand what people are saying. We don't have a social contract outlining acceptable codes of behavior, so no one hears anyone else, really—there are too many insensitive remarks, confidences aren't kept, and attendance is spotty. There is more of a sense of power tripping and power alliances versus operating on principle.

> One of our major blocks to success is Harry's role in the organization. When he [the director] does come to meetings, which is rare, he says nothing. He just sits there and doesn't seem to hear what we're saying. You wonder, does he think this is a waste of time and things will happen according to a grand plan he is controlling? He rarely speaks supportively or in a problem-solving way.

> There is unevenness of commitment here. No one listens to anyone. I am personally offended by people who fall asleep in meetings or say, "OK, it's time to go now, isn't it?" Harry does this. It seems like a favoritism thing. Some people get favored treatment. People are not behaving decently toward each other.

The results of poor communication in this organization included widespread distrust of management (especially Harry), rising rates of absenteeism, tardiness, and stress-related workers' compensation claims, and an increase in interpersonal conflicts that paralyzed the organization and made its performance mediocre. Everyone we interviewed was unhappy, and personal feuds and miscommunications were escalating as a result.

We facilitated a two-day retreat with Harry and the entire staff, who, to their credit, agreed to participate despite their doubts and distrust. The goal for the session was to have open and honest communication. We agreed on three ground rules—no-holds-barred honesty, confidentiality, and an agreement that there would be no retaliation for anything said during the session.

We surfaced the problems with Harry by asking everyone to identify what was not working in the organization. We reached consensus on a set of standards for effective communication that everyone agreed to implement. They proposed starting immediately, and as they did, we could feel the depression begin to lift. As the retreat progressed, everyone in the room gave one another feedback and received it in return. They specified the behaviors they could modify and the actions they could take to become better listeners and improve their communication.

We started with Harry, asking him to invite everyone who was present to give him their honest feedback, and to thank them for doing so. Afterwards, it became each person's turn to receive feedback from the others. We made sure the feedback was constructive and specific, and asked the group to practice new methods of communication during the feedback exercise. We interrupted occasionally to encourage listening, responsiveness, and speaking in nondefensive and nonjudgmental terms.

By the next quarter, productivity had increased remarkably, and morale had begun to return. One year later, people were actually happy to be working there. Harry had changed his behavior so completely that he was acknowledged by everyone in the organization and given a hearty, unsolicited round of applause at a meeting in which the organization's success was celebrated. In a client satisfaction survey completed eighteen months later, their work unit received high ratings in client appreciation and quality of client services.

It became clear over time that the problems they had been facing were responses to the frustration the staff felt as a result of having problems they could not communicate. This frustration led them to multiply their problems, perhaps in an unconscious hope that things would get so bad something would be done about them.

We often hear clients say that conflict resolution and effective communication take too much time, or that it costs too much to hold a retreat for employees to work on improving their communication skills or resolving their disputes. But consider how much time and money this organization spent *not* addressing unresolved conflicts, and how little time it took to set things right.

People rarely calculate the emotional and financial costs of living with conflict. They do not consider the time it takes to not communicate effectively or not resolve conflicts. They rarely include in calculations the time spent getting upset or sick over unresolved conflicts, the time dissipated gossiping or talking to others about them, or the time wasted not focusing on work. They do not weigh in the balance the customer satisfaction and future business lost as a result, or the amount of damage inflicted on relationships with friends, families, neighbors, and coworkers.

The two of us have worked with a number of organizations to assess the costs of unresolved conflict and miscommunication, using a device known as a "conflict audit." The audit consists of a set of subjective questions about conflicts within the organization and a collection of objective data, including the number of terminations, grievances, customer service complaints, stress-related illnesses, employee turnover, and similar data. This is in an effort to identify and measure communication problems within the organization and to put a price tag on them.

You can conduct a rough conflict audit in your organization by simply estimating the number of hours employees and managers spend each week miscommunicating or engaging in conflict, and multiplying that figure by their hourly salaries. The figure you come up with will be enormous. Then ask yourself, What is the *true* measure of this lack of listening? How many customers, valued employees, new ideas, and creative insights has the organization lost as a result of conflict and miscommunication? What would it be reasonable to do to stop paying that price? In the following sections, we offer a number of suggestions for how to reduce these costs, which are both personal and professional.

Clearing the Decks for Listening

Recall someone in your life who was a responsive and empathic listener, perhaps a parent or teacher who left you feeling you were valuable and had worthwhile things to share, or a favorite aunt or uncle whose visits were exciting because they spent time trying to find out more about you. It may have been a boss who mentored you, or asked hard questions that helped you understand how to become more successful. Or it may have been a friend or colleague who always seemed to be there when you needed to talk, nodding and making eye contact to let you know you were understood. What did these listeners do that made you feel heard?

As you reflect on your experiences, you will recognize that responsibility for effectiveness in any communication rests not only with the speaker to be clear in what is said, but with the listener to genuinely pay attention and hear what is being said actively, empathically, and responsively.

Effective listening means emptying your mind of all the thoughts competing for your attention—including what you are going to say in response—and surrendering your ideas about what the speaker should or should not do or be. It means being fully present and focused on what is being said—not just on the surface but underneath as well, with all your senses, your posture and body language, your emotions, and your mind. It means working actively to clarify whatever you have not understood.

The Different Ways of Listening

There are many ways you can become more active, empathic, respectful, acknowledging, and responsive when you are listening to someone speak. We often think of listening as a passive activity in which we sit quietly and take in whatever is said, but many forms of listening are highly active or interactive, requiring the exercise of initiative and energy on the part of the listener.

There is a fundamental difference, for example, between hearing, which is physiological, and listening, which is psychological—between listening *at* someone and listening *with* them. Anyone who has a teenage child will recognize this distinction. There is a difference between listening for what we want to hear and listening to what is important to the speaker, between listening in a role—listening, for example, as a manager or school principal—and listening as a human being. No one wants to be listened to by a manager or school principal. Everyone wants to be listened to by a human being.

There is a similar difference between listening passively and listening actively, listening guardedly and listening openly, even listening sympathetically and listening empathically. We know when someone is listening for facts and when they are listening for feelings, when they are listening collaboratively and when they are listening adversarially. We can improve our skills by listening not merely to the words but to the meanings, listening not just to problems but for solutions. In sum, we can engage in listening, or we can be committed to it.

Committed listening is what we do when we believe what is being said is vital to us, or when we are told a fascinating story that on the surface may have nothing to do with us—yet, on a deeper level, is *about* us. Committed listening is a reflection of the openness of our hearts, our willingness to act on what we hear, and our integrity in the face of answers we don't like.

The two of us observed a committed listener in action in a workshop we conducted for teachers who were selected to be leaders in a large urban school district. The district had hired a new superintendent, and we invited him to meet with the teacher leaders. We were surprised at the brevity of his opening remarks, expecting a speech full of promises. Instead, he sat in the audience with a pen and paper taking detailed notes and inviting the teachers to tell him about the conditions in their schools. He asked open questions and gave unguarded responses. He listened for feelings, meanings, and solutions, and the message he sent was clear to everyone. He genuinely valued their ideas, wanted their partnership, and was available to them as an active, responsive listener. His debut was an instant success.

You can become a committed listener simply by choice. If you choose to be fully committed to hearing what someone is saying to you at the deepest level of your being, and to listening as though it were you who was speaking, the quality of your participation in the communication will shift, as will your body language, facial expressions, and eye contact. Your questions will deepen and become more risky, your comments will become more empathic, and your relationship with the speaker will improve as you gradually increase your skills and dedication to the task.

Setting the Stage for Listening

To increase your skills and become a committed listener, it is important to begin by focusing on the physical and emotional environment in which the communication takes place. This means, to begin with, arranging the physical environment to encourage genuine listening. The sketch that follows illustrates how most managers arrange their offices, which is where most of their listening takes place.

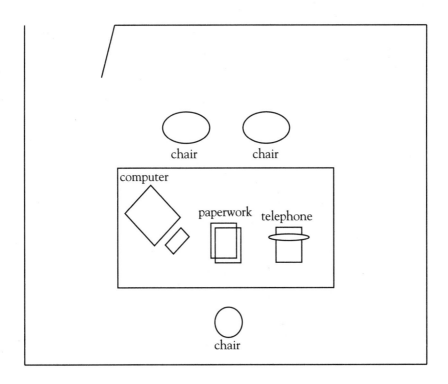

There are several problems with this picture. First, some conversations should not be held in the manager's office at all because, for many employees, being called to their manager's office portends discipline or rebuke. Second, in many offices, the manager has a distracting screen saver running on the computer, a telephone that has not been turned off, and piles of paperwork calling for attention.

Third, the arrangement of the chairs signifies who is in power and who is not. It establishes the listener sitting behind the desk as the authority, judge, and decision maker, rather than the coach, mediator, and facilitator. Fourth, the desk separates people from one another, obscuring much of their body language, which often communicates more about what they are feeling than the words they are using.

The next illustration shows two alternative arrangements for the same office, in which communication will be likely to take place more effectively.

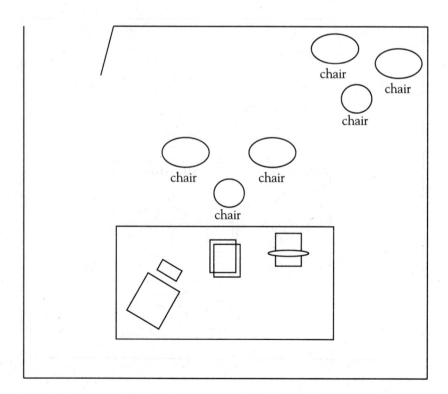

In either grouping of chairs in the second office layout, communication will be more likely to take place on an equal footing between participants. Telephones, paperwork, and computers will be less likely to get in the way, and responsibility for problem solving will be shared in more of a team atmosphere. The manager will be seen more as a participant, and employees will be able to speak more openly and naturally, allowing the listener to monitor body language for signals of consensus or resistance without a desk blocking full communication. Placing the chairs close to one another in a circle, at a distance that encourages intimate communication but far enough apart to respect personal space, conveys a message that communication is welcome. Try this in your office and experiment to see what works best. Make sure in arranging your chair that it does not communicate favoritism by being closer to one person than the other.

Communication, of course, does not consist only of arranging desks and chairs, but the whole atmosphere and ambiance of the setting. These are improved by natural or indirect lighting, refreshments, plants, art, and other details that encourage a friendly, open atmosphere so the communication can convey the message. You may not have enough space or room for these amenities in your office, in which case you may want to move the conversation to a neutral place such as a restaurant or park or living room where everyone can listen in a relaxed atmosphere.

The Elements of Communication

It has often been suggested that all successful communications consist essentially of a combination of the five fundamental elements shown in the following chart.

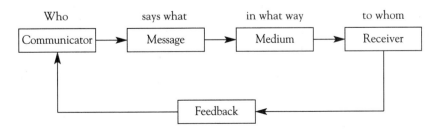

The difficulty with this typical description of communication is that we have all had the experience of being articulate communicators, expressing our message clearly and accurately, using a medium that conveys our ideas appropriately, having a receiver who is awake and listening, yet the communication fails. Most claims of wrongful work termination and sexual harassment provide excellent examples of how simply stating our message clearly and using a medium that reaches the listener may be inadequate to communicate meaning.

On the other hand, we have all had the experience of being in love, speaking incoherently, using a clumsy, ineffective medium— even speaking a foreign language to a listener who is half asleep, yet somehow our communication gets through. How do we explain these anomalies?

The Hidden Framework for Our Communications

Clearly, something else is at work in addition to the five elements in the diagram. That "something else" is the *hidden framework* of our communications. It includes the real-life roles, histories, and expectations of the speaker and the listener, the messages that are communicated by the medium, and the deeper meanings that are contained in the stories being told.

There are three important hidden frameworks for our communications: First, there are the *symbols and metaphors* we are using in the communication, which often constitute the real significance of the communication both to the speaker and the listener; second, there is the *process*, or how respectfully, responsively, empathically, appropriately, and reliably the message is communicated; and third, there is the *relationship* between the speaker and the listener, including each person's interests, needs, emotions, and unspoken expectations.

Each of these hidden frameworks helps define our communication more reliably than the literal definition of the words we use. Yet we focus most of our attention on the meaning of specific words, on their formal, dictionary definitions—which make up a part, but by no means all, of the communication. Few of us pay much attention to the subtle, symbolic meanings of the communication, or to the significance of the process by which we are trying to communicate. We miss the effect our relationships are having on the communication—yet these exert a powerful impact on meaning.

Even an innocuous word like "hello" can be interpreted in many different ways depending on the context, tone of voice, phrasing, speed, timing, location, and emotional relationship between speaker and listener. It can communicate rage or lust, friendship or enmity, admiration or disrespect, happiness or sadness.

As you listen to your own words and observe your gestures and emotions in conversation with others, search for the hidden frameworks that give meaning to your messages. What is the relationship between you and the person with whom you are speaking? If there is tension or unresolved conflict between you, is it seeping into your communication? Do you have unmet, unspoken expectations that are blocking your effort to convey meaning? Is there a perceived difference in your power or status? What is your history with each other? Is there an emotion, tone, or tension in your communication that is not matched by the words you are using?

How Communication Gets Distorted

There is only one test for the effectiveness of any communication, and that is what the other person *understands*. If we consider communication from the point of view of the person on the receiving end, we can see that there are many opportunities for distortion that arise between speakers and listeners.

Communication behaves like a wave or ray of light that is bent each time it passes through a different layer. Messages in organizations pass through many layers as they travel from intention through the hidden framework of symbols, process, and relationships to be translated into meaning by the person receiving them. Whether we are speaking or listening, we can learn to take account of these ways communication gets distorted, and adjust for the negative effect on meaning by noticing what has happened to the communication and correcting for it. In organizations, a message can be altered by being:

- *Refracted* or bent, as light that passes through water is distorted or refracted
- *Diffused*, by passing through so many layers that it becomes less focused or reaches people other than those for whom it was intended
- *Amplified*, expanded, or magnified by each of the layers through which it passes
- *Interfered* with, as conflicting messages, needs, and agendas alter or confuse its path to the listener
- *Diluted*, as the message passes through multiple layers and loses meaning in each one
- *Canceled*, as conflicting messages block it completely

As speakers, we need to be clear and strategic about what we say, how we say it, why we say it, and how we direct it to particular listeners. We need to be alert to what distorts meaning and act to avoid these distortions. As listeners, we need to be skillful in understanding what the other person means, taking account of these di stortions in communication, and testing the accuracy of our perceptions.

The Influence of Organization and Hierarchy on Communication

As a way of understanding the distortions that take place whenever we communicate inside organizations, consider the miscommunications that are generated by the hierarchical nature of most of our private and public sector organizations, and by the power inequalities and imbalances that permeate these structures.

Imagine, for example, a typical hierarchical organization in the form of a pyramid with vertical levels corresponding to divisions between executives, managers, supervisors, and employees, and horizontal functions (often called *stovepipes* or *silos*) corresponding to different departments. You may have spent most of your working life inside such an organization. If not, imagine for a moment how communication would be likely to work in such an organization.

Communications that take place inside these hierarchical structures are distorted in a number of specific, predictable ways. If the communication comes from the top down, there is a strong likelihood it will be twisted, diluted, and reinterpreted at each level of management and staff. If the communication comes from the bottom up, it will be simplified and compressed to reach its destination higher up in the chain of command. Many of these communications will never arrive.

Each level may add its own special spin to the communication, which will result in some messages being magnified in importance while others are minimized or nullified. Each department, as it competes with others for budget, manpower, and resources, may cancel, distort, suppress, or contradict information emanating from other departments. Competition within the organization will encourage people to see each other as adversaries rather than members of the same team. Because their relationship is *structurally* adversarial, listening will become doubly difficult.

An incident occurred recently at a meeting we facilitated that brought these distortions home to us. In the midst of a major corporate change involving a shift to self-managing teams and a flattened hierarchy, the chief financial officer met with his direct reports to inform them about a predicted shortfall in revenue. He assumed these managers would discuss the problem with their teams, brainstorm solutions, and let him know what they recommended to respond to the problem. They assumed he would decide and tell them what to do, or they would brainstorm solutions together at their next meeting. As a result, no one was prepared to deal with the problem—everything ground to a halt and the department could not respond to the crisis.

The context of their communication was a conflict between two expectations. One, appropriate to a hierarchy, was that the CFO would make the decisions. Another was that in self-managing teams, everyone needs to collaborate in finding solutions and moving the process forward. Either the CFO should have been more explicit in his request that the teams take the ball and run with it, or the teams should have sought clarification regarding how the problem was to be solved.

Contradictory messages and interpretations proliferate in hierarchical structures unless messages are simplified to the point of removing all the subtlety and complexity from them. As a result, official messages tend to be formal and obvious. A lot of time and energy is then spent filling the gaps through informal communications—including gossip and rumors—which are highly volatile, damaging, and imprecise.

For this reason, hierarchical structures intent on getting their messages across place a higher value on uniformity than diversity in communication, and on standing behind messages handed down from the top than on raising questions when they are inaccurate. For these reasons, they tend to limit creativity and individuality in communication. This dynamic has a profound impact on the culture of organizations, and leads to separating speakers from listeners, perceptions of incongruence in official communications, and lack of trust in those at the top.

A Commitment to Communication

The language we use contributes to the larger problem of how we behave when we are in conflict, how we respond to it, and how we communicate our feelings and intentions. To become more effective communicators, we need to have a better understanding of how to speak and listen, in order to communicate our commitment to genuine, honest communication and fair resolution of our conflicts.

Being a committed communicator means taking responsibility for observing and managing your own contexts, improving your skills, changing your behaviors, proactively seeking feedback and not waiting for others to volunteer it. This means inviting your coworkers, family, friends, and colleagues to support you in making good on your commitments, and call you on them when you don't.

For example, we worked with a small operations unit in a large corporation that led us to understand some of the ways even minor miscommunications can lead to serious misunderstandings. Mike, the manager, was described in interviews with the people who reported to him as follows:

> Mike's style is too much micromanaging and detail oriented. We get paralyzed if he isn't available.
>
> Mike's style is talking and not listening.
>
> Mike is unwilling to delegate to his managers.
>
> Management needs to be less negative, political, and confrontational.

Mike's aggressive, personalizing, controlling, disrespectful behavior and speaking style was getting in the way of people's ability to listen to him. As a result, a number of conflicts arose in the organization that made him look ineffective as a leader. We gave Mike strong and honest feedback about the feelings of his staff. We persuaded him to work on becoming more open and improving his effectiveness as a communicator.

We asked the people reporting to Mike to anonymously identify in writing to us the specific, concrete actions he could take to improve their relationship. They gave him some very painful, risky feedback. We prepared a written document summarizing their feedback. Mike was able to take the comments not as individual observations from his enemies, but as a group picture revealing how his communications were misfiring.

Before our intervention, no one was willing or able to give Mike honest feedback out of fear that he would retaliate against them. Yet, by their silence, they condemned him to continue making the same mistakes and themselves to continue misunderstanding his intentions. By ignoring the problem they paid a stiff price, until the issue demanded their attention.

As a result of the feedback, Mike improved his communications. He started by thanking everyone publicly for their feedback and meeting one-on-one with all staff to gather more information about how he could improve. He took all their suggestions seriously, and though he did not do everything everyone asked, he demonstrated a genuine commitment to changing his behavior. The group responded by giving him the support he needed to improve, and acknowledging him when he did.

Only by reality-testing your intention to change will you learn whether you are making good on your commitment to communicate. If your listeners don't see your commitment, it isn't real. Making a clear commitment to yourself and an open declaration of commitment to others is the first step. The second is learning the skills necessary to make good on your commitments and implement them. The third is giving feedback, making corrections, and acknowledging others for contributing to your growth and learning.

Effective Communication for Speakers

Effective communication includes not only listening but speaking as well. Even in extremely hostile confrontations, if you are the speaker, you can defuse misunderstandings through a variety of active, empathic, and responsive speaking techniques.

The difference between a communication felt by the listener to be authentic and believable and one felt to be inauthentic and unbelievable is the listener's interpretation—not only of your words and their dictionary meanings, but the congruity of your communication, your intentions, and the integrity of your commitments.

If these are weak or inappropriate, your questions—no matter how polite—will strike the listener as prying. Your statements of feeling will appear self-righteous, your assertions accusatory, your declarations egotistical, your requests manipulative, your contracts empty, and your commitments inauthentic. How can you speak in a way that avoids these problems and communicates your true intentions? How can you speak so as to encourage the other person to listen to what you *mean*, regardless of what you actually say? Here are some methods you can use to encourage the other person to listen:

- *Before you speak, draw out the other person's ideas.* Start speaking by listening, so your ideas will be targeted and presented to your listener effectively. This does not mean watering down what you want to communicate, merely recognizing there are a multitude of ways you can say what you mean so the other person will be interested.

- *Discover and manage your listener's expectations.* Make sure you do not base your comments on false expectations regarding what the other person wants or is willing to do. Do not encourage others to have false expectations of you.

- *Choose an appropriate form of speaking.* Decide what you want to communicate, and choose the form of communication that does what you want. If you want to make a declaration, make it an "I" statement rather than an accusation. Make sure your questions are genuine and not disguised statements. Be clear when you make a promise that you mean it.

- *Speak respectfully, responsively, and empathically.* Make sure you speak respectfully to the other person, *especially* when you disagree with them or disapprove of their behavior. Make sure you are responsive to the issues they have with you, and speak as you would want someone to speak to you.

- *Put the listener at ease.* Speak informally, or in a way that relaxes the listener and encourages their trust in what you have to say.

- *Demonstrate you have heard the other person's deeper needs and feelings.* Make reference as you speak to their issues and feelings, which may not be apparent at first glance. Demonstrate you are paying attention to what they have been telling you by summarizing their remarks without watering them down.

- *State your interests rather than your positions.* Rather than repeating what you want, explain in a personal way *why* you want it.

- *Anticipate objections and address them before they are raised.* Try to anticipate what the other person will say in response. Address those issues preventively before they do, as a way of demonstrating you understand their concerns.

- *Acknowledge differences and restate issues positively.* Acknowledge your differences openly and state them neutrally, then restate the issues positively so they can be resolved. Afterward, test for understanding, agreement, and disagreement.

- *Clarify and emphasize your agreements.* Do not lose sight of what you actually agree on. Start by thanking the other person for agreeing to discuss their issues openly with you. If they have done so, emphasize earlier points of agreement, whatever they are. There have to be some things you agree on, even if it is only your agreement to talk directly with each other rather than ignore the problem or take it to someone in authority.

- *Focus on developing solutions.* Address problems that can be solved rather than attempting to assign blame for unsatisfactory conditions.

- *Ask questions of the listener.* Asking questions is usually more powerful than speaking. At the end of your comments, turn the conversation over to the listener by requesting a response to what you said, or ask questions that could result in changing your mind.

- *Compliment the other person for listening.* Give positive reinforcement to the other person for listening and indicate your willingness to listen to them with an open mind.

Phrases for Miscommunication

Some of the miscommunications that trigger our conflicts lie in the phrases we use. As speakers, our communication will be more effective if we take time to reflect on the words and messages we plan to use and eliminate some of the phrases that most frequently trigger conflicts and miscommunications.

Recall the words you used in a recent conflict or miscommunication, or those someone else used with you. Was your communication successful, or did misunderstanding, disagreement, or conflict result? What might either of you have said differently? Here are some examples of phrases that often lead to miscommunication:

- *Ordering:* "You must—" "You have to—" "You will—"
- *Threatening:* "If you don't—" "You'd better or else—" "You'll pay a big price—"
- *Preaching:* "It's only right that you should—" "You ought to—" "It's your duty—"
- *Interfering:* "What you should do is—" "Here's how it should go—" "It would be best if you—"
- *Judging:* "You are argumentative (lazy, stubborn, dictatorial . . .)." "I know all about your problems." "You'll never change."
- *Blaming:* "It's all your fault." "You are the problem here."
- *Accusing:* "You lied to me." "You started this mess." "You won't listen."
- *Categorizing:* "You always—" "Every time this happens you do the same thing—" "You never—"
- *Excusing:* "It's not so bad." "It wasn't your problem." "You'll feel better."
- *Personalizing:* "You are mean." "This is your personality." "You are the problem here."
- *Assuming:* "If you really respected me, you would—" "I know exactly why this happened."
- *Diagnosing:* "You're just trying to get attention." "Your personal history is what caused this to happen." "What you need is—"
- *Prying:* "When? How? What? Where? Who?" "What are you hiding?"

- *Labeling:* "You're being unrealistic (emotional, angry, hysterical . . .)—" "This is typical of you—"
- *Manipulating:* "Don't you think you should—" "To really help you should—"
- *Denying:* "You did not—" "I am completely blameless—"
- *Double binding:* "I want you to do it my way—but do it however you want."
- *Distracting:* "That's nothing, listen to what happened to me—"

Effective Communication for Listeners

It is rare that our initial approach to conflicts involves sitting down with our opponents in open, honest, problem-solving dialogue, actually listening to each other and learning from our problems. Instead, we spend most of our time wondering how to win or defend ourselves, how to get our point across, how not to lose or suffer or be humiliated, or how to make the problem go away. As a result, we spend sleepless nights obsessing over surface issues in our conflicts, and planning responses to them without understanding their deeper truths.

If this is our approach, we will experience little other than the shame of being attacked, the fear of being defeated, the loneliness of not being listened to, the thrill and guilt of attacking others, the pain of lost relationships, and occasionally, the pyrrhic victory that comes from authoring our opponent's defeat. We feel, as Gore Vidal once wryly commented, "It is not enough that I succeed—others must fail."

In the process, we fail to realize that, like all self-fulfilling prophecies, our attitudes help create our reality. When we believe the other person is "out to get us," we behave with hostility toward them. Seeing our hostility, they reciprocate—proving we were right. On the other hand, as Mikhail Gorbachev demonstrated, even entrenched military opposition cannot continue when an opponent refuses to behave like an enemy.

When we avoid listening to our enemies, we also avoid being honest and empathic and are therefore unable to communicate effectively. Thus, we are condemned to doing battle or papering our conflicts over with temporary settlements. Listening is the first step toward working to resolve the underlying issues. It is crucial, since listening alone can lead to transformation.

Hearing is physiological while listening is psychological, and takes place even when the listener is physically unable to hear. Most of us hear and recognize the meaning of what is being said to us. We can even repeat it back word for word, in spite of the fact that we have not really been paying attention and do not care what was said.

Listening, like speaking, is a matter of *intention*. Its effectiveness depends on how important we think the information is to us. When we listen, we can do so in a variety of ways. We can listen only to the details of what someone is saying but not to their deeper meaning. We may listen only for openings or holes in our opponent's argument—picking out what is wrong with what they are saying so we can use it against them. And, we can listen while we wait for them to finish so it will be our turn to talk.

Active, empathic, and responsive listening happens when we genuinely care about what the other person is telling us and actively reach out to them with questions or body language. It takes place when we engage in conversation or dialogue that is moving back and forth and we are authentic in our responses. It occurs when we search for unidentified solutions or try to come up with new ideas or approaches to solving a problem. We experience it when we listen as though we are the one who is speaking.

The deepest level of listening happens when we listen as though our lives depended on our understanding what is being said, when we are no longer even aware of our existence as a listener and are completely merged with the speaker and the story. When we listen in this way with our hearts, we feel love for the one who is speaking.

There are many ways you can listen, ranging from going through the motions to communicating with your heart. As your listening moves deeper along this continuum, you will discover increasing opportunities for transformation—and improved listening skills.

We followed a client closely as he made this journey. Tim was a well-meaning, much-loved leader in city government who became isolated as a result of his communication problems. His staff, who respected and valued him but felt blocked in their communications with him, described him as follows:

> The volume of work is such and the number of crises and emergencies is so great that even if he were organized Tim would be pulled off constantly. Tim's meetings get interrupted by calls all the time. His availability to hear what we have to say is missing. It's hard to get his time and attention to focus on issues.

> Tim is marvelous, smart, and a good people person, but he is disorganized and lacks follow-up. He never has time to hear our problems.

> Tim is disorganized, and there often is no follow-up because his job is so overwhelming and challenging that no one can do it. Tim loses the points we are trying to make as we give them to him. He doesn't seem to hear us anymore.

We encouraged Tim to use the three easy steps that follow to more effectively listen to the city employees who reported to him. His consistent practice of these steps over a period of several months paid off in better relationships with his staff and a more responsive and community-based city government. The three steps to more effective listening are easy to articulate but extremely difficult to carry out consistently in practice. Take a moment in your next interaction to apply them, even one at a time. Notice if you grasp more of what is communicated, or find yourself in closer sync with the speaker as a result.

1.   *Let go of your own ideas, roles, and agendas, and try to understand what the other person is saying.*

The first step in communication is not speaking. It is not even listening. It is *preparing* to listen by emptying yourself of your own preconceived ideas, dropping your predefined roles, and letting go of your agendas, assumptions, judgments, and expectations—of everything that twists what you hear into something other than what was meant. The greatest enemy of learning is not ignorance, but what you think you already know. Ask yourself, "What is going on in my mind when a colleague is communicating with me? Am I open for learning and poised to understand what he is saying, or thinking about what I am going to say in response? Am I listening as a human being, or as a manager or relative or teacher? Possibly the greatest challenge you face is letting go of what you know to be true, yet your truths can prevent you from hearing theirs.

2.   *Search for the other person's meaning, especially if they disagree with you.*

After you empty yourself and let go of your judgments, genuinely listen to the words used by the other person and sense their deeper issues, hearing their assumptions, expectations, and hidden meanings. Ask yourself, "What do they really want?" "What are their real intentions?" "What is going on beneath the surface?" Are you aware of the subtlety hidden in the words being spoken? Are you listening to what is intended and not just to the words that are being used?

3.   *Respond respectfully and nondefensively, acknowledging and addressing the other person's concerns first.*

Respond by addressing the speaker's point of view, rather than immediately countering with your own and ignoring most of what they said. When people feel they have not been heard, they repeat their comments or become strident or angry. Try saying, "Thank you for your information. I appreciate hearing your point of view." When you respond seriously to what they say, they *feel* heard and are ready to make an effort to understand you. Put yourself in their shoes and walk a while along their path. Speak to them in ways that could make a difference, rather than replacing their ideas with yours.

In addition to talking less and listening more, there are a number of phrases, questions, and comments you can use to respond to what the other person says. Try to choose statements that are inherently respectful and encourage open communication.

Active and Responsive Listening

Being a committed listener includes being active and responsive during the listening process—not simply hearing, but participating actively in the communication. Using the active and responsive listening techniques that follow will support you in being more effective, and encourage others to listen when it's your turn to speak. They open up communications, invite the other person to share their feelings and points of view, and enable you to hear what is really being said.

Encouraging.   Encouraging questions and comments support the speaker in sharing their feelings, perceptions, and attitudes. Comments such as "Please tell me more," "I'm interested in what you are thinking and feeling," "I would like to know your reactions," "I hear what you are saying" are encouraging statements. You can even say, "Tell me more about why you hate me so much," which will encourage a more open conversation and dialogue. What statements could you make to your opponent that could be encouraging?

Clarifying.   As the discussion unfolds, ask questions that clarify the points being made by the speaker. Send a signal that you are interested in the speaker and in what is being said. Questions such as "When did this happen?" "Who else was involved?" "What did it mean to you?" elicit detail and meaning. Clarifying questions de-escalate emotions quickly by focusing the speaker on facts rather than feelings. Be careful not to interrogate the speaker with probing questions. Your tone of voice and *intention* establish the difference between probing and clarifying questions. What are some clarifying questions about a confusing or ambiguous situation you might ask?

Acknowledging. You can encourage greater openness by acknowledging, recognizing, and naming the feelings the speaker is expressing. Comments such as "I can see you feel angry about that" or "I can appreciate now why you might feel that way" give permission for greater depth of communication. Be careful not to assume you know what other people are feeling. You can use these expressions to give someone permission to say what they feel. Avoid popular phrases such as "It sounds like you are very angry right now," as they convey an impression that you are trying to manipulate the speaker. Statements like this betray a lack of empathy rather than a presence of heart. What acknowledging statements might you make when a coworker or friend gets upset?

Normalizing. As feelings are expressed and opinions offered, you may want to communicate to the speaker that it is natural and normal to have these feelings. Statements like "I think I might feel the way you do if that had happened to me" allow the person to feel accepted while expressing difficult emotions or critical thoughts. These statements will encourage the speaker to go deeper in their conversation with you. Can you think of a way of normalizing the feelings of someone with whom you are in conflict?

Empathizing. Put yourself in the other person's shoes to better understand their perceptions and feelings. Look inward, and find a time when you had a similar experience, reaction, or feeling. You might say, "I can understand why you feel strongly about this subject because I experienced something similar in my own life." Or, "I can appreciate why you might feel that way." Or just, "I understand." Do not say, "I know exactly how you feel." You don't. What are some empathizing comments you might make?

Soliciting. Ask questions to solicit advice and identify possible solutions such as, "I would like your advice about how we could resolve this." "What do you think should be done?" "Tell me more about what you want." "What would you like to see happen?" "Why do you think that would work?" What questions could you ask to solicit advice about a disagreement or conflict you are having?

Mirroring. Mirroring reflects back the emotions, affect, demeanor, body language, tone of voice, metaphors, even breathing patterns used by the speaker to encourage the speaker to feel they have a companion in their thoughts and emotions rather than a dispassionate observer. If the speaker takes a defensive posture, take one yourself, then move to a more open one, but do not make it appear that you are mimicking the speaker or being disrespectful. You can use mirroring to reverse a conflict metaphor, so if the speaker describes feeling "trapped," you can ask "What could we do that might open the door to a solution?" How might you reverse a metaphor in your conflict to suggest a solution?

Agreeing. If you disagree with a speaker about a topic, it does not mean you have to disagree about everything in life. It is useful in your disagreements to remember the issues on which you agree. You might say something like, "What I like about what you just said is—" or "I really agree with you about that. What I think we disagree about is—" What could you say to someone with whom you disagree that lets them know you have areas of agreement with them?

Supplementing. Instead of "yes, but" say "yes, and"—and convert adversaries into allies. Say something like "Let me build on that and see if I am on the same track you are—" or "Let me support what you are saying with another point—" or "Not only that—" What could you say to add to what your opponent said to supplement their basic points and distinguish them from disagreements?

Inviting Elaboration. Asking open questions lets the speaker know you respect their point of view. Ask wide-open questions such as "Why?" "What would you like to see happen?" "Why is that important to you?" Or more directed questions, such as "I'd like to ask a question about that" or "How would you—" or "Help me understand why you—" What do you really want to know from or about the person with whom you disagree? What could you ask that would get you that information?

Reframing. Reframing is preserving the content of a communication but altering its form so it can be heard and possibly result in a solution. Reframing or rephrasing transforms "you" statements into "I" statements and helps identify the reasons for disagreement. For example, change the statement "You are incompetent!" into a question, such as "What did I do that did not meet your expectations?" A format for reframing is: "I feel [whatever] when you [do whatever], because [reason]." Can you think of a way you could reframe a statement you don't like?

Responding. Listening respectfully means responding to what is said, not using listening techniques to manipulate the speaker. The speaker is entitled to a response that comes to terms with what was said. One approach is to say, "If I understand you correctly, you see the problem this way—[summary]. Here's how I see it." Or, "Would you like to know how I see it?" Make sure you do not respond defensively or angrily, but make your point clear. If your main purpose is to learn from your disagreement, you will not want to back away from the conflict or get sucked into it either. What could you say that would allow you to accomplish both these goals?

Summarizing. If you want the other person to know they have been heard, summarize what they said in your own words, for example by saying, "Let me see if I understand what you just said—[summary]. Is that correct?" This feedback helps the speaker *feel* heard, and provides an opportunity to confirm, correct, or change your understanding of the communication. It demonstrates your interest in what was said and your desire to grasp the essentials of the communication. It is useful to summarize at the end of a conversation to see if you have the same perception of what was said or decided. In doing so, you risk making a mistake, but it is better to be mistaken and gain clarity than to continue on the basis of a false assumption. How might you do this?

Validating. Recognize the speaker's contribution and thank them for communicating with you. Validate specific things the speaker said or did, or that you learned in the conversation. Use comments such as "I appreciate your willingness to raise these issues with me." "I learned a great deal from what you said." "I know it took a lot for you to be as open as you were and I want to acknowledge you for taking that risk." "I appreciate your willingness to talk to me about this." "I didn't know you felt that way before." What comments might you make to validate a speaker in a way that communicates your authenticity?

We hope you do not feel overwhelmed or daunted, and realize you don't always have to do all the things on this list to communicate effectively. The most important ingredient in improving your skills is to be conscious of how you are communicating, where you run into trouble or trigger responses in the listener you did not intend, and continually improve the skills you already possess.

None of these methods guarantee successful communication, and each can be used by an uncommitted listener to give the *appearance* of listening while holding fast to a private agenda. We call this "New Age manipulation" because all the words and techniques are right—but the listener does not really care about the speaker or the message they are delivering. Your challenge is to be deeply honest and empathic, to search your soul for your true interests and commitments, and to use language and communication techniques that reveal your authenticity.

Empathic Listening

The most important organ in listening is not the ear or the mind but the heart, and it is in your heart that the true meaning of the communications will be found. To listen with your heart, it is necessary for you to become one with the speaker and discover *their* truth within you.

Empathic listening, for this reason, is much deeper than mere active or responsive listening. It requires you, the listener, to focus awareness not just on the words the other person is using but on what they may be thinking or feeling. It means asking yourself what it would feel like to be in their shoes and what would cause you to make that statement or communicate that way yourself.

When we listen within a role—the way, for example, a manager listens to an employee who is complaining about a problem, or a teacher listens to a student conflict—we listen for the facts. But in addition to the facts, you can also listen for a wide range of information about the speaker and how they perceive the world, for indicators of what is really important to them. In addition to the facts, you can go deeper and listen for:

- Subjective experiences
- Roles
- Intentions
- Interests and positions
- Dreams and visions
- Fears
- Humiliations
- Defensiveness
- Denial
- Metaphors
- Universality
- Cries for help
- Openings to dialogue
- Requests for acknowledgment

- Interpretations
- Modes of perception
- Emotions and feelings
- Wishes and desires
- Family patterns
- Insults and stereotypes
- Self-esteem
- Resistance
- Prejudices
- Apologies
- Uniqueness
- Expressions of guilt
- Desire for forgiveness
- Need for support

The next time you listen to a colleague at work or family member, see if you can hear these elements in what they are saying. See what you can hear by listening with your heart and imagining what would lead you to make their statements or have their concerns.

Where Do We Go from Here?

After becoming committed, active, responsive, and empathic listeners, and learning to speak and act with integrity, the next challenge in resolving our conflicts is to work through the powerful emotions that block us from listening with an open heart.

We need to find ways of working through our emotions—both those we feel ourselves and those we experience from others in trying to resolve our conflicts. All our work on listening can be lost in a moment when a firestorm of feeling overwhelms us. To learn how to embrace and acknowledge the powerful emotions that fuel our conflicts and to reach deeper into the center of conflict where profound transformations take place, we invite you to read on.

Path Three

Embrace and Acknowledge Emotions

By embracing the inescapable, I lost my fear of it.
I'll tell you a secret about fear. With fear, it's all or
nothing. Either, like any bullying tyrant, it rules
your life with a stupid blinding omnipotence, or
else you overthrow it, and its power vanishes in a
puff of smoke. And another secret: the revolution
against fear, the engendering of that tawdry despot's
fall, has more or less nothing to do with courage. It
is driven by something much more straightforward:
the simple need to get on with your life. I stopped
being afraid because, if my time on earth was
limited, I didn't have seconds to spare for funk.

—*Salman Rushdie*

What do we do when listening results in an emotional outburst instead of calm and reasoned conversation? What options are available to us when we feel caught in a strong emotion, or others are, and the communication slips out of control?

Our emotions can be constructive or destructive, pleasurable or painful, positive or negative. They can distort or clarify our communications, escalate or de-escalate our conflicts, encourage us to act collaboratively or prevent us from doing so. They can blind us or allow us to see others as they truly are. They can leave us feeling exhausted or fulfilled. Most people experience the emotions they feel in conflict as exclusively negative, destructive, and painful. Yet these

emotions can be a powerful positive force for resolution and transformation, depending on how we approach them.

Just as conflict triggers negative emotions, such as hatred, fear,
shame and depression, *resolving* conflict immediately results in positive emotions, including love, courage, pride, and elation. Every
emotion has a negative and positive form, making it possible
for them to flip suddenly from negative to positive when we respond
to them in the right way at the right time. Our feelings are not fixed
states of mind; they are in constant motion, capable of moving
slowly or rapidly from one extreme to another.

How we respond to our own powerful emotions affects our capacity to hear and respond to those of others, and how available we
are for relationships with people who express intense emotions. It
is important that we think of emotions as teachers to be learned
from rather than devils to be suppressed. In spite of the ambivalence
of our emotions, we can all become more skillful in how we handle
them when they arise.

We invite you to directly address your emotional life, to look at
how your feelings direct your experiences, interactions, and relationships. It is always useful to become more conscious of the role
emotions play—not only in escalating your conflicts and shaping
your view of yourself and your adversaries, but in limiting your ideas
about what you can do to resolve your conflicts.

Emotional Lessons

We pay a heavy emotional price for unresolved conflict, including
pain and illness. Howard Friedman, a psychology professor at the
University of California at Riverside, has analyzed a hundred stud-
ies connecting people's states of mind with their physical health. He
found that being chronically pessimistic, irritated, cynical, de-
pressed, and anxious doubles the risk of contracting a major disease.
There is a link between the emotional centers of the brain, the immune system, and the cardiovascular system. When stress hormones

and brain chemicals produced during negative emotions flood the body, they hamper the ability of the immune system to fight disease, making us more susceptible to cancer, raising blood pressure, increasing cholesterol, and rendering us more susceptible to diseases of all kinds.

Emotions are always present in all our relationships, even when they do not appear on the surface or reveal themselves in obvious ways. The only question is whether we are personally and organizationally capable of acknowledging them and responding skillfully and intelligently to their presence.

There is always a risk of opening a floodgate of repressed emotions whenever we communicate openly and honestly with our adversaries or directly address our conflicts. It may seem initially that we are sinking into negative emotions and retreating from resolution. Yet the opposite is true—moving *toward* our emotions unlocks our disputes, while moving away gets us stuck. Why?

There are two fundamental ways of responding to any emotion, whatever the type of conflict, and whether the emotions are ours or our opponent's. We can

- Tighten up and turn away
- Relax and turn toward

When we withdraw from our emotions, we end up learning little or nothing about what gave rise to them, or how to experience them fully, or how to respond to them skillfully, or how to recognize what lies underneath them. When we relax, let go of our fear of expressing emotions, and engage them, we release ourselves from their grip and increase our clarity, creativity, opportunities for learning, and chances for resolution, transformation, and healing.

Suppressing, denying, and avoiding our emotions leads us away from solving the problems that caused them to surface in the first place. These strategies block us from understanding what our emotions actually mean, both to us and our opponents. Our emotions surface for a reason, and we need to discover where they come from in order to realize that we can communicate about what led to them in rational and constructive ways.

How Unexpressed Emotions Create Conflict

We were once asked to mediate a bitter conflict in the payroll department of a large organization. The atmosphere was so angry, rude, tense, and hostile that every employee in the department had applied for a transfer! They had been experiencing negative emotions for *eight years*, and the price had been enormous.

We started by asking how the conflict began, and were met with total silence as each employee tried to remember. Finally, Blanche said that eight years ago Frieda had made an insulting comment about her husband when he was dying of cancer. The anger, pain, grief, and guilt connected with her husband's death added to Blanche's injured feelings, leaving her so upset that there was no easy way to communicate it. As a result, she slipped into a cold, punishing, seemingly irrational anger.

Frieda was visibly shocked to hear that this was the reason behind their enmity. She told Blanche she had not known her husband was dying of cancer, and had no reason or desire to insult him. We asked her, "Since Blanche has believed for eight years that you meant to insult her husband, what do you want to say to her?" There is only one answer to this question. Frieda immediately and sincerely said she was sorry for any insensitive remarks she might have made.

We then asked Blanche: "Since Frieda has apologized to you and does not recall making the remark and you thought she did for eight years, what do you want to say to her?" Again there is only one answer, and Blanche apologized, admitting that she should have gone to Frieda and told her of the pain her remark had caused. Both women began to cry, releasing their pain and pent-up anger, and realizing the price they and their colleagues had paid for eight years of miscommunication.

Everyone in the department was shocked and speechless at how an innocent mistake could create such anguish. We asked each person, "Is there anything you want to apologize for, or any other mistaken communications you want to talk about?" As they spoke about related incidents, relief began to fill the air. At the end of the session, the two former arch enemies tearfully hugged each other and everyone agreed to communicate more openly in the future. Within six months, the performance record of the department increased 200 percent, the staff was happier. The department was so united they went on strike together when management tried to change their work rules.

These women were not alone in their inability to express their emotions in conflict. Many of us have great difficulty expressing intense emotions because we are afraid we will not be skilled enough to contain their destructive potential or communicate them constructively. Many of us feel inadequate listening to strong feelings, fearing we could be hurt or lose control over our responses. Yet the result of not confronting these fears can lead to years of pain and anger.

Unfortunately, most organizations have adopted an unwritten rule for the workplace: "Check your emotions at the door." The expectation that this can be done successfully—that human beings can function successfully while suppressing deep emotions over long periods of time—turns out to be false. In our experience, successful work teams acknowledge the reality of emotions and act to support team members who are in distress. By contrast, where emotions are suppressed, so are creativity, motivation, and morale.

In addition, it is virtually impossible to resolve many of the conflicts that arise in the workplace without delving into employees' emotional lives or their emotional responses to the events that fuel their conflict. For this reason, managers who try to resolve conflicts between coworkers often get stuck in impasse and feel inadequate as conflict resolvers. This is not surprising, since they have been asked to perform a task they have been neither trained nor authorized to complete.

The real problem with permitting the expression of emotion in most organizations comes from the traditionally masculine idea that emotions reflect weakness, and the fear that if we appear vulnerable in the face of our opponents, they will seize the advantage and crush us. In truth, expressing emotion makes us stronger while suppressing it makes us more fearful and brittle. Nobel Prize–winning Japanese novelist Kenzaburo Oe has written eloquently about our reluctance to face deep emotions, and what lies beneath them. He writes: "What was he trying to protect himself from . . . that he must run so hard and so shamelessly? What was it in himself he was so frantic to defend? The answer was horrifying—nothing! Zero!"

Instead of trying to protect ourselves and our organizations by suppressing the honest expression of emotions, we need to move toward and through emotions, responsibly express them, and give permission for people to openly reveal their hidden feelings. In saying this, we are not advocating out-of-control tantrums. We are suggesting that the responsible, empathic expression of feelings can lead us out of impasse and toward resolution, transformation, and reconciliation.

We require work environments that reflect and acknowledge our real human natures, that allow staff members to be present as whole human beings who have emotions as well as intellects. We believe it is possible to create organizational cultures in which employees can vent their emotions and clear the air without being destructive or losing sight of the main goal. These are environments where coworkers support one another in satisfying each other's emotional needs in ways that improve their ability to work together and produce better results. To learn how to achieve these ends, we need to return to the cauldron where emotional responses and attitudes were forged—our families of origin.

Families: The Origins of Emotional Life

We are all born with the innate capacity for experiencing pleasure and pain, desire and repulsion, satisfaction and frustration. As children, we gradually increase our capacity to communicate our feelings, based on observing the behavior of adults and peers engaged in conflict. We learn based on what succeeds in getting us what we want. These successful patterns are reinforced over time by parents, siblings, and friends, becoming almost automatic when we encounter conflict as adults.

Our emotions are not illogical. They are successful adaptations that are rational for reasons we may not immediately or entirely understand. They were shaped by the family and cultural systems in which we grew up, reflecting strategies that got us what we wanted or needed, even at the expense of pride, self-esteem, and love.

Our parents and childhood peers imprinted us with emotional patterns we carry with us the rest of our lives. In most cases, these patterns are communicated unconsciously, without responsibility or scrutiny, and accepted blindly, without choice or discernment. Generations of people who developed habits of anger, sadness, addiction, guilt, panic, manipulation, and withdrawal taught these behaviors to their children. The next generation, in turn, shaped their responses to manage or confront their pressures and taught the patterns to their children. Each generation brought these emotional lessons into the workplace and used them on others as their parents had before them. In this way the conflicts of the parents are visited on each new generation of children.

Counterposed to our families' responses are the strategies we learned from our peers. Our need for acceptance and approval from friends and colleagues began in childhood but extends into our adult lives, helping us adopt alternative models and patterns for resolving conflicts. Here again, we accepted these patterns for the most part without conscious choice, in automatic response to our environment.

One clear path to resolution and transformation lies in conducting a conscious, critical, affectionate examination of our emotional repertoire. It is possible to research our family histories, cultivate a capacity to separate ourselves from our peers, and make a determined effort to choose our own emotional path. In the process, we make ourselves responsible for our emotional lives.

Once we develop a successful strategy for responding to powerful emotions in conflict, we repeat it over and over, using it even when it cannot be successful. We give up learning how to develop other, equally successful approaches and ignore our weaknesses, thereby converting them into tragic flaws. Thus what we perceive as emotional success may lead to emotional failure.

We learn in our families not only how to express emotions but how to suppress them. In the process, we come to accept a set of ideas, myths, and assumptions about emotions that shape our responses throughout our lives. We use these myths and beliefs to justify our feelings about ourselves and others and create self-fulfilling prophecies of inadequacy, paranoia, and victimization. We learn to limit our expression of emotions, to construct intellectual defenses and explanations to rationalize our behaviors, and to avoid honestly addressing or communicating our feelings.

In every organization, whether we enter as employees, managers, customers, or vendors, we encounter a culture that dictates how emotions are viewed and handled. In the beginning, suppressing our emotions is not difficult. As our work life extends, more and more issues and feelings get swept under the rug, until we either shut down emotionally or leave.

Here are some of the most commonly held myths and assumptions about expressing emotion that shape our organizational cultures:

- Emotions are irrational.
- Emotions are negative.
- Emotions can't be controlled and will escalate if released.
- Emotions can safely be ignored.
- Emotions are not helpful in making decisions.
- Emotions are unnecessary.
- Emotions are for children, women, or the helpless.
- It's not proper to express emotions at work.
- Good, nice people don't feel emotions.

- It's okay to express emotions if I can justify my feelings logically.
- I shouldn't feel emotions immediately, but save them for later.
- I'll lose control or go crazy if I express my emotions.
- People will go away if I express my emotions.
- Other people have no right to express emotions to me.
- I'm responsible for fixing other people's negative emotions.
- If I express my anger to someone, it means I don't love or re-spect them. If they express their anger, it means they don't love or respect me.

Have these myths and assumptions hindered your communication with the people who are most important to you? How have they supported or undermined your relationships at work? How have they affected your family or others in your life?

Most of these myths and assumptions ask us to suppress our feelings, discount our emotional experiences, and avoid communicating what we actually feel. Our feelings do not go away as a result, they emerge elsewhere—often in the form of conflict, depression, suppressed rage, distrust, fear, self-doubt, apathy, or illness.

Many options are available to you when you experience powerful or intense emotions, and you choose not to act out old family patterns or cultural dictates in the workplace. You can change your responses any time you choose. To do so, you need to bring an even deeper level of awareness and acceptance to your emotional experiences, dissecting and separating out the jumble of components that make up your feelings.

Elements of Emotion

We often experience our emotions as a muddle and feel powerless to shape or control them. Yet if we can learn to experience them as separate elements that combine to produce what we feel, we can begin to understand and manage them. As you consider the following list of elements, reflect on the questions included to gain insight into your patterns.

- *Quality:* Is what you are feeling depression, anger, guilt, pain, shame, love, fear, or some other reaction?
- *Intensity:* Is it mild or intense? Barely noticeable or gripping?
- *Direction:* Is it inner-directed or outer-directed? Toward a specific target or generalized toward no particular person or situation?
- *Duration:* Is it momentary or long-lasting? Does it come in cycles? How did it start?
- *Location:* Where is it felt in your body? Where is its impact strongest? Is it a wave or a spot? Does it radiate? What is its shape?
- *Origination:* When have you felt this way before? What is it linked to? What makes it disappear? What triggers or causes it?
- *Meaning:* What does it mean to you? Why does it have that meaning? Where did you learn the meaning? What else could it mean?
- *Awareness:* How aware are you of each of these elements? Can you detect subtle movements in each? Are you blocking or impeding your awareness of what you are feeling? If so, why? What would happen if you didn't?
- *Patterns:* Take a few moments to review your emotional responses. Do they fit together in any way? Do you notice any patterns?
- *Change:* How often and easily do your emotions change? How open are you to consciously altering your emotional patterns?

The Stages of Emotional Response

You may have noticed that your emotional responses are not immediate, but take place over time. If you watch the flow of your emotions carefully, you can discern a number of discrete triggers, or stages, in their formation. You may also notice that some of these stages are over within seconds while others last months or years. It is possible to intervene consciously at any point in your response to transform what you are feeling and open up the possibility of resolution by moving to a different stage in the process.

As you review the following stages in the development of emotions, reflect on the places and times when you lose awareness or choice in your emotional responses to conflict, or go into "automatic pilot" and slip into old patterns:

- *Triggering action or event:* An action or event takes place and is communicated to us, becoming a fact in our lives.

- *Perception of emotional tone or intent:* We perceive an underlying intent, perhaps through body language, tone of voice, quality of action, context, or style of communication.

- *Stimulation of memories and subjective associations:* These perceptions trigger and connect with conscious or subconscious memories and associations, which have their own emotional content.

- *Interpretation or attribution of meaning:* We attempt to explain or interpret the action or event, together with its emotional tone, in a way that makes sense of our experiences.

- *Rise of emotional response:* Based on the meaning or interpretation we have given to what happened, we begin to feel fear, anger, shame, guilt, love, hate, or other emotions.

- *Suppression, repression, intensification, neutralization of response:* We become uncomfortable with our emotional responses, and decide whether to push them down, build them up, or turn away from them.

- *Action or inaction based on emotional response:* We respond to whatever triggered the emotion, either by taking some action or by failing to take it.

- *Internal consequences of action taken:* Whether we act or fail to act, we experience internal consequences and feelings that reflect our perception of whether we acted properly, and how we feel about ourselves as a result.

- *Reflection and reinterpretation:* After we acted or failed to act, we reflect on what happened, reinterpreting it after the pressure of the moment subsides and reconstructing it to fit a coherent pattern.

- *Learning and transformation:* We may learn something from our responses and be transformed as a result, or become more skillful in processing our emotions in the future.

As you reflect on these stages in your emotional response to conflict, consider: Where do you get stuck? What keeps you from having a complete experience of your emotions? We now turn to methods you can use to release yourself from the trap of powerful emotions.

Ways of Managing Strong Emotions

Expressing our emotions can provide positive opportunities for change. We are roused by conflict, and when our strongest emotions are triggered, we find we are able to say what we really think or feel or need, and be more authentic. By examining and expressing our feelings, we find out what caused them, which may have been hidden from us. We can learn to open these gateways more easily—causing less destruction to others—and allow whatever we have kept penned up, perhaps for years, to emerge in ways that are constructive and lead to deeper understanding.

While strong emotions can enhance intimacy and creativity and lead to problem solving, they can also become destructive and shift out of control. This may seem paradoxical, yet letting go and turning toward intense or powerful emotions, as opposed to running away from them, is the first step in learning to control them. When we cannot take this step as a result of suppressing our feelings, we easily get stuck in emotional conflicts, allowing the level of intensity to build until it is too high for us to manage. We thus move in an unending cycle, in which we are blind to our feelings, and then compelled to act irrationally.

If you have worked in the same organization over time, you have observed the undercurrents of hidden emotion in the workplace which remain just below the surface yet define and shape relationships, coloring all interactions. These undercurrents accumulate over time, as colleagues store away and continue to nurse emotional hurts they cannot express, release, or resolve. When an opportunity suddenly appears, the accumulation of powerful feelings may have become too great to release safely, or the employee or manager does not know how to do so. Observers, who know only the surface event and not the accumulation behind it, may see it as an overreaction or irrational response.

For this reason, it is important to learn how to manage intense emotions and find ways of expressing them clearly, calmly, and quickly, so that resolution and transformation can be achieved. There are five primary methods you can use to manage your feelings or those of others:

- *Experience your emotions fully, without suppressing them.* We need to start by giving ourselves permission to experience whatever we are feeling completely, without slipping into myths and assumptions that discount or suppress our feelings. When we experience emotions completely, they relax and release their hold.

- *Turn the spotlight of awareness on what you are experiencing and how you are experiencing it.* We need to monitor and observe our emotions carefully over time, trying to understand their elements more precisely and see them more clearly.

- *Accept your feelings nonjudgmentally and see them as sources of information.* We need to accept our deepest feelings without shame or suppression. Our ability to accept these feelings without being agitated by them allows us become more accepting of the emotions of others.

- *Turn the floodlight of analysis on underlying causes.* We need to recognize broadly what causes our emotions, understand their origins in our family patterns and past experiences, and recognize what makes them tick and stop ticking if we are going to communicate them rationally and calmly.

- *Communicate your emotions to others not as judgments or "you" statements but as information and "I" statements.* We need to honestly communicate even our strongest emotions to others and reveal what we are feeling without feeling ashamed, guilty, or pushy. We also need to own them, and not present them as other people's responsibility.

When we use this process of experiencing, observing, accepting, analyzing, and communicating, it becomes easier to release our emotions and see them as sources of learning, change, intimacy, organizational creativity, and transformation rather than triggers for loss of control and negative self-esteem.

These methods can also help your opponent manage and communicate their emotions. For example, by asking a series of questions, you can give the person yelling at you permission to completely experience whatever they are feeling, become more observant and accepting of their feelings, discover its causes, and communicate what they are becoming without yelling.

By asking these questions, you subtly shift attention away from parts of the brain that process emotions to parts that observe, accept, and analyze experience. If you nonjudgmentally accept yourself and what you are feeling and bring yourself to see your feelings as useful sources of information, you can communicate what you feel without becoming overwhelmed by its intensity.

In one conflict resolution session we conducted between a female manager and her male subordinate, we noticed a pattern in the words and phrases he used to describe her—she was "controlling," "punishing," and "bossy." He was unable to solve the problem because "she won't let me," "I have to ask for permission," and similar expressions. We read these words back to him and asked if they reminded him of anyone. He said, "Oh my god, it's my mother!" At that moment, the conflict literally disappeared. This allowed his manager to recognize that she was unknowingly responding exactly as his own mother had responded to him. They were then able to reach a number of agreements on working together that were successful. They reached a resolution—and the beginning of a real transformation—only by moving through their emotional responses to an analysis of their origins.

In this case as in others, the issues that upset us do not only concern the other person, but connect with unresolved issues from our past. Through analysis, we can reach a deeper understanding of why these emotions are so powerful. Strong emotions result from accumulated, unfinished conflicts that other people remind us we have not fully resolved.

The two of us once worked in an organization where the director had asked for feedback on her leadership skills by asking staff to complete 3x5 cards with anonymous comments. When she read their responses, she felt attacked and defensive. We spent considerable time listening to her pain and anger. We asked whether she felt she was in the right job, and she started to cry. She said she *knew* she was in the wrong job and couldn't seem to do anything to please her staff or her superiors. Her tears revealed her hidden sadness and shame. She admitted she had chosen the wrong career, was desperately unhappy, and resented having had to move from a city she loved to one she disliked.

Once she revealed her true feelings to us, rather than being defensive and angry toward her staff, she was able to thank them for their honesty. We reviewed with her different ways of managing strong emotions, and she was able to improve her responses. Unnecessary conflicts with her staff were resolved, and a problem-solving process was initiated that resulted in her being offered a more appropriate position in the organization in the city she loved. She was happy to return home, and her staff grew in understanding, teamwork, and skills as a result of working through these emotions.

Behind the Mask: Hidden Markers
in Emotional Communication

As conflicts escalate, emotions tend to spiral out of control. One of our clients described his feelings when confronted by his boss's anger as like "drinking from a fire hose." We can all learn to manage our emotions, minimize angry outbursts, and respond more skillfully when they occur. If we can sidestep a powerful stream of emotion or let it pass through us, we are able to see who is behind the hose and why it has achieved such force. We will then be able to act more strategically.

When we are confronted with intense emotion, we lose track of what is going on beneath the surface. This is partly the purpose of emotional outbursts. When we feel stunned, frightened, or trapped in a volatile drama, we are unable to see behind the mask, allowing those who express strong emotions to hide behind bluster and intensity and distract us from seeing what is hidden, or doing something strategic about it. People often become emotional because they are afraid we will see them as they fear they really are, or that their true, intimate, vulnerable feelings will be exposed.

We offer the following glimpse behind emotional masks to help you discover messages different from the ones presented by the speaker. See if you recognize the masks you wear, along with those worn by your opponent, and search for what is behind the facade when you communicate emotionally.

- *Accusation as confession:* It is often the case that people who feel guilty about something they have done accuse others of having done it, as a way of diverting (or even attracting) attention. Have you accused others of things you did yourself?

- *Insult as denial:* Every insult is a choice that says more about the insulter than the one insulted. For example, if X says that Y is lazy, it is likely X is hard-working and does not give himself permission to take time off or relax. The insult says more about the jealousy of the insulter than the character of the insulted. Think of the insults you use to describe your opponent. What do these insults reveal about you?

- *Anger as vulnerability:* Anger is partly a request for communication or connection and partly an effort to create distance or boundaries. Both result from being highly vulnerable, either to the person or the message. Are you vulnerable when you're angry? To what and who? Why?

- *Defensiveness as egoism:* Often when people become defensive, it is because they mistakenly assume the conflict or disagreement is directed at them, or because they are unable to separate their ideas from their identity. Have you ever thought someone meant something personal, only to discover it wasn't about you at all? How can you take responsibility for your role in the conflict without making it be about you?

- *Withdrawal as rage:* Those who withdraw from conflict may do so to silence uncontrollable rage, based on an assumption that there is no alternative other than withdrawal. Have you ever withdrawn in a silent, punishing rage? Can you think of a safe way of communicating your anger without withdrawing?

- *Passivity as aggression:* Public compliance often masks private defiance. Passivity does not mean agreement; it may instead be an aggressive act, using inertia to block momentum. Sometimes, the victim role is used to disguise a power play. Have you ever played the victim? Have you ever used passive behavior to gain power over others? Has this created satisfying relationships?

- *Attack as smoke screen:* Sometimes, people attack others to draw attention from their own failures. Children get into arguments or make blunders to draw their conflicting parents' attention away from each other. Do you use attack as a smoke screen to hide your vulnerabilities?

- *Apathy or cynicism as caring:* Apathy and cynicism sometimes "protest too much," revealing hurt feelings based on deep caring and frustration that so little has been accomplished. Have

you ever been cynical when what you wanted was the opposite? What would happen if you became vulnerable and
showed you cared?

German novelist Thomas Mann wrote in his novel *Buddenbrooks* about the connection between the energy of opposition and
a secret attraction for the very thing we are fighting against, writing: "We are most likely to get angry and excited in our opposition
to some idea when we ourselves are not quite certain of our position
and are inwardly tempted to take the other side."

Here we find managers who accuse employees of "goofing off"
but are unhappy at work and would secretly like to goof off themselves. We also see employees who oppose their supervisors' use of
power but would secretly love to exercise it themselves. We find
people who argue dogmatically when they know there is something
true in what the other person is saying.

Do you feel yourself drawn to the ideas or behaviors of those
you oppose? What masks do you use in your conflicts? Are you
using your arguments to achieve some result that is hidden? Are
you using a mask to hide some deeper emotion? How have masks
helped or hindered you in your conflicts? What would it take to
drop them completely?

Taking Off the Masks and Revealing Hidden Emotion

When we hide behind a mask or send confusing signals about our
real desires or intentions, we send distorted or double messages to
others. This causes considerable damage to ourselves and our relationships. It is difficult to hear our innermost voices when we mask
who we really are.

Masks produce distorted behavior partly because we are afraid
we are not good enough, and feel we need the thick skin of ego to
protect our deepest vulnerabilities. This motivates us to keep our
masks in place at all costs. Once we have them on, we become ac-
customed to them and even more frightened to take them off.

Jim, one of our favorite clients, has a brusque, blunt style—almost like a street fighter, with a quick wit and willingness to call things as they are. He asked his organization to become more empowered and self-managing, and was willing to give up his top-down, command-and-control behaviors. His frustration increased with the unwillingness of his staff to "accept responsibility" and "step up to the plate." As a result, he yelled at people, telling them to "get it or get out." He raised his voice to a fever pitch and delivered ultimatums, shouting that if they didn't get empowered they would be fired.

After a devastating meeting, we told him he was sending mixed messages, and that angry ultimatums were not encouraging his staff to do what he wanted. He listened carefully but did not respond. A week later, we received a call from a team member who had been at that meeting. She was in a state of shock. Jim had called a special meeting to apologize for his statements. In a softened, gentle voice, he revealed his passion for what they were all doing, his fear of letting go, and at the same time, his desire to do so and move on to more challenging work.

His mask of anger was a projection of his fear that failure would result if he released control. By opening up and becoming more vulnerable, he communicated his desire to turn control over to his direct reports. His willingness to take off his mask and stop blaming them set the tone for what followed. His staff took the reins and designed a series of meetings for the leadership group, then for the entire organization. This initiative dramatically shifted responsibility for leadership and results to the teams. Jim played a key role in these meetings, acting as a participant, leader, and fellow team member rather than a boss.

Jim broke through his anger by using "I" statements instead of accusing "you" or "them" of misdeeds. "I" statements help communicate strong emotion by labeling feelings as belonging to the person who has them, rather than blaming them on the person whose behavior accidentally or intentionally inspired them.

There is a vast difference between "You are a filthy slob!" and "Leaving dirty coffee cups makes me feel you don't respect me or my need to work in a clean environment." The second statement expresses real emotions and at the same time opens the door to negotiation and possible resolution. The first, by contrast, simply dumps our frustrations. It might cause the hearer to wash the cups, but it might also stiffen their resistance, perhaps leading them to break a few cups and putting the whole relationship at risk.

Using "I" statements gives us an opportunity to release ourselves from feeling controlled by our emotions. It allows the other person to hear the reality of their behavior's impact on us. It encourages us to put all the cards on the table, but not scatter them chaotically or attribute the blame to others. It encourages each side to take responsibility for their emotions and search for solutions to shared problems.

Virginia Satir, one of the founders of the field of family therapy, delved deeply into masks. She identified a series of behaviors she called "power plays." Power plays are surface actions intended to distract others from self-doubts they want to hide, both from themselves and others. Satir identified the deeper levels of emotion underlying each power play. She pointed to outward behavior, indicated the inner feelings that lay on the surface, and speculated on the deeper feelings hidden behind the mask.

What Lies Beneath the Mask

Behaviors	Expressions
Placating:	
Outward expression	I'm always doing everything wrong!
Inside, surface	I must keep everyone happy so they will love me!
Inside, deeper	I'm really unlovable. . . . If I don't placate others they won't love me.
Blaming:	
Outward expression	You never do anything right!

| Inside, surface | Nobody gives a damn about what I care about. Unless I keep yelling nobody will do a thing! |
| Inside, deeper | I'm really unlovable. . . . I'm the one to blame. |

Super-Reasonable:

Outward expression	One needs to face the fact that one makes errors in one's life!
Inside, surface	I must let everyone know how smart I am. Logic and ideas are all that count!
Inside, deeper	I'm really unlovable. . . . If I were not so logical, I would get lost in my emotions.

Irrelevant:

Outward expression	Hey! Anybody got a joke?
Inside, surface	I will get attention no matter what extremes I have to go to!
Inside, deeper	I'm really unlovable. . . . If I don't keep changing the topic, people will notice my faults.

In all of these cases, the deeper feeling is one of being unloved and unlovable. This is the core belief that drives our need to create masks and engage in power plays, and fuels the innumerable conflicts that fill our lives.

Behaviors That Trigger Anger

Anger is difficult to fathom, partly because we do not always understand its true source. The two of us interviewed a manager of a small entrepreneurial company who was well known for being angry and disgruntled. He quickly raised the temperature of his responses, becoming more and more angry for reasons we could not identify, and seemed unrelated to our behavior or comments.

We tried to respond logically, but—as you may have discovered— logical behavior can result in increasing anger rather than reducing it. We tried to uncover the source of his anger, but he wouldn't reveal it. Finally, we told him we would not continue the conversation if he could not control his anger. Once we set clear limits, he relaxed and calmed his voice. We probed to discover the source of his anger, and he recited several incidents in the business that left him feeling isolated and besieged. We initiated a group conflict resolution process that brought the management team together to agree on ground rules for their future interactions with one another, and jointly focus on building the company.

While it is true that other people engage in behaviors that trigger our anger, this does not mean we are not responsible for our reactions. No one can "make" us mad. There's always a choice, as in the experience with the manager. The two of us could have gotten angry and stormed out, but that would have proven we were hostile. Instead, we surfaced the manager's anger, expressed our discomfort with it, helped him calm down, established ground rules for our conversation, asked him respectfully what upset him, listened empathically while he spoke, and brought his colleagues together to address the issues that aggravated him.

What Triggers Your Anger?

We encourage you to explore your triggers or flash points, so you can say to yourself, "Here comes a trigger for my anger. I don't need to react. I have a choice. I can choose to respond indirectly rather than directly and discover the reason for my anger, which I may be able to do something about."

The Many Uses of Anger

There are many good reasons for getting angry that are legitimate and understandable, many of which we have mentioned. For example, it is reasonable to get angry when our personal space is invaded and we feel violated, or when we feel our needs are not being met or recognized by others, or when we are treated disrespectfully. Anger creates a boundary around us, commands recognition, even encourages respect.

Sometimes anger toward others is merely a projection of our own low self-esteem, anger at ourselves, or false expectations. If this is at the core of our anger, instead of openly and honestly communicating what we expect, or recognizing that our expectations are either unjustified or hidden and therefore unattainable, we suffer silently and blame others for not meeting them. When couples separate, they often use anger and anger-creating behaviors as a way of releasing themselves from the pain of losing their false expectations and admitting responsibility for the failure of their relationship. Paradoxically, anger is also a way of giving the other person permission to leave when they otherwise wouldn't.

Whenever anyone involuntarily leaves a place where they have worked for many years, anger is likely to explode. The employee is likely to feel mistreated, misunderstood, and betrayed, blame the organization for being unfair, feel their colleagues did not support them, and think their manager betrayed them. Often they are right. Yet these employees pay an additional price for never looking at their own skills, responsibilities, and complicities or recognizing their need to continue learning, growing, and improving even when they think their job is secure.

One powerful source of anger is its usefulness in creating intimacy. Anger strips away the mask and forces us into the present. It demands our attention, and is a deeply intimate emotion. It generates negative intimacy when positive intimacy has become impossible.

Another source of anger occurs when we feel bad or worthless. We may decide to relieve our misery and try to paint ourselves no worse than others, sometimes by forcing them into anger so we will feel or look better. When we speak judgmentally about others, it is often because we cannot accept the negative side of ourselves and want to bring them to our own perceived level.

In the workplace, anger is often simply a way of pointing out what needs to be improved or is not working. We use anger to gain attention, recognition, acknowledgment, affection, and results we are unable to obtain through our achievements. Anger can be a compensation for being paid or treated unfairly, and is often used to cement alliances and friendships with others in place of more positive interests, under the theory that "the enemy of my enemy is my friend."

Anger can be a distorted expression of fear, guilt, shame, or humiliation. When children do something dangerous, parents usually respond with anger instead of frankly acknowledging their fear, both as a way of forcing their attention to focus on safety and as a way of releasing their fear and guilt, which originated in caring. As we can see from this example, beneath anger is fear, beneath fear lies the possibility of pain and guilt, and beneath pain and guilt lies love.

These parental feelings lead to four entirely different conversations. For example, it is possible to yell angrily at your child, "Don't do that!" It is equally possible to speak from your fear, saying, "That scared the hell out of me!" Or to speak from your pain and guilt, saying, "It would make me feel terrible if anything bad happened to you." Or to speak from your love, saying, "I love you so much I would feel awful if anything bad happened to you, and that scares me so much I get angry and yell at you." Notice the difference between these alternative communications and the emotions they will elicit in the child to whom they're directed.

Anger is often a cry for help, a need to be heard when no one is listening. It can be used to cover a weakness or divert attention from a sensitive subject by distracting others from a difficult topic.

Getting angry is useful in getting one's own way—aggressive negotiators use it to throw the other side off balance, and "command and control" managers use it to secure a subordinate's compliance or divert attention from a failure. Anger is cleansing, helping us release negative feelings and the shame of victimization by dumping them on others.

Exploring Anger

Until anger is recognized and addressed directly, we cannot resolve the underlying reasons for it. Until we address those underlying reasons, giving it up will appear like surrender, we will be unable to resolve the reasons that gave rise to it, and the conflict may spiral out of control or never reach settlement or resolution.

Once people understand their reasons for being angry, they can successfully identify the behaviors that are triggering it. They can then communicate their anger to their opponent—along with requests for changed behavior and proposals for resolution. At that point their anger begins to dissolve automatically, and the conflict can become a source of learning and growth.

Hidden Assumptions and Beliefs About Anger

Behind our angry responses lie a set of largely unexamined beliefs, feelings, and assumptions. As you consider these underlying issues, notice which ones fuel your anger, and whether you are willing to give up the assumptions they rest on, or question their validity.

For example, we become angry when we believe we have been treated unfairly or unjustly. We assume the person with whom we are angry caused us to be treated badly. We believe our unfair treatment was not natural or inevitable or a result of our own actions, but was a conscious choice made by another. These actions seem wrong or evil to us, since there was a clear alternative. Yet when we examine the other person's underlying reality, we often discover this assumption is reversed.

When others claim they do not understand why we are angry or how they could have caused or contributed to our problems, we assume either that they are lying or that if they really understood these things, they would act differently. We believe they must therefore be evil or ignorant. Yet often they did not have a choice, or the choice was not apparent to them, or they had different interests.

Certain that others have acted deliberately against us, we use anger as a way of making them understand through direct experience what it feels like to be treated unfairly. Anger is an effort to communicate what we really feel, to get the other person to change their behavior and mitigate or correct their unfairness. In the process, we end up treating others unfairly and repeating the behaviors we find objectionable. We rarely clearly and honestly communicate our objections in words the other person can hear.

We have a hard time expressing our anger to someone who is superior to us in a hierarchy. Therefore, when we express our anger, we communicate that the other person is not our superior, but an equal, or inferior to us. If they express their anger back to us, they prove our point.

We feel we have no right to express our anger to some people, and others have no right to express their anger to us, based on the lack of depth in our relationship. When they do, we become angrier. Anger marks our perception that our relationship is broken, and signals to the other person that we need attention or affection, even as we drive them away.

We use anger to test our relationships, and deepen, solidify, or break them apart. We assume that if people respect us they will accept our anger, and that their anger toward us confirms the existence and importance of our relationship to them.

The closer the relationship, the more we believe we have a right to get angry without breaking the relationship apart. Yet we also use anger to drive away people who care about us, and do not see how awful we really are.

We experience anger as a barometer of caring, and as long as the anger is there, so is the caring. When our relationship is ending, we would rather the other person feel angry than indifferent, as we see this as a sign of caring.

When our relationship has really ended, we feel we no longer have a right to express our anger to the other person and no longer want their anger toward us. As long as we feel angry at them or they feel anger at us, we feel connected to them. When we stop being angry, we release ourselves.

When we feel powerless or helpless, or that we have no right to express our anger directly, we find indirect ways of expressing it. Satire, emotional withdrawal, passive-aggressive behavior, resistance to change, and noncooperation are all ways of expressing anger without admitting to it.

When we are angry, we receive attention from others and get what we want. We also feel powerful because they changed their behavior in response to our feelings. When others become angry in response, we feel less guilty about being angry at them. We are glad they have not made us look bad by being the only one angry. If others do not get angry in response, we feel guilty or become angrier because they seem to be saying they are superior to us, or that we don't have a right to express our anger, or that they don't care about us.

Our anger makes us feel righteous and important. It justifies our failures and diverts attention from our faults. It allows us to indirectly express our pain and fear without feeling vulnerable in the presence of people we do not trust. It motivates us to be true to our cause, and blinds us to the price we pay or the way it makes us less effective in achieving our goals.

While these beliefs and assumptions fuel our anger, most have little or nothing to do with the person with whom we are angry. Mostly our anger is based on our own issues. We are angry, for example, at behaviors we would secretly like to pursue ourselves, or behaviors we do not like in ourselves. We may want to prevent ourselves from doing what we dislike in others, or from tolerating other people's disrespectful behavior toward us.

Releasing anger feels better than holding it inside. The anger we hang on to turns against us. Expressing it directs the pain outward, but often ends up hurting the people we care about or want to reach the most. There is an alternative, which is to release the anger without inflicting it either on ourselves or others. To do so, we need to understand the deeper reasons for our anger, and why we should let them go.

Giving Up Anger

There are a number of paradoxes regarding anger. Just as it creates intimacy, it also sets up boundaries. It helps focus attention on solving problems, and it is a destructive force that leaves greater problems in its wake. Every one of the positive payoffs from anger or conflict can be achieved more skillfully and lastingly without it.

It is important to recognize the dark side of anger and not surrender to it. Our challenge is to find ways of getting people's attention, achieving results, creating intimacy, and securing assistance by asking for these things directly. Just as there are many reasons for anger, there are many reasons for giving it up in favor of more effective tactics. Here are some of the reasons to give up your anger:

- Anger is a form of ongoing connection with someone you dislike and probably do not want in your life.
- Anger always injures both its target and the person who directs it.
- Anger is often an externalization of anger against yourself. In this case, forgiving the other person means forgiving yourself.
- Anger creates the "other-as-enemy" and does not allow for empathy, or the "other-as-friend."
- Anger converts the person who uses it from being a victim to being a perpetrator, which undermines the sympathy otherwise due as a result of the original injury.

- Anger can be abandoned without giving up what we want; all we surrender are ways of getting what we want that are destructive to others.

- Anger is actually a reflection of weakness and vulnerability to others. When we rely on our internal strength, others' actions need not bother us.

- Anger creates a barrier against our own vulnerability, a defense against the most intimate and important part of ourselves.

- Anger is a kind of energy that lives in us, and destroys our lives from the inside.

- Anger saps the energy we need to live in the present and plan for the future, to be available for change and personal transformation. This energy is released when we let anger go.

Methods for Managing Your Anger

Being able to manage anger is an important life-skill that can help you dissipate its self-destructive effects and move toward resolution in your conflicts. Here are some techniques to manage your anger:

- *Own it.* Don't blame anyone else for your anger. Be responsible for your own intense feelings and for openly and constructively expressing them.

- *Discover the underlying reasons for it.* Ask yourself why you are angry, what triggered your emotion, and what deeper emotions or prior experiences are connected to it.

- *Share your feelings and perceptions nonjudgmentally.* Drop all self-justifications, defenses, and judgments you are using to support your anger. Consider avoiding statements such as "you are wrong" and clearly indicate what was done that made you mad. Use "I" statements, report your feelings, say where you think they came from in you, and identify what triggered your emotion.

- *Ask questions to discover whether your perceptions are accurate.* Without making judgments or fixing blame, ask questions to find out more about what happened, so you can get to the bottom of what triggered your anger. Ask if the other person *meant* to treat you disrespectfully, and if so, why.

- *Focus on solving the problem rather than blaming others for it.* Define the problem as an "it" rather than a "you." Brainstorm possible solutions with your opponent. Take a problem-solving approach to the underlying reasons for your emotional response to the conflict.

- *Avoid responding defensively.* Do not fall into the trap of defending your behavior. Consider the possibility that you may have been wrong, or that you and your opponent may both be right. Explore these possibilities openly. At the very least, if the other person doesn't understand, recognize that you did not communicate your feelings skillfully.

- *Ask clarifying questions.* Ask the other person—keeping your own tone nondefensive and avoiding hostility—to clarify what they meant. Ask if your assumptions about what they are saying or doing are correct, and allow them to explain. Listen more carefully if you were not correct the first time.

- *Clarify your expectations.* Say exactly, specifically, and in detail what you expect. If the other person cannot meet your expectations, you can always negotiate more realistic expectations, so they will be clearer about what you really want.

- *Take a time out.* Step away from the interaction for a few moments to reflect on whether it is getting out of hand. Determine whether it is possible to say the same things in a way that can be heard.

- *Ask for help.* Ask a third person to mediate or facilitate your communication. People are often more polite when company comes to dinner.

- *Apologize and start over.* An apology is a declaration of ownership of what is not working, and a request for improvement. Your apology is an acknowledgment that your relationship with the other person is more important than being right.

As you consider these methods and possible ways of using them in your conflicts, notice which ones are the hardest to swallow. The ones where you balk may require focus and work. The last, apologizing and starting over, takes considerable skill. What would it take for you to apologize to the other person in your conflict? Consider the following alternative ways of doing so.

Alternative Ways of Apologizing

A little apology goes a long way. Sometimes, the best way of defusing anger is to apologize for misunderstandings or miscommunications that occurred, and for any discomfort your opponent experienced as a result of your anger. Apology does not mean you were wrong or bad. It means you understand what the other person experienced, and are sorry for anything you may have done to contribute to their discomfort. An apology is a way of saying "I value our relationship more than I value being right."

An apology signifies willingness to take responsibility for your behavior and contribution to the conflict. Your acknowledgment of responsibility enables your adversary to follow suit, and lead to a resolution of the dispute and a melting away of the anger that kept it going. Here are a number of different ways of apologizing from which you can choose.

- Make your regrets about what happened completely clear. "I am very, very sorry for what I did to cause the problem." Include specifics.
- Take full responsibility for what happened. "It was totally my fault."

- Specify the behaviors that were wrong or offensive. "I really apologize for having—" Again, be specific but neutral. "I'm sorry I embarrassed you in front of your staff" is a statement that works; "I'm sorry I let everybody see what a horse's ass you are" doesn't.

- Focus on the events and results that you regret. "I'm sorry you weren't told about this in advance. It must have upset you."

- Indicate your understanding that there was an alternative. "I could have handled it differently."

- Acknowledge the feelings that resulted. "I'm sorry for the pain this must have caused you."

- Ask for forgiveness, and wait until you receive it. "Can you forgive me?"

- Indicate what you could have done to prevent the problem. "I wish I'd spoken to you before this happened."

- Recognize the positive results of the error. "This has been a real learning experience for me."

- Make good on your promises quickly so the other party will see an immediate result. "I will see that your name is put on the distribution list today so this doesn't happen again."

- Ask what they need from you. "What can I do to make it up to you?"

- Negotiate an agreement for future forgiveness. "What would it take for you to forgive me?"

Once you have chosen one, consider why you chose it, and rate it on a scale of one to ten, with ten being highest in authenticity, humility, and forgiveness. If you did not choose an apology that was a ten, ask yourself why it is so difficult to make an apology that is strong and unambiguous.

The only way out of strong emotions is through them. By running away or suppressing them, we create internal knots. These knots sap our energies, keep us focused on the past, and diminish our capacity to live in the present or plan for the future. We then get locked into behaviors we do not like and are unable to transcend.

The primary purpose of working through emotions is to transcend them. Genuine transcendence comes when we own our emotions, and by owning them, release ourselves from their grip. As writer Milton Glaser has eloquently stated, transcendence is the primary task we are given in life: "All life is about transcendence. If you're ugly you have to transcend your ugliness; if you're beautiful you have to transcend your beauty; if you're poor you have to transcend your poverty; if you're rich you have to transcend your wealth. . . . You get nothing at birth except things to transcend."

If we want to transcend our problems, learn our life lessons, and take on a more advanced level of conflict, we need to release ourselves from their emotional grip. Once we have become free of their fiery control, we can use them to probe more deeply beneath the surface of our conflicts, and in the process uncover their hidden meanings—as we explore in the next chapter.

Path Four

Search Beneath the Surface
for Hidden Meaning

An autobiography is the truest of all books, for
while it inevitably consists mainly of extinctions of
the truth, shirkings of the truth, partial revealments
of the truth, with hardly an instance of plain
straight truth, the remorseless truth is there,
between the lines.

—*Mark Twain*

Resolving conflict is like unearthing an archeological treasure, painstakingly brushing away the surface to reveal deeper layers that have lain hidden under dust and mud. It is like looking beneath the water's surface to discover an iceberg, most of which cannot be seen.

We rarely take time to carefully excavate the deeper truths in our conflicts, mostly because our attention is focused on the mistakes and misdeeds of others, or on our own emotions and victimization. Most of our communications and nearly all of our conflicts are *not at all* about the topics we are urgently arguing over. The deeper we go, the more there is to see.

There is a vast difference in conflict between surface appearances and hidden realities, what we talk about publicly and what we secretly think or feel, the issues we address and those we conceal. It is not the superficial layers but the deeper, more mysterious ones hidden from view that unlock our conflicts and catalyze our transformations. When we reach below the surface and find the source or center of our conflict, it opens up, revealing its hidden truths, and enabling us to resolve it and break free of its grip.

In novels, plays, and movies, authors often use a narrator or character or chorus as a "third voice" to clarify inner thoughts, deeper motivations, and hidden feelings. In conflict, we need a third voice to remind us of our own deeper issues and reveal the hidden truth of others' experiences. The purpose of this chapter is to help you discover and develop your third voice, so it will guide you the next time you are in conflict. The path we are proposing may seem perilous to you. We only ask that you honestly observe yourself while you are in conflict, holding nothing back. Observation, acceptance, and skill are the means by which you make yourself free.

When you argue over trivial issues, such as who is responsible for a mistake, you may actually be arguing about something else. You may be responsible for the error, yet feel the other person is being hypercritical, or asked you to do something demeaning, or did not request your input beforehand. On the other hand, they may be responsible for the error, yet feel you are being disrespectful or not listening to them, or they may be too embarrassed to admit making a mistake. You may both be responsible, yet remind each other of difficult family members, or trigger memories of similar disputes in the past, or behave in ways that make each other angry or uncomfortable.

Regardless of which is the real reason, you will have become involved in an argument over superficial issues, rather than engaging in open, honest communication about real problems. These arguments often appear silly even to participants, because the surface disputes are trivial, superficial, and pointless compared to the real issue.

What is at stake when we fight is not the dirty coffee cups or who gets what kind of chair to sit in, but our capacity for mutual respect, integrity, inner truth and honest relationships with others. What is also at stake is our learning and growth, and the possibility of transcending our conflicts and using them to transform our personal and organizational lives.

The Iceberg of Conflict

One way of picturing the hidden layers and complexities of conflict is through the metaphor of the iceberg, as depicted in the following chart. You may want to identify additional layers besides the ones we cite, to reveal what is below the surface for you.

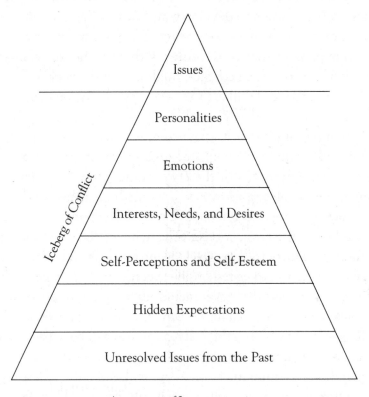

Awareness of Interconnection

Exploring Your Iceberg

Each level of the iceberg represents something that does not appear on the surface, yet adds weight and immobility to our arguments when we are in conflict. Beneath the iceberg, the chart identifies an "awareness of interconnection," meaning that we all have the capacity, when we go deep enough and are not stuck on the surface of our conflicts, to experience genuine empathy and awareness of our interconnection with each other—including the person who is upsetting us.

To understand the deeper layers of your iceberg and get to an awareness of interconnection, consider a conflict in which you are now engaged. Try to identify the specific issues, problems, and feelings that exist for you at each level of the iceberg. As you probe deeper, notice whether your definition of the conflict changes, and how it evolves. Become aware of any emotions that emerge as you look deeper. Fear or resistance to these feelings can keep the conflict locked in place and block you from reaching deeper levels. Allow yourself to experience these feelings, whatever they are, and identify them to yourself or to someone you trust, so you can let them go. Try to answer the following questions for yourself and your opponent:

- *Issues:* What issues appear on the surface in your conflict?

- *Personalities:* Are differences between your personalities contributing to misunderstanding and tension? If so, what are they and how do they operate?

- *Emotions:* What emotions are having an impact on your reactions? How are they doing so? Are you communicating your emotions responsibly, or suppressing them?

- *Interests, needs, desires:* How are you proposing to solve the conflict? Why is that your proposal? What deeper concerns are driving the conflict? What do you really want? Why? What needs or desires, if satisfied, would enable you to feel good about the outcome? Why is that important? What does getting what you want have to do with the conflict?

- *Self-perceptions and self-esteem:* How do you feel about yourself and your behavior when you are engaged in the conflict? What do you see as your strengths and weaknesses?

- *Hidden expectations:* What are your primary expectations of your opponent? Of yourself? Have you clearly, openly, and honestly communicated your expectations to the other person? What would happen if you did? How might you release yourself from false expectations?

- *Unresolved issues from the past:* Does this conflict remind you of anything from your past relationships? Are there any unfinished issues remaining from the past that keep you locked in this conflict? Why?

Notice whether your understanding of the conflict changed as you moved through different levels, and how your feelings about it, yourself, and your opponent might evolve further if you continue. Now ask yourself, "How much of my answers have I shared with my opponent?" If there is anything you have not shared, why have you chosen not to share it? Is there any way you could share it?

Applying Your Knowledge of the Iceberg

Picture a conversation, however difficult, in which you share your deeper thoughts and insights with your opponent. Practice both parts of the conversation in your own mind or with a colleague, or write them down on paper. Notice any shifts in your feelings as you envision each part of the conversation, and how the other person might respond. After rehearsing, try it in reality, and see how close you get to the way you imagined it.

Most people who are at impasse have never met with their opponent to have an open, honest discussion—even of the surface issues in their conflict. When we ask people who are in conflict why they have not communicated important information about the deeper levels of their iceberg to their opponents, they say it is because the other person is unwilling to listen, or would not be interested in the information, or is untrustworthy. We then ask the following question: "Are you withholding your information because of who your opponent is, or because you are unwilling to risk becoming vulnerable in their presence?" Often, it is ourselves we are protecting, precisely because we fear what will be revealed in the honest communication that, at a deeper level, is what we want most. We cover our fear and vulnerability with rationalizations of lack of interest and lack of trust, and in the end deprive ourselves of an authentic communication with someone who may be as afraid of vulnerability as we are.

Consider another question: How will they ever start to listen or become interested or trustworthy if we don't provide them with information, so they can understand who we are and why we're upset? Getting to the real issues has to start with someone, and it might as well be you since you're the only one you can control. When you do, the other person usually starts to listen, becomes interested, and behaves in a more trustworthy way. If they don't, at least you feel better and more self-confident, because you know you acted with integrity.

It is always difficult to know what is going on below the surface with yourself, let alone with others, particularly when you are mesmerized by conflict and operating in a semiconscious state. In your confusion, you can easily become defensive or aggressive. Your best option in getting below the surface is to probe your own iceberg, and be willing to reveal your deeper issues to the other person. By revealing yourself, you invite similar behavior in return, thereby breaking the conflict system.

Even then you may not succeed. Each of us is so well defended that the information we need to resolve the conflict is often unknown or unavailable to us, and we cannot describe what we do not know. You may hide this information even from yourself because it is connected to some highly charged issue or unresolved conflict from your past that you do not want to face. You may think you are in touch with what is going on, yet be completely off-track.

Hypnotized by Conflict

The past is powerfully present in all our conflicts and communications, yet we are false historians in describing our conflicts. We frequently do not even know what we are angry about, which may have originated in some incident that happened years ago. We become angry at others when we are frightened, in pain, or are trying to protect ourselves. We may want to divert attention from shameful incidents in our past or heal our wounds, but find it difficult to say what is on our subconscious minds.

Instead, we operate semiconsciously much of the time, especially when we are in conflict. We react to unseen forces that are detectable only because our reactions are out of proportion to what caused them. We have all been socialized from infancy into ways of experiencing and interpreting the world around us. We live in a hypnotic trance, beginning in childhood. In our early years our families shape and color what we see and blind us to everything else. Growing up means removing our blinders and seeing for ourselves.

Our families are not the only places where we engage in trance-like behavior. Many of us function in semi-hypnotic states at work, with friends, while driving, exercising, even reading this book. We are easily hypnotized by emotions in conflict, and our attention distracted from the real issues. We may be unable to think or speak about them or even remember what they are until we go below the surface.

Steps to Get Below the Surface

Novelist Ursula Hegi chronicled the rise of fascism and life in a small village in Germany before and during World War II in her novel, *Stones from the River*, where she describes the difficulty of telling the truth when silence is the norm: "It took courage for the few, who would preserve the texture of the truth, not to let its fibers slip beneath the web of silence and collusion which people—often with the best of intentions—spun to sustain and protect one another."

How do we break this web of silence and collusion and discover what is beneath the surface when everyone is behaving emotionally, and no one is willing to risk honestly saying what is going on? Here are some ways of getting below the surface of your conflicts:

- Start by focusing on yourself and understanding more about your own iceberg of conflict.
- Use curiosity, open-ended questions, and empathic listening as probes to take you beneath the surface.
- Take a risk by bringing a deep level of honesty to what you see, hear, and observe, recognizing that the more honest you are with yourself, the deeper you can go with others.
- Be willing to accept whatever you find beneath the surface without shame, anger, or judgment.

As you gain more perspective on your own subterranean issues, you will grow more confident and skillful, and be ready to take the next step, which is to ask questions of your opponent so you can move together to address the issues that lie below the surface.

A simple way of doing so is to simply become curious and willing to ask naive, even silly questions. You may avoid asking questions that appear stupid or seem to have obvious answers—but these are the best questions, and posing them can dramatically alter the conflict. We suggest you not censor yourself but let your questions flow, with only one warning: a probing, attacking, prying style of questioning will prove counterproductive. Begin by asking permission, use a gentle, respectful, empathic approach, and listen nonjudgmentally to the answers. Invite your antagonist to join you in exploring underlying issues, and welcome the resulting insight, no matter which of you comes up with it.

Here are some questions you can ask to deepen dialogue and turn the attention of the person being questioned toward solutions. These questions can be asked by managers or employees, teachers or principals, parents or children, neighbors or officials, or anyone who wants to get below the surface:

- "What do you think I did that contributed to the conflict?"
- "Can you give me a specific example?"
- "How did you feel when I did that?"

- "Can you tell me more what bothers you about what I did?"
- "What did you do to contribute to the conflict?"
- "Would you like to know how that made me feel?"
- "What did you mean when you said—?"
- "Why is that a problem for you?"
- "What is the worst part of what happened for you?"
- "Why don't you tell me your experience and I will listen, and then I would like to tell you mine."
- "I hope you can hear what I am saying without getting upset or angry or confused. Will you let me know if this starts to bother you so I can communicate with you better?"
- "If you had it all to do over again, what would you do differently?" "Why?" "Would you be willing to start over again right now and do it differently?"
- "What is most important to you in solving this problem?"
- "What would you suggest I do to solve my part of the problem?"
- "Can you think of any solutions that might be acceptable to both of us?"
- "What would it take for you to let go of this conflict and feel the issues have really been resolved?"
- "How would you like me to communicate with you in the future if there are any more problems?" "What should I say?"
- "Would you be interested in hearing how I would like you to communicate with me?"
- "What kind of relationship would you like to have with me?"
- "How would you like this to end?" "Why?"

Discovering the Invisible

One of the effects of conflict hypnosis and superficial awareness is that even explicit and overt behaviors can be ignored and suddenly become invisible. When we are locked in conflict, we hear and see only whatever supports our position and ignore everything else as though it were invisible or nonexistent. We may even pretend the other person does not exist, and look right through them, as if we were passing a stranger in the street.

Our lack of awareness of these "invisibles" occurs in small ways in everyday life. For example, look around you right now. What do you see? Perhaps you see a table and chairs, a desk and telephone, grass and trees. Here are some of the things you may not have noticed, a set of elements, forces, and connections that are *invisible*, yet nonetheless link you to your environment, to others, and to your conflicts:

- *Empty space:* The open spaces in the room that allow you to feel free to move, the spaces between your words that allow their meaning to be understood, and the emptiness in your mind that allows you to hear your opponent

- *Processes:* The process of reading in which you are engaged right now, or the process of communication with your opponent

- *Relationships:* The relationship between you and the subject matter of this book, or between you and your partner in conflict

- *Emotions:* The fear of searching below the surface of your conflict, or trying out some of the ideas we are suggesting

- *Ideas:* The idea that something might exist in a room yet be invisible, or that there may be more to your conflict than proving you were right and your opponent was wrong

- *Intentions:* The intention to not let anyone get away with treating you this way, or to resolve your conflict or become a better communicator

- *Expectations:* The expectation that the other person will listen to you calmly, or that they will not be receptive

- *Symbolic meanings:* The hidden meanings you associate with what your opponent did or said, or with being in conflict

- *Values:* The value of respect or honesty in your communications, or aggression in responding to someone's insults
- *Histories:* The past organizational, family, and personal histories associated with your conflict
- *Opportunities:* The opportunity to try out new techniques in your conflict that might lead in a new direction
- *Time:* The time that passes as you read this page, your memory of the past, vision of the future, or sense of the present, and the influence these have on your conflict communications
- *Changes:* The changes that have taken place in you since the conflict began, or since you started reading this chapter

None of these are visible, yet each is present wherever you are, powerfully influencing your life and conflicts. You probably behave as though they are not there, even when their impact leaves you with an identifiable result. So how can you enter the invisible world where these forces are created, shaped, and resolved?

Identifying Invisible Issues

Here is an example of how the two of us located an invisible issue and used it to unlock a conflict. Sally, vice president in charge of programs, and Ted, vice president in charge of operations, were embroiled in a bitter conflict. In interviews, they blamed each other, as did the people who worked for them, each group identifying the other group as the problem. The entire organization was polarized.

Sally felt undervalued by the president of the company, with no voice in executive decisions, and stuck with the responsibility of making Ted's bad decisions work. Ted felt he was losing the president's favor, was not respected, and that his only power was to resist or sabotage Sally, his main competitor. Each was convinced they were right.

We began our intervention by asking about family backgrounds. Sally said she was the youngest girl in a family with three older brothers, and Ted said he was the oldest boy in a family with three sisters. They realized they were re-enacting ancient sibling rivalries, stopped personalizing each other's behavior, and the conflict disappeared. They rapidly reached a number of agreements on how to support each other, and we all went together to ask the president for help.

The president agreed to include Sally on the executive decision-making team, and reassured them of the vital role they each played in the organization. They began working together as allies, and while they continued to disagree, their conflicts were contained and creative.

Using Empathy and Honesty to Probe the Iceberg

Empathy is one of the most powerful methods available for resolving conflict. With empathy, we are able to access deeper layers of the iceberg, develop an "awareness of interconnection," and discover that we all share a common set of emotions, interests, and perceptions. We learn we can understand and identify with each other, even when we differ in language, culture, and personality.

Empathy is a skill you can develop and practice in all your interactions, though it is not as easy as it appears. To begin, you will need to give up all judgments about the other person in your conflict. Judgments are a defense against empathy, since they convince us we already know the truth and do not need to ask any more questions.

To exercise empathy, we need to hold two opposite ideas at the same time. First, we need to realize that the other person is a separate, unique individual whose ideas, feelings, and experiences we can never fully know. Second, we need to walk in the other person's shoes and understand their feelings and point of view, and see that we share an enormously rich set of human conditions.

Empathy is different from sympathy, which is feeling sorry for someone. In sympathy, we are absorbed in the other person's feelings, whereas in empathy, we are using our feelings to understand what the other person *might* be feeling. In a strange way, sympathy ignores the real person, and by offering consolation to a *victim*, places them in a power-down position.

Empathy treats the other person as a separate individual, entitled to their own feelings, ideas, and conflict experiences. In sympathy, there is always a kind of consensual boundary violation, which leaves the "victim" feeling less secure than before. There is no violation of emotional boundaries in empathy, which leaves people feeling more secure.

To help us understand the power of empathy, and how we can accomplish this complex emotional feat, it is useful to read the eloquent Sufi poet, Rumi, who described a way of creating empathy even in the face of silence. He asked:

> *"What if a man cannot be made to say anything?*
> *How do you learn his hidden nature?"*
> *"I sit in front of him in silence,*
> *and set up a ladder made of patience,*
> *and if in his presence a language from beyond joy*
> *and beyond grief begins to pour from my chest,*
> *I know that his soul is as deep and bright*
> *as the star Canopus rising over Yemen.*
> *And so when I start speaking a powerful right arm*
> *of words sweeps down, I know him from what I say,*
> *and how I say it, because there's a window open*
> *between us, mixing the night air of our beings."*

Empathy is a part of all acting and role-play experiences, allowing us to vividly imagine someone else's life, and begin to feel what it might be like to *be* them. While we know we are pretending, our emotions ring true. They feel genuine—and are often accurate for the person we are role-playing.

As you attempt to resolve your conflicts, you can use empathy to identify with your opponent and thereby discover how it might be possible to create a bridge between you. One reason you may reach impasse in your conflicts is because you find it difficult to imagine what it might be like to be on the other side. One way you can get unstuck is by reaching out to the other person with understanding and empathy.

Empathy takes us deeper into ourselves to find the internal places where we understand each other. We are all capable of feeling what it might be like to be angry or afraid or in pain, and we can always recognize the deeper levels of their iceberg by understanding more about our own. We recommend following a simple, consistent empathic rule: speak and act *as though it were you*, and not some other person in the conflict.

Creating Empathy Through Role-Reversing Dialogue

To practice empathy as a path to resolving your conflicts, try the following exercise. Get a sheet of paper and pen or pencil, and complete the following steps. You can also do this exercise orally, by shifting from one chair to another and saying what you think the other person might say, or role-playing their part in the conflict and asking a friend to role-play you.

1. Write down or state orally what you would most like to say to your opponent.
2. Write down or state what you would say back, if you were that other person.
3. Write or state your response to what "they" wrote or said to you.
4. Write or state their response back.

Look at what you wrote or said to see if you honestly expressed both sides of the conflict, and presented them equally. If not, start over again. If so, did you learn anything you didn't know before you started about how the other person felt or what they thought? To make the exercise more powerful, try it in real life. Suggest that your opponent take your side in the argument for a few minutes while you take theirs, just to see what it feels like to be on the other side. In organizations, you may want to do a reverse role-play and temporarily redistribute titles or positions in the hierarchy or sides in the dispute. Afterward, debrief to see what everyone learned. The results can be profound, and we have found that participants in this exercise often emerge with lasting empathy for each other's roles.

While consulting with an information technology (IT) organization, we observed that the staff were engaged in numerous conflicts with a business unit over what they perceived as unrealistic demands, while the business unit complained about IT bureaucracy, unreasonable rejection of requests for help, poor service quality, and miscommunication.

We asked both groups to participate in a strategic planning session where it was agreed that some staff members would exchange work locations to better understand conditions in each other's offices. In each business unit, one person was assigned to work in the IT office, and one IT person was assigned to each business unit team, as liaison. After a year the conflicts were over, and both groups asked to remain in their roles so they could continue to coordinate delivery of services. As their empathy increased, they were able to develop a strategic vision for the company that improved customer service.

Honesty and Empathy

Empathy alone is not enough. Once we place ourselves in another person's shoes and discover something about their deeper truths, we need to honestly communicate what we learn. Empathy that is not combined with honesty becomes sentimental, cowardly, and ineffectual. Honesty that is not tempered with empathy becomes brutal, aggressive, and judgmental.

If empathy consists of discovering the other person within ourselves, honesty means communicating what we discover so the other person can reach a similar level of self-understanding through our questions and responses. Honesty means not turning away from what we see, but speaking fearlessly and openly about it so we can learn the lessons held within it.

In this way, empathy and honesty are intertwined. To reach a deeper level of honesty and successfully communicate what we believe is taking place beneath the surface of our conflicts, we require a more profound level of empathy. As we reach new levels of empathy, we require deeper levels of honesty.

Really honest communication is not easy. Like many of us, you have probably learned to "play it safe." We all participate in "conspiracies of silence" based on unspoken agreements to communicate superficially, without honestly saying what is true for each other. Yet in doing so, you may have cheated yourself—and your opponent— out of learning and growth through confronting your issues honestly. If so, you may end up mistaking your internal conflicts for conflicts with others.

There are high risks associated with the use of honesty as a conflict strategy. Yet honesty is what differentiates conflict *resolution* from conflict *suppression* and *settlement*. It is easy to settle a conflict by avoiding the issues that lie beneath the surface. While honesty gives the impression that we are intensifying the conflict, it is essential to discovering the hidden content of the conflict.

It is difficult to be deeply honest. It is risky, and can backfire. You can lose the empathic connection you need for deep listening. Yet to settle your disputes without touching the underlying reasons for them, to search for self-justification rather than self-examination, to allow the downward spiral of rage and shame to block authentic communication, is to cheat yourself out of learning and intimacy, and the other person out of opportunities to change.

By settling for shallow communications, you run the risk of creating a culture of conflict that imprisons both of you and sets a standard for dialogue within your organization that is defined by superficiality. This is the true risk, as opposed to the risk we face when we honestly plumb our conflicts for opportunities that lead to growth and transformation.

Real Honesty Is Real Difficult

In nearly all organizational cultures, rules and sanctions are directed against honest communication, and rewards are given for suppressing true feelings and honest dialogue. We rarely discuss openly and honestly what is really going on inside us, especially with those with whom we are in conflict—partly because we want to be kind more than we want to be honest, partly because we want to protect one another from the harshness of the truth, and partly because we think honesty will make us vulnerable to our opponents.

You may well be operating in an organizational culture that does not support or value honest communications. All organizations generate rules for deciding when it is safe to be honest and when it could cost you your job. Yet all organizations are vulnerable to honesty, since most of the behaviors that keep us locked in impasse work covertly and thrive on silence. By calling attention to these behaviors, we automatically discourage them.

The two of us have worked with many people who were trying to shift their organizational culture in the direction of deeper honesty, and these efforts have largely been successful. But there is always an element of risk-taking in these ventures, for many of the reasons that follow. If you feel the need to shift your organizational culture, you will need to find internal allies who will stand with you—and often external consultants to support you in developing new norms and consolidating new behaviors.

It is especially hard for any of us to be deeply honest with those we dislike or who dislike us, because superficiality, lies, secrets, and silence appear less risky and more powerful than vulnerability, honesty, shared responsibility, and open communication. Aggression and self-defense are instinctual and difficult to control. At the same time, our willingness to take responsibility for our own actions and self-esteem is distorted by our need for sympathy and support.

When we hide our true thoughts and feelings, we condemn ourselves to silent suffering and self-doubt. In this state, we may repress our feelings because they are too frightening or powerful to discuss openly. Or, we may externalize them, and see them only as responses by our opponents, and from the outside-in rather than the inside-out.

Honesty is difficult because we want to avoid blame and make ourselves appear good or right by making others appear bad or wrong, yet the negative consequences we direct at others ultimately return to us. If we make someone lose, feel bad, or accept blame for what went wrong, our relationship and communication will suffer.

It is dangerous to speak honestly because to do so is to accept the possibility that the other person will speak with equal honesty to us. Hence, we are reduced to silence or banality or nonengagement, fueled in part by a fear that honesty will not be held in check by either side, because we lack the willingness to be honest with ourselves, or sense we do not have the skill to manage the chain reaction of anger that could take us out of control.

This is connected to a deeper reason for not being honest. We take deliberate steps to protect ourselves from hearing the truth because we know that serious life consequences may result. We suspect that these consequences may force us to change our behaviors and redefine ourselves, compelling us to leave the comfortable—albeit dysfunctional—ruts we have created for ourselves. We know intuitively that honesty is the precondition for transformation.

Rationalizations for Not Being Honest

We are all skilled at rationalizing our behavior. Each of us has our own list of perfectly good reasons for avoiding honest communication with bosses, colleagues, friends, and family, not to mention our opponents. Entire organizations can easily find themselves committed to cultural norms of dishonest, self-serving communications.

In one organization with which we worked, the staff were so focused on customer sales that they treated each other with unflagging superficial banality and never communicated their deeper truths. They asked us to help them figure out why, in spite of their superficial joviality, there was such low morale in the organization.

As the conflicts they kept beneath the surface began to emerge they realized that suppressing honest communication doesn't make it disappear, but renders it more powerful. By creating a happy-face, have-a-nice-day norm for communication, they prevented themselves from addressing issues that had to be addressed to improve their morale and ensure continued growth.

Here are some of the rationalizations they used to justify keeping communications superficial and not risk honest dialogue. Notice the ones you use when you want to hide honest feelings from the other person, and protect yourself from the risk of open and honest interactions.

- "I don't want to hurt their feelings."
- "They will misinterpret what I say."
- "They won't be receptive."
- "It will put our relationship at risk."
- "I will become open to retaliation or counterattack if I open up."
- "There's nothing in it for me, because we can settle our issues without it."
- "It could escalate and I should not increase the conflict."
- "I will be out on a limb and won't be supported."
- "Nothing will change anyway."
- "I always take the risks and this time it's their turn."
- "In the past, I haven't found it useful."
- "I could lose my job, or the respect of others."
- "It's not me, they're the ones who are stuck."

Reviewing this list, consider what would happen if you abandoned each rationale. By being deeply honest and empathic with your opponent, you will become more authentic and encourage their open communication. You will live more comfortably with yourself and improve your work life if you allow yourself to address issues that are important to you. Make an agreement with yourself to abandon the rationalizations you use most often.

Rationalizations for Being Honest

If you are still unwilling to abandon your rationalizations for not being honest, consider the following set of contrary rationalizations that are equally valid, yet encourage you to communicate more honestly.

- "It's possible for me to communicate honestly without hurting anyone's feelings, if I do so empathically."
- "It's possible for me to communicate accurately so there will be less possibility of misinterpretation."
- "They can't be receptive unless I give them something to receive."
- "Without honesty, there can't be an authentic relationship between us."
- "If I act collaboratively, they will find it more difficult to respond defensively."
- "I increase my own self-esteem and skill as well as their opportunities to change through honest communication."
- "The problem will get worse if I don't communicate honestly."
- "If it escalates, I can use conflict resolution skills or mediation to resolve the conflict at a deeper level."
- "If I risk being honest the other person may take that risk also."
- "Things will begin to change when I communicate honestly."
- "I can't live with myself if I don't speak my own truth."
- "I could improve my job and gain the respect of others."
- "We will both remain stuck unless I do something to end the impasse."

Consider using these sets of rationalizations and counter-rationalizations as an organizational checklist, asking teams and departments to identify the phrases they use most often, and use the information they gather to create a strategy for encouraging authentic communication. Survey yourself or colleagues in your organization. Which do you accept? Why? Are you using rationalizations to cover your fear? Are your negative experiences a result of being honest, or of inadequate empathy in communicating what you think? Ultimately, where will avoidance of honesty get you? Is that where you want to be as an individual or an organization?

Taking Responsibility for Actions and Inactions

It does not matter how creatively we deny responsibility for the effectiveness of our communications and the resolution of our conflicts. None of our conflicts *could have happened* without our active or passive participation. We can obscure but never eliminate the truth, that responsibility for our conflicts extends not only to those who acted and should not have, but to those who did not act and should have.

We recognize that responsibility for any act, even an unspeakable horror such as the Holocaust, belongs not only to those who did it, but to those who ordered it done. It also belongs to those who proposed it, those who profited from it, those who supported it, those who justified or applauded it, and those who defended it. It belongs to those who obscured, denied, or covered it up, those who knew about it and did nothing to stop it, and those who ought to have known, but chose to sit in silence and ignore it—in other words, to *everyone* within conscious reach of it. It is the same in our conflicts.

The primary reason for honesty in conflict resolution is that it makes each of us responsible for our own lives. It does this by asking deep questions, seeking permission to give honest feedback, presenting feedback as though we were the ones receiving it, supporting and applauding the willingness of others to hear it, modeling and being authentically who we truly and ultimately are, and accepting, even embracing the things for which we are responsible in our lives.

The act of taking responsibility for what we have done and not done in our conflicts, paradoxically, allows us to stand up for ourselves and at the same time for others. It allows us to experience our lives as within our control, and to appreciate, learn from, and live with our choices. This extends not only to what we think or say, but to whatever our lives silently stand for.

Taking Responsibility
for Our Conflicts

We work closely with a highly successful mediation project, the Centinela Valley Juvenile Victim Offender Reconciliation Program in Southern California. Headed by Steve Goldsmith, this program brings young people accused of crimes face-to-face with their victims in mediation. Both sides are encouraged to communicate honestly about what happened, about the impact of the crime on the victim, the responsibility of the juvenile who committed it to provide restitution to the victim, and the responsibility of the victim to release, forgive, and reconcile with the offender.

This program produces extraordinary results in keeping adolescents out of prison, teaching them to communicate honestly about their crimes and be responsible for their actions. Their recidivism or re-arrest rate is substantially lower than that of juvenile offenders who have not gone through the program, and their success in rehabilitation is nearly 90 percent, primarily because of the honesty and responsibility encouraged by the mediation process.

Taking responsibility for your conflicts starts with acknowledging your contribution to the conflict, and the pain you may have caused others. Here are several steps you can take to encourage responsibility for conflict in your organization and work life:

- Start by giving yourself an honest appraisal and identifying what you contributed or are responsible for in the conflict.
- Do not take critical comments personally.
- Tell the truth. Speak the unspeakable.
- Listen to and acknowledge honest responses.
- Express a willingness to reassess your own position.
- Surface and discuss covert behavior, including any you may have fostered or accepted.
- Be unwilling to engage in covert behavior yourself.
- Help others take baby steps toward honest dialogue.
- Look for ways of reconnecting and reintegrating with others.
- Search for forms of honest expression that allow others to save face.
- Unhook yourself from judgments about other people's personalities and motives, and describe their *behavior* in nonjudgmental terms.
- Surface alternative ways of achieving what both of you want or desire.

By taking not just 50, but *100 percent* responsibility for your conflicts, you close the door to blaming others. You discover hidden opportunities to learn from your mistakes, become more skillful in future conflicts, and free yourself from the feelings and behaviors that led you to impasse. We encourage you to enjoy whatever treasures you may find along this path.

Path Five

Separate What Matters from What's in the Way

Plantagenet: The truth appears so naked on my side
That any purblind eye may find it out.
Somerset: And on my side it is so well apparell'd
So clear, so shining and so evident
That it will glimmer through a blind man's eye.
—*Shakespeare*, King Henry VI,
Part 1, Act 2, Scene 4

We now enter the path of action, creative problem solving, and separating what is important from what stands in the way of resolution. In earlier chapters, we focused on listening and learning—from ourselves, our adversaries, and our conflicts. In this chapter and the ones to follow, we focus on finding solutions for our problems, overcoming resistance, responding to difficult behaviors, learning to live with paradox, and committing to action.

Committing to Action

Orienting ourselves to open, honest communication and active, empathic listening puts us in a position to take committed action. As our stance shifts from adversary to seeker, we move from a mode of *being* that is preparatory and poised for action, to one of taking *action* based on who we authentically are.

People often feel paralyzed by their conflicts. One teacher described herself as "sinking into quicksand of negativity." Unresolved conflicts block us from acting intelligently, strategically or with genuine commitment. We become incapable of seeing ourselves clearly, understanding our adversaries or feeling they understand us, reaching the issues we need to address, perceiving openings for constructive action, or committing to what we know we should do.

Yet the hidden truth of conflict resolution is that *every conflict already contains its own resolution*. The secret is to unlock it and discover its hidden opportunities for resolution and transformation. If we can unlock our conflicts by listening for the magic moments, cryptic signals, secret structures, and hidden gateways that reveal what it is really about, we can then act to bring these possibilities into the open and resolve them.

This may sound easy, yet the first step in clearing a path for action and resolving our conflicts requires us to let go of what keeps us hooked, including our need to be right. In the process you will see how what you think of as "The Truth" keeps you from discovering an even greater truth. Before you take two steps forward, you need to take one step back.

Locked in Positions and Trapped in "The Truth"

When we are in conflict, we always share one thing with our opponents: we *know* we are right! We assume the truth will be clear and apparent to every unbiased listener, as Shakespeare had Plantagenet and Somerset claim. Yet our opponents have no difficulty rejecting our ideas, any more than we do rejecting theirs, in spite of the fact that our ideas clearly represent The Truth.

Rather than claiming to represent The Truth, which reflects our experience, we need to understand that our experience is *true for us*, and that our combined experiences create a larger truth than either of our separate truths standing alone. The perspective that ours is the single truth gives rise to *positions*, which represent what we want, based on our truth. Understanding that there are multiple truths helps us identify *interests*, or the reasons why we want what we want, which permit us to combine our truths into a larger truth, a composite of both our experiences. When we shift from single to multiple truths, our process is transformed from one of debate over who is right, to dialogue and a search for solutions that will satisfy everyone.

We helped a group of thirty sales representatives in a large commercial bank organize into self-managing teams. Before the team initiative, each salesperson was rated every month based on their individual sales performance. These ratings were published throughout the organization, creating intense competition to see who could achieve the highest score.

The newly organized teams wanted to eliminate individual monthly rating lists and report only team results, but the head of the organization wanted to keep the individual lists in place. In one session, a conflict flared between a woman who spoke in favor of team-based lists and the head of the organization who defended individual reporting. Neither would budge from their position, because each was certain they were right.

It took the team members some time to recognize that the head of the organization wanted individual results reported because he was afraid others would see teams as places where they could slack off, become irresponsible, and blame other team members for nonperformance. Everyone on the teams was able to understand his legitimate concerns and respond with alternative suggestions.

It also took the manager time to understand that the reason the teams wanted results listed together was to motivate their members to collaborate—not give themselves room to slack off or become irresponsible or blame others. They wanted to support each other in making their work succeed and change the culture of the organization to encourage collaboration. The head of the organization was able to see their goals as legitimate, and that they all had similar interests at heart.

Thus, they were able to negotiate a compromise in which both sets of results were listed, with an agreement to assess the sales they produced in the next quarter to see which plan worked best. This decision motivated the teams to produce extraordinary results. On average, the teams produced 130 percent of their *annual* goals in only six months!

Another example of the damage caused by being certain of The Truth occurred when we facilitated a strategic planning program for the senior staff of the mayor of a large city. The mayor's staff and the city council were at loggerheads, with each side not only knowing they were right, but convinced the other side was irrational, or operating from a hidden agenda. One staff member put it this way, from the mayor's point of view: "The city council is our main obstacle. They've decided to defeat the mayor's programs so he won't get credit, to the point of being irrational. It's a power struggle."

A city council staff member saw it differently: "There is an ideological war between the mayor and the city council. There is an issue of respect also, both politically and in terms of behaviors. We are criticized for not being consensus oriented in our relations with the mayor, but the mayor's office is far more isolationist than the council is. We don't have an independent way to accomplish our goals and we need each other but they are too arrogant and don't want to work with us."

Everyone in this drama was frustrated and unable to find common ground, so they continued holding on to their positions, refusing to acknowledge the other side's point of view. When each group realized it could not achieve what it wanted without the cooperation of the other side, a change began. The mayor's office created a task force and assigned a staff member to work with each council member to build a closer relationship. They agreed to stop acting unilaterally and develop programs in partnership with the council, rather than coming in with fully developed proposals and demanding approval.

In both these examples, the protagonists were locked in positions and prepared to defend them to the death if necessary, because they knew they were right. Argumentation and debate solidified each side's stance, and prevented them from listening to the truth on the other side, or even trying to meet the other side's legitimate interests. What was needed in both cases—as in every conflict—was to separate what works from what doesn't.

Creating Separations in Conflict Resolution

In conflict, we tend to lump issues that upset us into a mass of indistinguishable complaints. As long as they are intertwined, it is difficult to negotiate, fix, or resolve them. As strange as it may seem, simply creating distinctions—separations between the elements in our conflicts—can produce a significant shift in our ability to approach them constructively.

These separations can transform our attitude from passive, reactive, and powerless to self-possessed, proactive, and strategic. They signal our transition from focusing on listening and emotional processing to focusing on problem solving and negotiation. With them, we break down seemingly monolithic issues into easy-to-handle parts, using a set of uncomplicated tools. In doing so, we discover solutions and prepare to implement them.

The following "separations" should allow you to see your conflicts more clearly, identify strategies for tackling each piece separately and make it easier to transform the whole.

- Separate positions from interests
- Separate people from problems
- Separate problems from solutions
- Separate commonalities from differences
- Separate the future from the past
- Separate emotion from negotiation
- Separate process from content
- Separate options from choices
- Separate criteria from selection
- Separate yourself from others

As we separate these aspects of conflict, we do so recognizing that, in an ultimate sense, *nothing* can be separated from anything else. When we view things as separate that are inseparable we can lose sight of what they have in common. The deepest truth is that there is no separation between ourselves and the people with whom we are in conflict, other than the illusion that our fundamental interests differ.

When we discover common ground and unite elements we thought of as separate, we are able to see each other as parts of a whole. In that moment, we understand that our conflicts are actually expressions of an underlying unity. We start with separations so as to come to a point where we can see these unities, which are more difficult to grasp.

While the separations cited may seem obvious, there are complexities and subtleties in each, and it is easy to lose sight of them when we are caught in conflict. To successfully apply them and make the distinctions between them clear, we have provided an analysis of each one, followed by a set of questions to help you explore your personal conflicts.

Remember as you proceed that the basic idea is to move beyond settling your conflict on a superficial level. If you identify the deeper issues that are involved in the dispute and work through them completely, you will achieve a resolution that prevents the conflict from resurfacing in a different guise. We hope these tools of analysis and perspective will stimulate a deeper understanding of your conflict and help you discover a way to resolve it.

Separate Positions from Interests

When we shift from debate to dialogue, not only does our process change but the substance of our communication changes as well. In debate, we declare positions, whereas in dialogue, we identify interests. Interests are based on our needs, wants, thoughts, and feelings, and are the *reasons* for our positions. Positions are what we want or think, while interests express why we want what we want, and why we think as we do.

Roger Fisher and our friend Bill Ury, in their classic book on collaborative negotiation strategies, *Getting to Yes*, develop the idea of interest-based negotiations, and Ury, in *Getting Past No*, advocates using interests to resolve disputes in a process that keeps people from getting stuck in mutually exclusive adversarial positions.

Here is an example: Say you are meeting in a room with several people in your organization, and some of them want the air conditioning off, while others want it on. Assuming the air conditioning unit can only be on or off, there are three fundamental ways to resolve this dispute:

- *Power:* If you resolve this dispute on the basis of power, whether in the form of physical force, coercion, money, status, position, organizing ability, or political connections, each side will be pitted against the other, inevitably producing winners and losers, and dividing the group against itself. The most powerful faction will be able to turn the air conditioning on or off at any time, regardless of what the powerless faction wants, encouraging an abuse of power. Accumulated power can be used to gain advantages or protect privileges, resulting in corruption, instability, and the use of negative forms of power by the powerless faction to get their interests met.

- *Rights:* If this dispute is resolved on the basis of rights, as through lawsuits, voting, or negotiation, a compromise may result in which the air conditioning is on, for example, from 10 to 12, and off from 12 to 1. There are still winners and losers in rights-based contests. Corruption and abuse of power are reduced, but continue to exist. The group remains divided and adversarial, and no one has their interests met completely or solves the underlying causes of their dispute.

- *Interests:* If the same dispute is resolved on the basis of interests, we find out why people want the air conditioning on or off. If they want it off because they can't hear due to its noise, we can use a microphone or speak louder. If they want it on because they need fresh air, we can open a window or take a break. If they are cold, we can bring in a directional heater. If they are having trouble breathing because the air is stuffy, we can bring in a fan. In the end, everyone is able to feel like a winner, there is no abuse of power, and the group is united. In short, there is no fundamental reason why one has to feel stuffy so another won't feel cold.

For thousands of years, we have resolved disputes on the basis of power proving the truth of Lord Acton's remark, "All power corrupts and absolute power corrupts absolutely." For this reason, over the last several hundred years we have shifted from power to rights based processes. Rights are *limitations* on the exercise of power. Every word in the Constitution is a limitation on the power of an absolute monarchy to do as he or she wishes. Yet rights originate in, and depend on power. Only in the last several years have we begun to create effective mechanisms for making decisions on the basis of interests.

The easiest way to separate positions from interests is simply to ask *why* the other person has that position. Here are some additional questions you can ask to elicit the other person's interests, or discover your own:

- "Why does that seem like the best solution to you?"
- "If you could have any solution, what would you want?"
- "Help me understand why that is important to you."
- "What concerns do you have about this?"
- "What's the real problem here?"
- "What would be wrong with—?"
- "Why not do it this way—?"
- "What are you afraid would happen if we—?"
- "What would you do if you were in charge?"
- "What are your goals for the future?"
- "Why not just accept their proposal?"
- "What would your proposal be if they were willing to meet your interests?"
- "What would it take for you to give up that proposal?"
- "What could they do to make their proposal acceptable to you?"

By asking these questions, you shift from assuming there will be a win-lose outcome to assuming you can both win. By identifying interests, we make it possible to consider multiple options that are not mutually exclusive, and satisfy everyone's legitimate needs.

Fisher and Ury give an example of the difference between positions and interests which we have modified to relate to conflict resolution. Assume you have two children, Sally and Freddy, who are fighting over an orange. What do you do? When we ask this question, most people say they would cut the orange in half, while some would take it away, and a few say they would eat it themselves. Assume you cut the orange in half, and when you check to see how the children are doing, you discover Sally squeezing the juice out of her half of the orange and throwing away the peel, and Freddy grating the peel off his half of the orange and throwing away the inside. What have you done?

First, you have missed an opportunity to create a win-win solution by failing to discover what their real interests were. Worse, your behavior taught them these lessons about resolving disputes in the future:

- They do not have the ability to resolve conflicts themselves.
- Therefore, they need someone to intervene to solve it for them.
- The intervenor will be someone in a position of power or authority.
- The person who is in a position of power or authority will not care what their real interests are.
- As a result, they will at best get half of what they really want.
- This result will be imposed on them as a kind of punishment for disagreeing with each other.
- Conflict is dangerous and pointless.
- There is no reason to believe they could collaborate to get everything they both want.
- There is no reason for them to believe they could learn from their conflicts.

An alternative scenario would be for you to ask Sally and Freddy why they want the orange. A more skillful approach would be to suggest that Sally ask Freddy why he wants the orange. In this example, you would teach them a very different set of lessons about resolving their disputes in the future, including:

- They do have the capacity to resolve conflicts themselves.
- They do not need anyone to intervene to solve it for them.
- They can find out themselves what their real interests are.
- The way to find out is to ask a "why" question, or some other question to identify interests.
- It is possible to get everything they want.
- It is possible to collaborate and get what they want.
- Conflict can be creative and useful.
- They can learn from their conflicts.

Let's assume Freddy is extremely angry about the orange, that we ask why he is so angry, and he says: "Sally is the older sister and she always gets the orange first." Now we know the conflict was not about the orange at all, but about sibling rivalry! By cutting the orange in half, we settled the superficial issue and pushed the deeper problem under the rug, where it will fester until it emerges in a new set of disputes until it is finally addressed and resolved.

Freddy's answer now allows us to talk about the real issues, and possibly transform their relationship. We might open the real issue for dialogue by saying: "Terrific, Freddy. Thank you for making the issue clear. Why don't you tell Sally *directly* what it feels like to be the youngest child and always get the orange last?" or "Sally, how would you feel if you were the youngest child and always got the orange last?" Finally we are directly talking about real problems and able to identify real solutions, such as:

- "Now that you've identified the real problem, what solutions would each of you suggest?"
- "Sally, what if you take the inside of the orange and Freddy takes the peel?"

- "Sally, if you're thirsty, what about apple juice?" "Freddy, if you want to cook with the peel, how about using a lemon instead?"

- "Sally, since Freddy feels you always get to choose first, how about letting him choose first this time and you choose first next time?"

- "Let's all go to the store together and get more oranges."

- "Great. Sally, you make the juice, Freddy you make the cookies, and let's have a party!"

This conversation, of course, will take much more time than cutting the orange in half, but consider the time you will spend over the next twelve years cutting oranges in half. And wouldn't it be worth the time if you could help Sally and Freddy improve their communication and make their relationship more collaborative?

Shifting from positions to interests reduces the perception that we have to compete aggressively to satisfy our needs, and makes it possible for us to successfully collaborate and still get what we want. It allows us to directly address the issues that lie beneath the surface of our disputes. It wakes us up by not allowing us to continue pretending we care about oranges when we know that there are more important issues at stake.

The difficulty is that all the little Sallys and Freddys grow up some day and come to work with you. Whether you are a manager or employee, school principal or teacher, coach or parent, you will probably have dealt with a number of Sallys and Freddys. For most such people, conflict creates the desire for a parent or authority figure to come in and resolve the dispute for them. This may stop the fighting, but it will also prevent them from growing up and learning how to resolve their own disputes.

Separating interests from positions, it is possible to take the first step in helping people grow up and take charge of their conflicts. Consider the following questions, which will help you identify your interests and those of others:

- What is your position? What do you want, and what are the points that demonstrate you are right?
- Why have you taken this position? What are your interests?
- What is the other person's position? What do they want, and what are the points that support their position?
- Why have they taken this position? What are their interests?
- Is there anything about your interests that would block achievement of the other person's interests, or vice versa?
- If not, what could be done to satisfy both sets of interests?
- What are some ways you both might win?
- Have you gained any insights into your conflict by making this distinction?

Bringing conflicting interests out into the open seems to run counter to our desire to hide our disagreements, to minimize them or sweep them under the rug. You may feel if you accept the legitimacy of your adversary's interests, yours will not be met. In our experience, if you do not clearly distinguish positions from interests, you end up forcing solutions on people who feel their basic needs have not been met. By openly stating and eliciting interests, you encourage dialogue about what is really important to each side. You can then identify interest-based substitutes for positions, as in the example of the air conditioning dispute, and allow each side to drop their position in exchange for satisfying a deeper set of interests.

Separate People from Problems

We tend to demonize our opponents. We are quick to label them, find evil in their hearts, and believe they are unjust, dishonest, disagreeable personalities. We personalize their behavior toward us, even when it clearly has more to do with them and their unresolved issues than it does with us. In our experience, it is rare that people *intend* to do each other harm. Usually they have important goals and are willing to do harm in order to achieve them. While the harm you experience is the same in either case, the motivation is different. You do not need to take it personally to put a stop to it.

In this separation, you want to focus your energy and anger on the *problem,* understanding that the *person*—no matter how despicable their behavior—has some redeeming human qualities you ought to be able to recognize and appreciate. If you cannot, you will begin to behave toward them as they behaved toward you, demeaning yourself and making it more difficult to discover solutions to your problems.

Consider the following logical progression. If your hostility is directed toward someone, they are likely to become aware of it. If they detect your hostility, they will begin to see you as the enemy, act hostilely toward you, and be unwilling to listen to you or find common ground. You will then do the same to them, and the cycle will continue. In this way, confusing the person with the problem becomes a self-fulfilling prophecy. When you feel personally insulted you withdraw, which they interpret as hostility and withdraw from you, which you see as rejection, justifying your withdrawal.

Only by recognizing the human being within your enemy while not accepting or condoning what they did to you, can you open pathways to resolution and transformation. In the following chapter on difficult behaviors, we will investigate this distinction in greater detail and suggest a number of methods for separating people from their actions. If we follow this process to its conclusion, we come to release, forgiveness, and reconciliation—not for what was done, but for the person who did it.

The truth is, no matter how much you hate someone, they are not the problem. The problem is what they are doing, together with your own lack of skill at responding to what they are doing. When you identify the problem as one of behavior and response, you position yourself to act more powerfully and effectively. You then listen and thereby encourage the other person to listen to you. You can give honest, empathic feedback without provoking a defensive response, and learn ways of responding more skillfully in the future. Paradoxically, you can be harder on the problem when you are soft on the person. Otherwise, your natural compassion may get in the way, and you may find yourself being soft on the problem so as not to hurt the feelings of the person.

In resolving organizational disputes, begin by asking both sides to agree on common goals for their relationship, a vision for their work together, a set of ground rules for their communication, or a set of shared values. Ask them to respond to a question that makes them appear more human, such as recalling why they originally wanted to work for the organization, or setting out their hopes and wishes for the future.

This process reminds both sides of the ideas they share, and the qualities they can genuinely appreciate in each other. You learn your opponent has the same desires you do. The personal dislikes, individual attacks, and factional infighting begin to melt away when you agree on what is important. Try answering the following questions to identify the human qualities of your opponent. Notice the ones you find hardest to answer, try to gain some insight into why, and consider how you might respond to your opponent's difficult behaviors more skillfully.

- What do you most like about your opponent?
- What are three admirable qualities this person possesses?
- What do you want or expect from them? Why do you want it?
- Are you comparing yourself to them? Are you comparable?
- What do they do that bothers you?
- How do you respond when they engage in this behavior?
- Is that working?
- Why is your response not working?
- What could you do to respond more skillfully?
- Are you, in some indirect way, rewarding the behaviors you don't like?
- What are three things you could do differently to respond more skillfully to their difficult behaviors?

The fundamental premise behind these questions is that we are all responsible for our own behaviors. By separating behaviors from people, we shift the locus of responsibility from "me" or "them" to "us," both for creating the conflict and for discovering and implementing solutions. We will be more successful if we address our problem together, which we can only do if we identify it as an "it" rather than as a "you." At the same time, we all need to take 100 percent responsibility for solving our conflicts. When we do, clear commitments, workable solutions, and transformational learning often result.

Separate Problems from Solutions

When we are in conflict, we are so busy focusing on our disagreements, bolstering our positions, and searching for quick solutions that we fail to listen to the conflict and involve our opponent in a collaborative search for answers that meet both our needs. As a result, we propose solutions for the wrong problem, or our solutions are received with suspicion and distrust because both sides did not participate in creating them. We become locked in a mountainous dispute over a molehill, unable to propose solutions without replicating the problem.

It is important to stop for a moment and analyze or understand your problem before trying to solve it. You need to discuss the problem in detail with your opponent before even thinking about coming up with a solution. Try to reach agreement on the origin and nature of your problem. Determine whether it is linked to other problems, and trace the extent of its impact and depth of its effect on yourself and others. We explore this issue in greater depth in a later chapter on the path of problem solving.

Research on problem solving indicates that the effectiveness of solutions increases 85 percent once the real problem is identified. Most creative problem-solving techniques advocate spending most of your time analyzing the problem. Resolution emerges effortlessly once a well-defined problem has been mutually identified by all interested parties. In analyzing your conflict, consider the following questions:

- What *exactly* is the conflict about? Why is it about that?
- When did the conflict begin? Why then?
- Who does it involve? Why them?
- What kind of conflict is it? Why that kind?
- What aspects of the conflict have you overlooked? Why those?
- How has your understanding of the conflict changed over time?
- What caused the conflict?
- How would you analyze the conflict? What type of conflict is it?
- Can you break the conflict down into separate parts?
- How would you prioritize these parts?

It may seem counterintuitive to begin problem solving by putting aside solutions and staying with the problem, but it works. We often advise organizations that are stuck in conflict to meet in small teams to analyze and prioritize their problems, and observe them laughing cheerfully while listing twenty or thirty major problems. When we ask them why they're enjoying themselves, they say they feel relieved to be finally talking about what they all know but have been unable to discuss. Some feel relieved to meet others who have the same problem. Others are excited because discussing their problems implies the possibility of solutions.

We then ask them whether they experienced any of the twenty or thirty problems they came up with while working on their analysis, and no one ever says they did. We ask why, if their problems are so deep and all-encompassing, they did not experience them during this process. They are then able to see that problems disappear when we face them together. Problems are easier to resolve when we include everyone in the effort to solve them, when we work in teams, set clear process rules and identifiable goals, and talk openly about the root of the problem without having to come up with quick solutions.

Separate Commonalities from Differences

When we work with labor-management groups to resolve conflicts, improve cross-departmental relationships, or develop skills in collective bargaining, we often ask each side to meet separately to identify their goals for their relationship. We always find that even bitterly antagonistic groups share common goals. When they take the next step and commit to making these goals a priority in their communications, they can talk about their disagreements without feeling overwhelmed.

In conflict, we focus on how different we are from each other. Our differences are important to understand and work through, but it is equally important to recognize how focusing on our differences makes it difficult for us to recall what we have in common. We share many interests as human beings—and if we cannot bring them to mind in the midst of our conflict, we can at least recognize that we have our conflict in common. The paradox is that at the very moment we are poles apart, we are also inseparable.

In recognizing that we have similar wants and desires, a bond begins to develop between us, we become more aware of the need to talk about our problems with one another, and we are able to collaborate on finding solutions. This does not mean eliminating or understating your differences. Our differences are important, but we need to discuss them openly in the context of what we share. These questions can help you discover your context of commonalities and differences:

- What are three things you have in common with your opponent?
- If you were unable to identify three, what made it difficult?
- How much do you actually know about your opponent?
- How much have you assumed about them without trying to find out what is true and what is not?

- What are three values, beliefs, or principles you and your opponent share?
- What are three solutions to your conflict you both might accept?

To discover what you share with your adversary, identify your core values. These values link you to people in general, and whatever values you share with everyone, you share with your opponent. This does not force you to forgive what they did, but it can prevent you from giving yourself permission to do the same to them. An enemy is anyone you allow yourself to exclude from your core values.

In this way, identifying what you share with your enemy is transformative. This happens not only because you see them differently, but because doing so allows you to fight more powerfully against the problems their behaviors create. Simultaneously holding on to your commonalities and differences with others forces you to redefine the nature of your conflict, your opponent, and yourself. It ultimately forces you to give up the false idea that your conflict can be defined in terms of "either/or." More likely, it can be defined more completely and accurately as "both/and."

Separate the Future from the Past

The world has seen countless bloody conflicts fueled by the accumulation of generations of pain, humiliation, anger, and retaliation. The carnage of centuries lives on through succeeding generations. The price of failing to distinguish between past and future is paid years after the events that triggered it have passed into history and their details forgotten. If, in these conflicts, combatants could agree on what they wanted for their children or hoped for their future, they might more easily find a path to resolution.

In the realm of conflict, the past always weighs on the present. We once resolved a dispute in a school where the faculty had rejected three principals in less than six months. The divisiveness was so great that even the factions had factions, and their anger and bitterness at one another made the entire community miserable.

We began by asking everyone to introduce themselves, and offer one idea for how they could make this the best school in the state. We wrote their ideas on flip charts and posted them around the room. We then asked whether anyone disagreed with *any* of these ideas. No one did. We then asked, "What would you rather spend your time on today: proving you were right, or working on these ideas and making this the best school in the state?" The response was unanimous. They wanted to put the past behind them and focus on their future. We still had to spend time addressing the underlying issues and cleaning up the past so it would not leak into their future, but we ended the day with high morale and enthusiasm for working together.

We sometimes ask people who are arguing bitterly if they think they will ever convince the other person they are right. They always say no. The only healthy, intelligent thing to do then is to give it up! In truth, we *never* succeed in convincing the other person in *any* of our conflicts that we are right. This is partly because we are describing what is right *for us*, not for them, and partly because what we think of as "right" is tied to blaming them for who they are or what they did in the past, without considering the future.

We can disagree forever about what happened in the past, about who said or did what to whom, who did it first, and who was at fault. None of this gets us anywhere. We each have our own stories to tell based on what we perceived, filtered through our own emotions, preconceptions, and needs. We sincerely believe our stories to be true, because if they weren't, we would see ourselves as wrong or bad or at fault. We do everything we can to avoid these outcomes, yet none of it ultimately matters.

Recall a conflict in your organization, and how radically people's stories differed from one another. You might wonder whether you worked in the same organization! Each person recalls different facts and draws different conclusions and identifies different heroes and villains. You all wear different lenses and perceive events differently based on your vantage points, needs, and roles at the time. You each come away with wildly different memories you feel passionately about years later.

You will be better able to resolve your disputes when you release yourself from debating endlessly over who is to blame for the past and focus on how to solve your problems in the present, or on what each of you wants in the future. The following questions may help you examine the areas on which you might be able to agree in your past, present, and future:

- What have you been unable to agree on about the past?
- Are your disagreements about the past concerned with who is at fault or to blame for what happened?
- Is it likely you will ever succeed in resolving these issues, or that the other person will ever agree with you?
- If not, what would it take for you to give up your effort to convince them you are right?
- What would the consequences be for either of you if you could agree on the present or the future?
- What might you have to give up? What might you gain?
- What do you both want for the present? For the future?

Focusing on the past or seeking revenge for the pain you have experienced will prevent you from releasing it. Holding on to the past brings its pain into your present and future and denies you resolution, closure, and inner peace. Creating dialogue in the present or a vision of the future will give you a framework in which you can share your present realities and explore your hopes and dreams.

Separate Emotion from Negotiation

We are all emotional. When we suppress our emotions, they do not disappear, but submerge and pop up elsewhere, preoccupying our conscious and unconscious attention. Unresolved emotion distracts us and makes it difficult to focus attention on finding logical or strategic solutions to our problems.

At the other extreme, when we dump emotions on others, we escalate our conflicts and become unable to identify or stick to our priorities. We fail to see the forest for the trees, and have difficulty remembering what is really important. As a result, we cannot behave constructively, quickly reach impasse, and believe it is impossible to solve our problems.

While it is important not to suppress or negotiate your emotions, it is equally important not to negotiate emotionally. Emotions should be acknowledged, not negotiated—and then released so you can solve your problems without being tempted into making emotional decisions that are not to your long-term benefit. The goal of emotional processing in conflict resolution is to communicate your emotions and hear them acknowledged—not as an end in itself, but as a transition to non-emotional problem solving, in which you are both able to set emotion aside, realistically assess what is best for you, and come to agreement. If you suppress your emotions, you will not be able to make reasoned choices. Instead, you will act emotionally when you need to think logically.

People who cannot express their emotions are generally unable to work free of them. Repressing any deep feeling forces you to focus considerable energy on keeping it in check, which prevents you from paying attention to what is happening around you. Internal blindness always leads to external blindness, and vice versa.

In conflict, one person is often more emotionally expressive than another, and it is difficult for more than one person to express their emotions at a time and still feel heard. In these situations, it is important to encourage some form of emotional release, acknowledgment, dialogue, or grieving to take place, because if it doesn't, these unexpressed emotions will leak into the negotiation process and generate silly, pointless arguments about things that do not really matter in the long run.

The following questions may help identify the emotions in your conflict. We hope they will encourage you to express them constructively, and say or do whatever you need to say or do in order to let go of them and negotiate non-emotionally.

- What emotions are you feeling about your conflict?
- What do you need to say or do to let go of them?

- Have you tried communicating your emotions to the other person in the conflict? What was their response?

- How could you express your emotions constructively?

- Do you know what the other person is feeling emotionally? What have you done to find out?

- What level of permission have you given them to express their emotions to you?

- What would it take for you to give them more permission?

- What could you do to encourage them to express their emotions so they can let go of them and negotiate more logically?

- Have your emotions gotten in the way of your ability to negotiate logically? How?

- Have the other person's emotions gotten in the way? How?

Separate Process from Content

Conflicts that concern content—the accuracy of information, data, facts, chronology, recollections, or other matters of substance—are difficult to resolve when we cannot convince the other side. On the other hand, conflicts that concern process—*how* we go about working together—can be defined more flexibly, and provide us with enough common ground to reach agreement.

In international negotiations, process is enormously important. In the talks that ended the Vietnam War the parties argued endlessly over the size and shape of the negotiating table, who was entitled to speak, how many days of discussion there would be, which points would be on the agenda, and what would be said to the press. They knew that if they could reach agreements on these process issues, they would create a starting point for agreement on content.

In organizational disputes as well, reaching agreement over process rules can help us reach agreement on content. Many corporate departments, schools, partnerships, and government agencies have been able to negotiate their differences and improve communications by developing ground rules and process agreements. Process agreements have the following advantages:

- They build areas of trust between people who do not trust each other.
- They create a boundary around the conflict that safely contains it.
- They allow people to settle the rules of combat that will operate within these procedural boundaries.
- They eliminate small, petty conflicts that would otherwise get in the way of resolving larger ones.
- They encourage a sense of order and predictability about the process.
- They provide a sense of fairness and equity.
- They encourage a feeling of ownership of process.
- They help people identify issues that need to be solved or negotiated, and in what order.
- They normalize having a conversation about what is not working in the relationship.
- They encourage constant monitoring of process issues and continuous improvement in negotiation skills.

In our conflict resolution sessions, the first agreements we reach are ground rules concerning process. We do this because it is easier to agree on how people will talk to each other than on what they will say. Small agreements gradually increase the level of trust and communication between adversaries, paving the way for dialogue over content.

Here are a number of common process or ground rules from which you can choose. We have listed a number of optional ground rules, many of which will not apply to your situation. Before beginning your next discussion, propose that you mutually agree on some of the following ground rules:

- To be present at each session voluntarily
- To make no retaliation or reprisal for anything said or done during the session
- To agree on who will participate in the discussion
- To agree on when and where to meet
- To keep all communications in the sessions confidential, except for those specifically identified as not confidential
- To agree on which issues will be discussed and in what order
- To reach all decisions by consensus
- To publicly support all consensus decisions
- To agree on time lines for each meeting, and when to take breaks
- To begin, end, and return from breaks on time
- To allow one person to speak at a time without interruptions
- To focus on issues, situations, and behaviors rather than on personalities
- To sincerely try to listen objectively, openly, and nonjudgmentally
- To break into caucuses or separate meetings on request
- To accept that whatever is said in caucuses or separate meetings will not be confidential to other participants, unless the person making the statement specifically requests it
- To agree on how to handle public announcements
- To agree on what will happen if no agreements are reached
- To agree on what will happen if confidentiality is breached
- To agree on how to select mediators or arbitrators, if needed
- To be present in a spirit of good faith and problem solving
- To be honest and address real problems
- To act with courtesy and not engage in disruptive behavior
- To maintain a "cease-fire" during these sessions—or, if that is not feasible, to agree on a specific list of actions to be avoided

- To resolve all disputes over process or interpretation of these ground rules by mediation before a mutually agreeable mediator

In most cases, it should be relatively easy for you to reach agreements on a minimum number of ground rules. If you run into difficulty, first decide whether you really need that ground rule. If you do, try brainstorming alternative language that addresses both sides' legitimate interests. If this fails, try reaching agreement on an interim ground rule that will at least allow you to discuss the reasons the proposed ground rule is unacceptable, then tailor a new draft to the reasons that are given.

Reaching process agreements helps resolve disputes by encouraging trust in the process and building momentum toward resolution. For example, we resolved a dispute between two managers who were competing over office space in a new wing of a building in which they were housed under cramped conditions. One manager was unwilling to agree to meet because she was afraid the other manager would not keep the conversation confidential. We asked the other manager whether he was willing to do so, and he said he was. We asked him if there was anything he could say to her that might convince her of his willingness to keep the conversation confidential. He told her that if he didn't, she could have as much space in the new wing as she wanted. She immediately accepted, and after that, they had no problems negotiating a fair agreement. See if you can separate the process and content issues in your dispute using the following questions:

- How could the process by which you are communicating be improved?
- How might changing the process affect the content of your communications?
- Do the process conflicts you are having reveal content issues? How? What are they?
- Do the content conflicts you are having reveal process issues? How? What are they?

- Which of the process rules we have suggested might be agreeable to you and your opponent?
- What might you do if they are not?

If at any time you get stuck negotiating the content of your dispute, shift your focus to process. If you are able to transform your process, the content of your dispute may automatically resolve as well.

Separate Options from Choices

Before you choose a solution, expand your range of alternatives. Do not assume your options are limited. Play with ideas and brainstorm all the alternatives you can think of. If you select a solution before you consider all the possibilities, you could reduce your chances of finding the best way of resolving the dispute or discovering options that appeal to everyone.

Options are not fixed choices but creative possibilities. Rather than pointing to a single choice that will lock you into a final position before you are ready, open the possibilities by jointly listing all your options. Creativity comes into play when you search for new ways of solving problems rather than arguing over whose solution is best.

The most effective way of generating options is to give your imagination full scope. This means not evaluating or rejecting anyone's suggestion until all ideas have been expressed. It also means encouraging wild, funny, and creative ideas. As you each come up with new ideas, piggyback on each other's suggestions and improve earlier proposals. Above all, go for broke—ask for everything you want. Here are a variety of processes you can use to brainstorm options:

Brainstorming:

- Group members call out their ideas spontaneously.
- A recorder writes down the ideas as they are suggested.

Round Robin:

- Each member in turn expresses their ideas.

- Anyone may pass on any round.
- The session continues until everyone passes.
- Ideas are recorded as they are suggested.

Secret Ballot:

- Everyone writes their ideas on a slip of paper.
- The ideas are collected and organized.
- The ideas are exchanged, so each person or group has some other person's or group's ideas. These are discussed, prioritized, and presented by someone different from the one it came from.

Subconscious Suggestion:

- Each person thinks of words that may seem unrelated, but can be used to generate ideas about the problem.
- Everyone forgets about the problem entirely and talks about a dramatically different topic.
- Someone picks an object around you, and everyone describes it in terms that can be applied to the problem.

Each of these methods has its benefits and detriments. While brainstorming is quite spontaneous, it has the disadvantage that a few vocal individuals can dominate the conversation while others remain silent. Round robins involve everyone, but take longer to complete. Secret ballots are useful when there is a high degree of distrust, but allow people to take cheap shots and not own their ideas. Subconscious suggestion is extremely creative, but can strike some people as a diversion, or too "touchy feely" for practical work. Any of these methods will help identify the alternatives that lie somewhere between those that each side has suggested. The following questions may also lead to creative options:

- What are the options that might resolve your conflict? (List everything you can think of, as quickly as possible, without considering whether the ideas are realistic or acceptable to your opponent.)

- Of these, which are your top three possibilities?
- What are three silly, outrageous, or impossible options, and how might they apply to your problem?
- How is the problem like an object you see in front of you? What options can you derive from this list?
- What ideas might your opponent suggest for resolving your dispute that you have not considered?
- What do you think would happen if you searched for solutions together?

You will be able to imagine many more solutions if you disengage yourself from thinking about whether they will work or be successful. There will always be time after brainstorming to analyze your choices. We suggest you do so only after you have examined all the options.

Separate Criteria from Selection

One way to resolve your conflict is for you and your opponent to agree on a set of criteria for a successful outcome, or the elements that meet both of your interests. If you can discuss and agree on appropriate criteria before selecting a solution, you will be able to judge beforehand the viability and success of the option you choose.

Many conflicts are not resolved because people cannot agree on criteria or standards to use for selecting among multiple options. Some of the criteria we have found most useful in our work include:

- Jointly seeking the advice of an expert
- Equality of treatment or outcomes
- Agreed-upon ethical standards or shared values
- A ranking and weighting of priorities
- The least costly alternative
- The least time-consuming alternative
- Barter or exchange of one thing for another

- What the likely legal outcome would be
- Tradition or precedent
- What it would cost to buy or replace
- An agreed-upon mathematical formula
- Chance (for example, a coin toss)
- Whoever has the greatest emotional commitment
- Letting each side take turns picking based on subjective preference

Asking people who are at an impasse to agree on the criteria they will use to decide which outcome is best often unlocks the conflict. Although Fisher and Ury in *Getting to Yes* refer to "objective" criteria, we believe there are some highly useful, mutually acceptable criteria that are purely subjective, or based on chance.

What is important is to move the decision-making process to a higher level of abstraction and mutuality. Allow people to select a process they think will be fair *before* they decide who will get what. This helps them feel they are acting with integrity and encourages them to accept the outcome even when they lose. Using the following questions, identify the criteria you could use to select the best solution to your conflict:

- What are all the available criteria for selecting the best option to resolve your dispute?
- What would make any solution seem fair?
- How could you accomplish what you both want?
- How have other people handled the problem?
- What would happen if you went to court?
- What expert opinion would be useful?
- What ethical or value considerations might influence your choice?
- Why do you think a particular suggested criterion will not work? Do your reasons suggest a way of modifying the criterion so it will work?

- What would make you both feel you won?
- What insights about your conflict have you gained by making this distinction?

Separate Yourself from Others

All conflicts create boundary confusions. We are confused by the boundary between what we think and feel and what the other side thinks and feels, between our anger and our compassion, between what the other side does that touches us and what we cannot fathom, between who we are with our opponent and who we are without them. The emotional exchanges that take place during conflict blur the line that separates us from others. When we are in conflict, we can easily lose sight of who we are, of the distinction between what is ours and what belongs to them.

By arguing for our solutions, we appear to be trying to run others' lives or telling them what to think or feel or do. When they argue back, we feel they are trying to do the same to us. It is crucial in resolving our conflicts that we recognize what legitimately belongs to us and what actually belongs to others. Here are some questions and statements that may help you make this separation in conversation with your opponent. They are all phrased in terms that demonstrate acceptance of responsibility for the speaker's role in the conflict:

- "What is it I did that you are upset about?"
- "I understand that's what you think. Would you like to hear what I think?"
- "Here is what I understand you are asking for: [specific statement] Is that correct?"
- "What do you think I'm asking for?"
- "Here's where I believe you're right, and here's where I disagree with you." [With specific statements for each.]
- "Instead of using the word 'you,' could you make that statement using the word 'I?'"

- "What do you see as the main differences between us?"
- "What do you see as our main similarities?"
- "What role would you like me to play in this conversation?"
- "I can hear that you feel I am being controlling. Would you like to know what I'm really worried about?"
- "Thank you for your ideas. I appreciate your concern. I will think about what you said and let you know my response tomorrow."

It is important that you make it clear, both to yourself and your opponent, what you want and feel. Tell them directly what your ideas are, and listen in the same spirit. Avoid making assumptions about what someone else wants or thinks or feels. If this effort fails, it may be necessary to communicate directly about your confusion regarding boundaries. You may need to actually stop the conversation and say something like this: "I'm sorry for interrupting, but I find it very difficult to listen to you when you make judgments about me, because I find myself becoming defensive and angry. I want to hear what you have to say, and would appreciate it if you would focus on the problem or what I did, rather than who I am. If you cannot do that, I will not be willing to continue this conversation."

We suggest you consider asking these questions to discover what you need to do or say to separate yourself from others in your conflict:

- Do you feel there has been a boundary violation in your conflict? In what way? How?
- Have you done anything to encourage or give permission for this kind of boundary violation?
- Have there been similar boundary violations in your past? If so, how are they related to what is happening in your conflict now?
- What defines the boundaries, definitions, and distinctions between yourself and others in your conflict?

- What could you do or say to more clearly define the boundaries between yourself and others?
- Is it possible that the other person in your conflict feels you have violated their boundaries? How could you find out?
- If you have, would you be willing to stop?
- What insights about your conflict have you gained by making this distinction?

These questions assume your willingness to take responsibility for your role in your conflicts. They demonstrate that you are willing to give up the victim role or the righteous position, and separate yourself from the person on the other side of your conflict. This means accepting the idea of standing alone together, and forming positive rather than negative connections. If this is not possible, it means moving on and connecting with others.

We are all able to form bonds through love, acceptance, and affirmation or through pain, rejection, and negativity. When we are in conflict, the fear of separating from others, of being less when the conflict disappears, of being judged for what we have done can seem overwhelming and keep us from resolution. We hope you will have courage, trust your innate worth, and reach out to other souls—which, though separate, are not unlike your own.

Reminder

As you review the insights you have gained through these separations, pause to recall that none of them actually exist. We live a paradox in which we clarify our identities, set our boundaries, analyze the distinctions between us, and make separations. Yet all the while, if we watch closely, we can recognize and live in the knowledge that we are actually one, and that only together do we create a whole.

Path Six

Learn from Difficult Behaviors

If you feel guilty, you invent a plot, many plots.
And to counter them, you have to organize your
own plot, many plots. But the more you invent
enemy plots, to exonerate your lack of
understanding, the more you fall in love with them,
and you pattern your own on their model. You
attribute to the others what you're doing yourself,
and since what you're doing yourself is hateful, the
others become hateful. But since the others, as a
rule, would like to do the same hateful thing that
you're doing, they collaborate with you, hinting
that—yes—what you attribute to them is actually
what they have always desired.

—Umberto Eco

It may not be enough to focus attention on listening, emotions, interests, and separating issues as discussed in earlier chapters. In spite of all our strategies, our attention is drawn to the *person* whose unreasonable behavior triggered our anger, deepened our frustration, blocked our achievements, kept us at impasse, and justified our distrust. In our fantasies, we feel that if only we could make that person disappear, our conflicts would be over.

Think of the most difficult person in your life—yes, the one who comes to mind immediately. Consider that by accepting the challenge of working through your conflicts with that person, you could experience a transformation, not only in your conflicts with them, but in your ability to resolve *every* conflict for the rest of your life. It is our aim in this chapter to enable you to do so.

Defining the Problem *Is* the Problem

The way we look at a problem has an immediate effect on the range and variety of options that occur to us in trying to solve it. Some options will not appear unless we define the problem correctly. There are three main ways of defining the problem of our relationship with the other person in our conflict. These involve identifying the problem as the person who opposes us, their personality, or their behavior.

Identifying the Problem as a "Difficult Person"

Many of us refer to the people with whom we are in conflict as "problem people." We label our opponents "dishonest" or "negative," or describe them as "controlling," "mean," "manipulative," "lying," or "incompetent." We may use even less pleasant words to label and diminish them.

The effect of these words is to shift our attention from what someone *did* to who they *are*. When we do so, it becomes more difficult for us to resolve our conflicts. How? If we define the problem as a *person*, the only remedy is to shoot them, or remove them from our presence. The first is illegal and immoral. The second is impossible or ineffective, as it only transfers the problem somewhere else, leaving us feeling powerless and frustrated.

Worse, identifying the person as the problem creates a justification for acting against them in an inhuman, antagonistic way, dismissing their concerns and humanity as we feel they have dismissed ours. Ultimately, this gives us permission to engage in some variety of annihilation of the Other, including character assassination and even murder, because by definition, nothing less will solve our problem.

Whenever we define a group as the problem, we automatically create a justification for genocide. Historically, genocide has always been preceded by a campaign of vilification and stereotyping directed against a group of people with the purpose of identifying the entire group as a problem. It is the "person as the problem" as a way of thinking that has always produced revengeful, inhuman, murderous, genocidal solutions, which have been rationalized by saying our targets were "evil" or "naturally inferior" people who "brought it on themselves."

The difficulty with this way of thinking is that, on a personal level, we have all, at some time or another, been "bad" or "problem" people. For this reason, there can never be a limit to our revenge or a barrier to our participation—if not in large-scale genocide or acts of revenge, at least in small acts of annihilation, mini-genocides, that take place every day in all organizations.

The attitude that the person is the problem, which can be found in some form in nearly every conflict, is based on a stereotype nearly identical in operation to those that support every prejudice from racism and anti-Semitism to sexism and homophobia. Stereotyping means transforming people into caricatures of themselves by taking one of their real characteristics, exaggerating it out of proportion, ignoring the diverse ways it manifests itself, collapsing the individual into the group or category, and omitting the complexity of the real human being.

When we stereotype our opponents, it is usually because we cannot find any convincing justification for the pain or fear we have experienced at their hands. We are afraid they will retaliate for the injustices we have done to them and are angry at them, even for the pain they have caused us by being on our conscience.

Our logic in stereotyping our opponents is ordinarily quite simple: If we are basically good and they intentionally hurt us, they must be bad. Or: If we want to end the conflict and are unable to, it is because they are being unreasonable. The value of this way of thinking is that it simultaneously lets us off the hook from having to improve our behavior and gives us permission to act aggressively while still claiming the role of victim.

Identifying the Problem as a "Difficult Personality"

If we define the problem not as the other person, but their difficult *personality*, we will have identified what needs to be solved as the product of inherited genes and decades of family and peer conditioning, which even long-term psychotherapy may not fundamentally alter. In essence, we have defined ourselves into a corner, except in terms of a set of tricks that may allow us to escape injury at their hands.

Labeling our opponent's personality as the problem or judging their character as defective does not automatically lead to annihilation or genocide, but does allow us to permanently dismiss someone and act aggressively or in a manipulative way against them. It also has the advantage of absolving us of responsibility for creating the problem and allowing us to let ourselves off the hook from meeting with them, or doing anything to solve it.

Both these ways of thinking give us permission to stop asking honest questions, to defend ourselves against our own empathy or compassion, and to give up our search for solutions. We need to reconstruct these chains of reasoning backwards to see that they are rationalizations for doing nothing. The real reason we think the person or their personality is the problem is that we don't know what to do to solve it and have given up trying to change anything.

Yet when something shifts in the conflict and empathic communication begins, or when a resolution takes place or creative solutions are discovered, we no longer see our opponents as bad or unreasonable—and they immediately become human to us. Logic compels us to recognize that it was not they that changed, but our attitude toward the conflict. We are then compelled to conclude that our entire mental construct about who they were was fallacious and self-serving.

We get into conflicts with people whose personalities we define as difficult because their behaviors are difficult *for us*, because they trigger something in us that we have not resolved, or that makes us feel powerless in their presence. In other words, we have chosen a way of relating to them that is unskillful or unsuccessful and don't know what else to do, and in this way, have become part of the problem.

We were recently asked to help resolve a highly emotional dispute within the board of directors of a major labor union representing tens of thousands of people in the transportation industry. While the union was fully engaged in bargaining for a new multiyear contract, the directors were busy attacking one another. One of the officers of the union had simply had it with the personal attacks directed against her, and began to respond in kind, with dismissive, smug, challenging, and provocative statements to the board.

As the exchanges grew more heated and tempers flared, paradoxically, they moved further away from addressing the real issues, which were lost in a fog of recrimination, defensiveness, and punishment. The real issues had to do with the dysfunctional way the organization was operating, the failure of the officers to respond to telephone calls from directors, a perceived lack of respect for members of the board, conflicts over style and strategy in raising issues with the company, and differences in union philosophy over how militant or collaborative they should be.

All these issues could have been resolved through informal discussion, or argued about without getting personal. The conflict had gotten so far out of control that several directors refused to participate in a facilitated informal problem-solving process to work on finding solutions to these problems until *after* they had officially reprimanded and punished an officer for disobeying a resolution of the board. The focus of their attention was on trying to change or punish her for what they saw as her "hostile personality." Instead, they needed to address the difficult problems in their relationship, and her disrespectful behavior.

There are, of course, people with "borderline" personalities who are difficult to work with, whom we label crazy because they are difficult for us to reason with. But there is an enormous difference between being crazy and being "crazy like a fox." Most people we think of as crazy are engaging in behaviors that work for them and produce some of the results they want.

R. D. Laing transformed the treatment of mental illness in families by recognizing that many of the people called crazy were simply using strategies that helped them survive in dysfunctional family systems. The same can be said of crazy behavior in organizations. We have seen many employees labeled "difficult personalities" who were simply—but unskillfully—trying to survive in a dysfunctional work environment.

Identifying the Problem as a "Difficult Behavior"

The alternative to labeling the problem as either a "difficult person" or a "difficult personality," is to see it as a "difficult behavior." By shifting the way we describe the problem, we discover how to solve it, since everyone can change their behavior. Simply ask (rhetorically of course) if the person who is engaging in difficult behaviors has learned to speak. If so, they have changed their behavior, and can do so again.

By ceasing to identify the problem as the person or their personality, we allow them to look at what does not work in the way they are acting without thinking of themselves as bad or fundamentally flawed. This shift implicitly makes us more powerful and responsible for solutions, since we can all learn more skillful ways of handling other people's behavior.

When you confront difficult behaviors, ask yourself three questions. First, has the behavior been rewarded in any way by others, by you, or by the system in which they are working? The chances are good that it has, if only by giving them the attention they crave but have been unable to get through positive behavior.

Second, is the behavior a coping mechanism, a way of adapting or surviving in a dysfunctional system? What you may experience as difficult behavior may be a diversion to draw attention away from the fact that they are working beyond their capacity or skill and are afraid of being fired. It may also be that it is the organizational system that is dysfunctional rather than the person, and they are being blamed for not fitting in to an environment that meets no one's needs.

Third, can you become more skillful in your responses so as to diminish support for behaviors you see as a problem? Your negative response to difficult behaviors may simply reinforce or perpetuate them. In work organizations as in families, "misbehaving children" and "squeaky wheels" receive the most attention, are rewarded for difficult behavior, and sometimes succeed in drawing attention to problems and issues everyone else has been ignoring.

Why People Engage in Difficult Behaviors

We tend to see the difficult behaviors of our opponents as irrational, yet they merely appear irrational because we haven't understood the reasons behind them. We need to find out why people are behaving as they are, and what rewards or benefits they are receiving for behaviors that bother us.

Every difficult behavior represents a *why* question we haven't asked. As a result, every honest question we ask someone who is engaged in difficult behaviors will lead to a more accurate description of the reasons they are engaged in those behaviors. And every accurate description of behavior will lead to a strategy for stopping it.

This lesson was made clear to us as we tried to help a group reach consensus on the design of an employee coordinating committee. One person refused to go along with the group, refusing to accept the design. Her "difficult behavior" created considerable conflict and criticism, but she held firm, seemed to enjoy the conflict, and smiled as she stood her ground.

We discovered by open-ended questions that her real issues had nothing to do with the coordinating committee, but were with her own work group, where she had been unsuccessful in raising or resolving problems. We realized she was trying to draw attention to these issues in a roundabout way. We talked about the problem, and in another forum gave her a chance to address the issues that concerned her. She accepted the design, solved many of her problems, and became a leader of the coordinating committee.

There are many reasons people engage in difficult behaviors. Sometimes they are upset because of personal problems at home, unfair criticism at work, an action of which they are ashamed, a topic they can't discuss directly, poor self-esteem, repressed anger over past injustices, or feeling no one likes them so they decide to reject others before they are rejected.

One of our clients is president of his own business, and judges every action of his executives and managers in terms of loyalty to him. If they make their family life or health a priority, he sees it as a rejection and evidence of disloyalty. Yet his greatest unresolved issue is his own commitment, dedication, and loyalty to his employees! He guards himself against commitment, creating conflicts with his staff on a regular basis. He would rather distance himself from commitment and use his staff's alleged disloyalty to rationalize his distancing behavior than confront his issues regarding fear of commitment head-on.

Not Rewarding Difficult Behaviors

In any system, whether at home or at work, you can take the initiative in shifting the focus from blaming or scapegoating to problem solving by changing your own behavior. You can start by not blaming people personally for their problems and initiating a search for practical solutions that satisfy both your interests.

There are substantial payoffs for dysfunctional behaviors in most organizations. These payoffs include becoming the center of everyone's attention, being placated, reprioritizing issues to focus on those being complained about, controlling the group's decisions through negative power and influence, creating a fear of confrontation, diverting attention from mistakes, bringing everyone down to the same level, and being promoted as a way of getting rid of the problem.

Take a moment to analyze how you may be feeding or rewarding behaviors you find difficult. Think of a person whose behavior causes problems for you, and answer the following questions:

- What is the specific behavior you find most disturbing? (Try to describe it in precise words.)
- Why is that disturbing to you?
- Why do you think they are engaged in it?
- What benefits are they deriving from their behavior?
- How are you responding to their behavior? How are others responding?
- Have your or others' responses been successful in stopping the behavior?
- How is the other person benefiting from your reaction?
- How could you change your own behavior to stop rewarding them for behaviors you find unacceptable?
- Have you given them honest feedback about their behavior? If so, how did they receive it?
- Has the group as a whole given them feedback?
- What feedback have you not given them about their behavior? Why not?
- What would it take for you to give them honest feedback?
- What could motivate them to change their behavior?
- How could you reward them for behaviors you find more acceptable? How could you support them in changing?

Changing Difficult Behaviors in Organizations

Managers and employees often point fingers at one another, each claiming the other is difficult or crazy, and citing this as the reason the organization is not more successful. We heard finger-pointing responses like these from staff at a large county agency seeking to "reinvent government":

> My manager is the type that doesn't level with people. Giving a straight message is not part of how he does business. Things happen to people and they don't know why because there's no communication from the powers that be.

> We have difficulty as a management team working together as effectively as we should. There is too much discomfort among the personalities that are present. The majority of people are open to carrying on a dialogue, but one person has a strong personality. She either makes pronouncements or doesn't say anything. Socially, she's delightful, but when things are pushed or tense it's very difficult to talk with her. She thinks she's right and is not open to coaching.

These complaints identify important problems and pinpoint ineffective behaviors. They also attribute the problem to a specific individual based on personality. The comments reveal, however, that it is not personalities but behaviors, and the responses to them, that are the real problems. None of the interviewees took responsibility for their part in creating or continuing the problem. They did not go to the person they were accusing to impart the honest feedback they gave us. Once they labeled the problem as one of personality rather than behavior, there was little they could do to solve it.

In response, we suggested they shift the way they were defining the problem from seeing it as an issue of difficult personalities to seeing it as one of behaviors they had difficulty handling. We recommended that they focus on the actions other people were taking, on the responses they might use, on giving timely, honest, and empathic feedback, and on not feeding or rewarding behaviors they didn't want to continue experiencing. Finally, we suggested they take responsibility for improving their communications rather than giving up, expecting someone else to solve the problem, or trying to change other people's personalities.

Practical Strategies to Change Difficult Behaviors

By focusing on actions and behaviors and what we can do in response, by giving feedback, and taking responsibility for finding solutions, we move from feeling hopeless to being strategic about our problems.

In the county agency we described earlier, we were successful in helping the parties change their difficult behaviors and powerless responses by getting them to assess the unseen rewards they had created that encouraged people to engage in difficult behaviors. To help you become more strategic about the behaviors you find difficult, consider the following list of the steps we took as part of an overall strategy to shift the focus from defining the problem as a "you" to defining it as an "it":

- *Surfacing the conflict:* We began by surfacing the behavioral issues and putting them on the table for discussion. We interviewed people, noted their comments and typed them up verbatim. We deleted names and identifying characteristics to preserve confidentiality and distributed them to everyone without censoring or watering them down.

- *Coaching:* We coached the leader of the organization in how to respond to these issues, to model direct and honest communication, ask others for honest feedback, thank them for it, and set a tone that encouraged openness and empathy.

- *Teamwork:* We conducted a group conflict resolution session in which we assigned people to random teams and asked them to read through the interview comments and reach consensus on the top five behavioral problems. We then asked them to indicate five possible strategies for responding to them more effectively.

- *Process awareness:* We asked each small group whether they experienced any of the problems on the list while working in their groups. No one did, in spite of the fact that all the "difficult people" who had created the problems were present.

They hadn't engaged in problem behaviors, because the group approached their problems strategically in small teams. Everyone was listened to and acknowledged, instructions were clear, and they were addressing issues that were important and real to them.

- *Constructive feedback:* We handed everyone a checklist of positive and negative behaviors, and asked them to identify ones they wanted to develop, minimize, or eliminate for themselves. They read their checked behaviors to their coworkers, starting with the leader of each group, and asked each person for honest feedback on the changes they needed to make. Everyone assessed themselves and received honest feedback about their behaviors from everyone else. This resulted in far more open communication than had existed before.

- *Problem solving:* As the large group discussed ways of improving their behaviors, the issue of diversity was raised. They agreed to hire more diverse staff, and the group brainstormed strategies to increase respect for diversity—not only at the top, but throughout the organization. We complimented them on tackling their problems strategically and discussing sensitive issues without slipping into difficult behaviors.

- *Shared responsibility:* The problem with the "strong personality" of the woman described in the second of the two quotes was addressed by the group, not only in her team, where everyone gave her feedback, but in the large group afterward. When she heard identical feedback from all her coworkers, she became aware of a consistent, coherent pattern in her behavior—something that was perceived not only by people she saw as her enemies, but by her friends as well. Several people said the fault was not entirely hers because no one in the group had given her honest feedback or supported her in changing her behavior.

- *Support for change:* She asked the group for help. Rather than being coached by her supervisor, which would have made her defensive, she agreed to work with several people she respected, who volunteered to help her. With several on-the-job mentors to meet with her every day to focus on specific action items, she was able to change her behavior and reduce tensions considerably in the department.

While the group started out thinking nothing could be done to change her negative behaviors, she was able to change as a result of open communication, honest feedback, group dialogue, and support. The same can happen in your organization and in your life, when you shift from blaming people to solving problems.

The Family Origins of Difficult Behaviors

Consider whether there is a hidden pattern in what you find difficult—that is, whether there is anything that connects the people with whom you have worked or lived with those behaviors you have found difficult. Consider whether their difficult behaviors may in some way match issues you have carried with you from your childhood.

Your opponents' difficult behaviors began long before you became involved in their lives. Most of these difficulties are in fact patterns that were forged in response to unresolved issues or unmet needs from early childhood. If you are not rewarding the behavior, and if the dysfunctional behavior does not appear to have any rational relevance to the present situation, the chances are good that you are dealing with someone who is living out a pattern that has nothing to do with you—something left over from their past, probably from their family of origin.

These behaviors often originate in our inability as children to get our needs met, either because we were deprived and didn't get enough, or because we were smothered and got too much. Children who are unable to satisfy their needs or whose needs are oversatisfied develop compensating behaviors that remain with them for the rest of their lives. As in tuning a musical instrument, excessive tightness produces a high, shrill sound, while excessive slackness produces a thick, dull one. Each of us carries wounds from our families of origin, and as we adapt to our pain, we learn to engage in difficult behaviors we carry into our adult lives without understanding why.

If our parents or peers responded to our needs in ways that were inadequate or excessive, we were likely to adopt patterns of compensating behavior that limit our ability to participate in beneficial adult relationships. If, for example, we needed closeness as a child and didn't get enough, we experience loss, and as adults may be unable to commit to a team or develop close relationships with colleagues. We may be plagued with constant fear of loss, and appear rejecting, distant, and defensive to others.

We may also respond in opposite ways to those we experienced in childhood. Lack of closeness can produce a fear of loss so great that we become clingy and dependent. Our fear of becoming dependent may lead us to avoid intimacy through protective distance, or to become excessively vulnerable to signs of dependency in others.

The people whose behaviors we find most difficult to handle may conduct themselves in ways reminiscent of the parent with whom we have not fully resolved our differences. Often, they are people who developed patterns of compensating behavior exactly opposite to ours, or who engage in behaviors we had to struggle to overcome, or who simply remind us of the difficulties we had as children in getting our needs met.

Regardless of the reasons for the difficult behavior, our responses are a mirror pointing directly to our own childhood issues. Because conflict is a relationship, other people's behaviors point to problems we have not resolved in our own lives. When we fully resolve these issues, their behaviors do not bother or entrap us, and we become skillful at handling their idiosyncrasies.

Many managers want to help their employees, yet fear they are doing too much, and worry they might rob them of the experience of helping themselves. On the other hand, they may also fear that cutting off support could force them to accept choices that are not theirs so they send a message that they do not care about their staff or their problems. The real issue in this dynamic is less the employee's need for help than the manager's internal vacillation between overindulgence and underindulgence.

In one organization where we worked, two women managers had been asked to create a fast-forming team to develop a new product for a premier customer. Corporate management was about to pull the plug on the project because the two were locked in conflict and could not collaborate. We asked April, the senior engineer, whether Sharon, the team leader, reminded her of anyone in her family. She said as a child she felt she had never been good enough to meet her parents' standards. They were distant and judgmental and she felt she would never gain their approval because they couldn't acknowledge who she was. Not surprisingly, she had a similar complaint about Sharon. April felt everything she did was criticized by Sharon, and her work was devalued through personal distance, cool objectivity, and formal review. She wanted Sharon's praise, support, and recognition for being creative.

Sharon, on the other hand, had an alcoholic parent who filled her life with destructive uncertainty, lack of respect for emotional boundaries, and instability. She complained that April was unreliable, never cleared plans with the team, always came up with unexpected reactions, and was needy. Sharon wanted April to work with the team and be more predictable.

At a team retreat, we asked everyone to tell a story from childhood that shaped their team expectations. Their stories revealed the core issues between Sharon and April, and they saw the emotional buttons they pushed in each other. Their team gave them honest feedback, and agreed to coach them when they started to slip into old behaviors. They were each able to say what the other could do to avoid pushing their buttons, and in a written agreement, planned new strategies for communicating and working together. With support from their team, they became a powerful product development group, and among the most satisfied employees in the company.

It's Your Button

We all have emotional buttons that are pushed from time to time by difficult behaviors. Some of our buttons are obvious, and the people who want our attention or are trying to trigger a conflict will learn our buttons well. Anyone who has lived with an adolescent knows how skilled teenagers can be in locating our buttons and knowing exactly when to push them!

In an organization where we once consulted, a woman who was favored for a position became insensitive to an interviewer's buttons during the hiring process. During the interview, she was informed about some of the pressures of the job, and responded, "You don't need a marketing analyst, you need a psychoanalyst." When they told her about the needs of their customers, she said, "You should just give them Prozac."

As it turned out, a member of the selection team was on Prozac and deep in psychoanalysis. He was furious with the candidate and rejected her out of hand. Other team members thought her comments were flip, but did not reject her. These disparate reactions created a conflict on the team. When the team showed empathy for the person whose buttons were pushed, he was able to join them in agreeing to give the interviewee constructive feedback and reevaluate her for the position. She apologized sincerely for her insensitive remarks and was given the job.

We all need to be able to identify the specific behaviors that push our buttons, focus on defusing them, and become less troubled when someone touches them. We increase our energy, health, mental focus, and strength when we talk openly about behaviors that trigger our buttons, especially with the people who trigger them.

Always remember, however, that even though someone has pushed your button, it is still *your* button, and it is your choice how to respond. Choosing your response reduces the other person's ability to control you because you gain power with every choice. Before responding, consider: How did you expect the other person to behave? Why? What would make you engage in their behaviors? Do you know anyone who is *not* bothered by their behavior? Why not? How do they do it? How could you respond to them more skillfully? What skills could you develop to feel less vulnerable to them?

Techniques for Working with Difficult Behaviors

Heraclitus wrote that "character is destiny"—meaning, for our purposes, that we may not have a choice about whether we encounter people who engage in difficult behaviors, but we always have a choice about how we respond to them. Each encounter can be seen by us as a test of our character. We can respond as though it is their fault and wash our hands of the problem. Or we can see it as a challenge and work hard to increase our level of awareness, understanding, acceptance, and skill. When we choose the second, we discover opportunities for personal growth and character development that are not available when we choose the first.

There are two fundamental ways you can respond more skillfully to people who engage in behaviors you consider difficult. First, you can be responsible for your own attitudes and behaviors, including those that trigger difficult behaviors in others. Second, you can communicate honestly to them that what they are doing is hard for you to handle. These steps will encourage both of you to learn how to improve your process, communication, and relationship.

When you focus your attention on increasing your level of skill, you become less vulnerable to the behavior of others, and encourage them to change their behavior by changing yours. If you cannot inspire change in them, you can at least achieve internal peace by honestly confronting the real issues. If there is nothing to do, you may still learn how to live with the problem without losing sight of your long-term goals. In any event, you will feel better about yourself for trying.

Learning techniques to handle difficult behaviors is a lifelong process. We recommend you consider the following checklist of techniques and attitudes we have found useful in relating to people who are engaged in difficult behaviors:

- Accept the other person and their view of the issues that divide you as legitimate from their perspective, without preconceptions or agendas of your own. Next, focus on their behavior and the deeper reasons why it is bothersome to you.

- Do not try to unilaterally determine either the process or the content of your communication about the conflict. Do not start by indicating how it should be resolved, or how the other person should change their behavior. Begin by entering into dialogue with them about the issues.

- Be willing to collaborate in defining what is wrong with your communication and relationship. Take responsibility for your participation and contribution to what is not working between you.

- Express curiosity about the reasons for their behavior, the sources of the conflict between you. Do not assume you already know the answers.

- Search for a deeper, more empathic understanding of the other person. Focus on behaviors you are least able to understand. Ask yourself what would make *you* behave that way.

- Be willing to observe and release hostile feelings and judgments. Openly acknowledge your own lack of skill in responding to behaviors you don't like.

- Work collaboratively to find solutions. Start by thinking of something you can do to improve the situation.

- Express your desire to get beneath the surface of the conflict and discover the real issues and problems. Tell the truth about what is happening, and express a desire to improve your relationship.

- Take responsibility for your false expectations. Ask questions to uncover their interests, expectations, and desires.

- Rigorously respect personal boundaries and differences, including your own. If you or they can't, it may be time to distance yourself from them.
- Accept paradoxes, enigmas, riddles, and contradictions in others' behaviors, as well in as your own.
- Strive for perfect integrity in your behavior.
- Model the degree of openness to introspection, feedback, and evaluation that you want from the other person.
- Keep an empty, open mind. Give the other person the benefit of the doubt, without necessarily agreeing that what they are doing is right.
- Be consistently respectful, courteous, acknowledging, and hospitable, regardless of the other person's allegations or behaviors.
- Hold on to your sense of humor, irony, and play. Most conflicts are not as important as they seem.
- Reach for completion and closure with the other person and for yourself. Make your agreements, understandings, decisions, and responsibilities concrete.

All these techniques and attitudes have a common core, which becomes especially important when we confront someone engaged in difficult behaviors. The core is to center yourself in who you really are, behave responsibly toward others regardless of how difficult they become, and cultivate your capacity for compassion and empathy. As you become more aware of your own contribution to the dance of conflict, you can be more deeply honest and give others feedback about their behaviors. This insight will help you coach and support your opponent, as best you can, to become more effective and authentic in their dealings with you.

As you follow this path, we believe you will discover that you can resolve even the most difficult conflicts, and transform your life. These techniques encourage you to focus less on your opponent and more on building your own capacities through practice, attention, awareness, empathy, and commitment. It takes time—but the time will be well spent, particularly if you consider all the time you have spent being upset about other people's behavior and feeling power-less responding to it.

Responding to Difficult Behavior in Organizational Cultures

As noted in the first chapter, culture exercises an extraordinary influence in shaping how we think about and handle our conflicts. Many organizations have developed cultures that foster and reward difficult behaviors. Even if you build your skills in responding to difficult behaviors, manage how your buttons get pushed, and heal un-resolved wounds from the past, if the culture in your organization does not support cooperation and honest, open communication, you will continue to struggle for balance.

Every organizational culture includes a set of norms for accept-able behaviors, unspoken expectations regarding interactions, and hidden rules for how to work together. Most often, these are invis-ible to people inside the culture, yet they shape everyone's thoughts, feelings, and behavior. It is common for cultural values to clash and even contradict one another.

When we want someone to change, we give them advice or try to get them to do something that fits *our* expectations or needs, but not necessarily their own. We are like the monkey in the African story, who places the fish safely up in a tree so it won't drown. If you want to end the difficult behaviors in your organization by increas-ing opportunities for skill development, resolving chronic conflicts, and improving cooperation, you will need to reshape the culture to welcome and support efforts, so people will not behave like the monkey in the story.

Our definition of organizational culture is *what everyone knows and no one talks about.* And you can't change a culture if you can't talk about it. Indeed, every culture defends itself against change, creates obstacles to new ways of thinking, and resists alteration of its values. This is what gives cultures their staying power. Here are some of the primary obstacles we have encountered in the organizational cultures in which we have worked:

- Conditioned passivity and reactiveness
- Rewards for competition, individualism, and selfishness
- Stories of victimization and demonization
- Reliance on formal rules, policies, and external discipline
- Isolation and social fragmentation
- Conflict avoidance and rewards for aggression
- Acceptance of covert behavior

One powerful tool for creating dramatic cultural change is simply to talk about the shared values, ethics, and standards that people in the organization want to live by, and secure everyone's agreement to honor and promote them. By clarifying values and standards and committing to them, we learn what is expected, what is important, and how our behaviors are perceived by others.

If you can work with others in your organization to create a set of shared values, ethics, or standards, it will be much easier to differentiate the behaviors that undermine those values from those that support them. You can then work to develop an environment that discourages the former and encourages the latter.

Nearly every organization has at least one member who regularly engages in destructive or difficult behaviors. Yet everyone in these organizations has the capacity to act in unison in such a way as to publicly identify, and thereby either minimize or transform, these behaviors.

As mediators and consultants, we have the advantage of being outsiders and are permitted to design and implement group processes that differ from—even contradict—key elements of the organization's culture. Even cultural insiders can have a substantial impact on difficult behaviors if they approach them in the right way and do not slip into responses that reinforce theose behaviors.

It is possible for anyone in any organization to speak up during a meeting, and simply ask, for example, whether everyone in the group is comfortable with what is happening. At the end of a meeting, anyone can ask if it would be possible to take turns and have each person make one suggestion for how the next meeting could be made more effective.

It is possible to stop someone as (or after) they engage in behavior you find difficult, ask their permission to give them some honest feedback, and then describe—using "I" statements—how their behavior affected you. Anyone can ask members of their team to write down what is working and what is not, or ask if it would be possible to hold a meeting where everyone gives everyone else honest feedback.

Often, we find the person engaged in difficult behavior feels isolated and alone. By drawing them in and acknowledging their needs and interests, you can shift their attitude and style without rewarding their problem behaviors. Classroom teachers know "problem children" often give up antagonistic attitudes toward the class when they are included or given a role or job that is valued by others. As the poet Edwin Markham wrote, we can draw them in:

> They drew a circle to shut me out,
> Heretic, rebel, a thing to flout.
> But Love and I had the wit to win,
> We drew a circle that took them in.

Several years ago, we worked with a team of teachers from a school in Chicago having tremendous difficulty with one team member. Fred, the only male on a team with four women, refused to take part in team meetings; he sat to the side grading papers while the others tried to draw him in. He routinely expressed his contempt for the team process, which he called "touchy-feely" and regarded as an interference with his right to teach in whatever way he wanted.

Toward the end of a team meeting, Fred announced that he was leaving early because he had been called to the principal's office to meet with a complaining parent. The other team members stopped him as he got up and said that since they were a team, if there was a complaint it should be directed to the team as a whole. They adjourned the meeting and went together to the principal's office, where they spoke to the parent about Fred's outstanding teaching abilities. After that, Fred became an active team member and an ardent supporter of the team process. They drew him in.

Giving Feedback and Evaluation

One way of discouraging or preventing difficult behaviors that lead to conflicts is to give each other regular, honest, open, timely feedback about what is working in your relationships and communications and what is not. Relationships are living, changing organisms that are highly sensitive. Like all living things, they require feedback to grow—or simply stay alive. When feedback dies, so do the relationships that rest on it.

Feedback is an honest, nonjudgmental, personal response to another person's communications or behaviors. It is most effective when it is

- Opened with a self-assessment by the person giving it
- Done with permission
- Delivered as an "I" statement
- Reciprocally exchanged
- Given by one's peers
- Offered constructively
- Specific and detailed
- Balanced and fair
- Communicated in real time
- Delivered without anger or judgment

- Supportive of learning, growth, and change
- Accepted with sincere thanks from the person receiving it

Evaluation is a more objective, less personal response, and is also useful in jointly assessing what worked and what didn't and reaching closure. Unlike feedback, evaluation focuses on events or actions rather than behavior or feelings. When applied to people, evaluation implies judgment, grading, or an exercise of power or control over another. When applied to strategies or actions, it is a way of discovering why one approach worked or didn't, and correcting it in midstream. Feedback and evaluation should be reciprocal and collaborative, so no one feels they are in a one-down position, immune from learning, or not responsible for assessing what's working and what is not.

It is always best to start the process by giving yourself feedback, then invite the other person or members of the group to respond. In this way, you indicate the level of honesty and nondefensiveness you expect from them, and your feedback will be received more openly when it is their turn. Afterwards, thank them for their comments, and ask for permission to begin giving your feedback to them.

When you have completed the process, evaluate together what worked and what didn't about the conversation you just had.

Responding to Difficult Behaviors in Meetings

People who work in organizations spend considerable time in meetings. With collaborative group processes, team building, conflict resolution, and other change initiatives, we end up meeting frequently with peers and coworkers as well. The number, variety, and pace of meetings has increased steadily, while our skill in conducting effective meetings has lagged behind.

Difficult behaviors blossom in meetings, where they leave us feeling frustrated and powerless. You have doubtless experienced meetings in which you felt trapped or held hostage by behaviors that were difficult or painful. We once consulted with an organization undergoing a massive change process in which meetings seemed designed to increase frustration and distrust. The group's manager, Cathy, was a "nice person" with few organizational skills. She meant well, but she seemed unable to create a clear agenda, delegate tasks, or answer important questions. Ted, the organization's comptroller, loved dominating meetings and using them for attacking, criticizing, and blaming staff. Everyone dreaded meetings, and spent time in them ducking barbs from the comptroller and holding back their anger.

We were told this behavior had to stop or "the organization will implode." We began by asking each person to offer one suggestion for making their meetings more effective. Most of the suggestions were for Ted to stop his dominating behavior. Ted agreed to do so if they would agree to take responsibility for making their meetings work. In the discussions that followed, Ted became one participant out of many and unable to dominate the meeting. As the issues emerged, we asked volunteers to draft a set of procedures and ground rules for their next meeting, facilitate it themselves, and spend five minutes at the end discussing how to improve their next meeting. Finally, they had a structure for their meetings, and were able to control their comptroller.

There are many ways we can respond to difficult behaviors in meetings. Most do not require advance agreement and can be implemented unilaterally. In doing so, it is important to distinguish between people who disagree with the direction a meeting is taking or with some policy or decision being made by the group, and people who are being intentionally disruptive.

The former need to be heard out. Efforts need to be made to satisfy their interests, which are expressed through disagreement. This is especially the case when they feel passionately about a subject or issue. Passion is often experienced by others as an obstacle to open dialogue, as a judgment of the other side's integrity, and a block to consensus.

If you are facing problems with people who are exhibiting genuinely difficult behaviors, try bringing the following suggestions to your next meeting, and asking everyone to select the ones they want to follow. This will raise the issue of difficult behaviors openly, and reveal ways of limiting or managing them.

- Prepare the person who regularly engages in difficult behavior *before* the meeting, by discussing how they could help make it a successful session.

- Inform this person that one of the topics on the agenda will be a discussion of what happened at the last meeting. Ask them to say what they think should be done differently in the future so meetings will be more satisfying to them and others.

- Interview them and model empathic and responsive listening. Be explicit about what you want to accomplish. Tell them you are listening as you would like them to listen to you.

- Meet with other group members before the meeting. Ask them to be willing to include this person and acknowledge and validate their contributions. Ask them to calmly and honestly confront the behavior, keep to the agenda, and refuse to engage in diversionary arguments.

- Negotiate ground rules for the meeting.

- Create listening teams, in which everyone pairs with someone with an opposing or different point of view, and each presents their partner's perspective to the group, to build understanding for diverse positions.

- Create a "fishbowl" discussion of issues where pairs of opponents discuss the issues for ten minutes while other group members observe the process and give them feedback. Call time-outs so observers can offer feedback on the process.

- Draw out their motives and respond directly to these, rather than to their behavior or the content of their issues.

- Give them your honest personal, emotional responses to their actions. For example, say, "I feel powerless to accomplish anything when you get so angry or talk so much during the meeting."

- Give them a special task or role in the meeting that is valued by the group, such as facilitating, recording, or keeping time.
- Ask them to summarize their critics' arguments. Ask the critics if the summary was accurate, and to correct it if it fell short.
- Suggest a role reversal. Ask those who have been silent to do all the talking for five minutes, and those who have talked to be silent, and then debrief. Or ask the critics to argue in support and the supporters to criticize, then debrief.
- Create a moment of silence so everyone can think about what just happened in the meeting, then ask people to share their thoughts.
- Find some basis for agreeing with the person engaging in difficult behavior. Ask, "If everything else were acceptable, would that still be an issue?"
- Support or agree with the interests being expressed, and limit your disagreement to the process or the content.
- Reframe their statements, to show how they might communicate them more constructively.
- Acknowledge their feelings and ask whether others share them.
- Allow for only clarifying questions first, and debate afterward.
- Post issues neutrally on a flip chart to defuse ownership and political opposition.
- Post opposing points of view so everyone knows they've been heard and the point does not need to be repeated. Ask for a straw vote on their point of view to see if there is any support for continuing the discussion.
- Post the significant contributions people make during the meeting to create a sense of group ownership. Use names to record the contributions, lack of contribution, or domination of the meeting.
- At the end of the meeting, ask everyone to suggest one way of making the next meeting more effective.
- Agree on ground rules for the next meeting, and sanctions if they are violated.

- Ask a professional to facilitate the meeting.
- Bring in a mediator to resolve issues separately with those who engage in difficult behaviors.

Before you move too quickly to silence difficult behaviors, consider whether you may not have engaged in some yourself, and whether the real reason for the behavior may not be the meeting itself. Walk in the other person's shoes for a while in your imagination and consider how you would feel before putting a stop to what may actually be a healthy response to an unhealthy situation.

Difficult Behavior as Resistance to Change

Personal and organizational changes occur constantly in our lives, as many of us struggle with sweeping changes. As we search for the sources of difficult behavior, we discover many that are disguised forms of resistance to change and a result of the failure of leadership to involve people from the beginning in defining both the process and the content of change.

We once watched a cynical vice president in a telephone company overwhelm a creative, innovative, and enthusiastic department director with demands for meaningless paperwork as a way of resisting her effort to restructure the organization into self-managing teams. We witnessed an entire staff in a public school sabotage a school reform effort because their ideas, suggestions, and contributions had not been solicited or respected. We saw the department chief of a large government agency undermine the efforts of his social work staff to provide more responsive customer service by resisting meeting with a planning delegation and dismiss them by opening his mail as they tried to present their plans to him.

Rapid, constant, and disruptive change is now a fact of organizational life. The difficult behaviors that emerge during the change process often take the form of resistance and a fear that change will lead not to improvement but to loss. The result is often conflict, because every change involves loss, insecurity, and fear. Yet we know that change takes place more smoothly when

- Everyone is involved in planning it.
- There is a clear vision.
- People know where it is headed and what it will actually do.
- Goals and outcomes are collaboratively and clearly identified.
- Small changes are tried out first.
- People who resist the change are won over or moved to neutrality or support by having their objections answered.
- Conflicts are addressed openly and resolved.
- Feedback, evaluation, and self-correction are built into the process.

The difficult behavior you are experiencing may actually be an expression of fear that the change will result in unacceptable loss, or anxiety that the person may not have the skills to succeed under the new system, or worry that something valuable may get thrown out by mistake. It may simply be a lack of opportunity to grieve for the loss of old relationships that are about to be dismantled.

If you can welcome the person engaging in the difficult behavior, if you can affirm and even celebrate the resister's gift of a different perspective, if you can see their resistance as an opportunity to improve the substance as well as the process of change, if you can actually *encourage* criticism and see dissent as a contribution to deeper understanding and growth, then you will be able to see your enemies as allies and do battle against what made you enemies in the first place.

Imagining a World Without Difficult Behaviors

Every difficult behavior represents a lesson we can learn, a challenge we can rise to, a skill we can develop. By suppressing the people who engage in difficult behaviors, we may actually eliminate our opportunity to learn from them. This idea lies at the heart of the following story by Anthony De Mello:

There was once a rabbi who was revered by the people as a man of God. Not a day went by when a crowd of people wasn't standing at his door seeking advice or healing or the holy man's blessing. . . . There was, however, in the audience a disagreeable fellow who never missed a chance to contradict the master. He would observe the rabbi's weaknesses and make fun of his defects to the dismay of the disciples, who began to look on him as the devil incarnate. Well, one day the "devil" took ill and died. Everyone heaved a sigh of relief. Outwardly, they looked appropriately solemn, but in their hearts they were glad. . . . So the people were surprised to see the master plunged in genuine grief at the funeral. When asked by a disciple later if he was mourning over the eternal fate of the dead man, he said, "No, no. Why should I mourn over our friend, who is now in heaven? It was for myself I was grieving. That man was the only friend I had. Here I am surrounded by people who revere me. He was the only one who challenged me. I fear that with him gone, I shall stop growing." And, as he said those words, the master burst into tears.

Carlos Castaneda, author of the Don Juan chronicles, has written of the value of having a "petty tyrant" in one's life, because only through a petty tyrant does one learn patience, endurance, and perseverance. What would we be without the difficult behaviors of others? Who would we become without enemies, troublemakers, boat-rockers, and gadflies? What one person finds difficult, another finds useful, or indicative of integrity or determination. Literature, drama, and popular culture would be bland and boring without the tension of difficult behaviors. History would cease, and social progress would come to an end.

In some Native American cultures there were people who did everything opposite to the way it was supposed to be done. If everyone danced clockwise, they danced counterclockwise. If everyone cried, they laughed. They did so to preserve the harmony and balance of the universe, which is not one-sided but composed of opposites. Just as there cannot be an up without a down, there can be no easy behaviors without difficult ones.

Charles Swindoll has written powerfully about the importance these attitudes have in determining how we live our lives:

> Words can never adequately convey the incredible impact of our attitude toward life. The longer I live the more convinced I become that life is 10 percent what happens to us and 90 percent how we respond to it.
>
> I believe the single most significant decision I can make on a day-to-day basis is my choice of attitude. It is more important than my past, my education, my bankroll, my successes or failures, fame or pain, what other people think of me or say about me, my circumstances, or my position. Attitude keeps me going or cripples my progress. It alone fuels my fire or assaults my hope. When my attitudes are right, there's no barrier too high, no valley too deep, no dream too extreme, no challenge too great for me.

Our final recommendation to you on this topic is that instead of focusing on eliminating difficult behaviors, you focus on learning from them. Every difficult behavior is difficult *for you*, for reasons you can learn to appreciate. You can investigate your own discomfort, develop your skills, monitor your behaviors, and improve your relationships by confronting and working through your difficulties rather than blaming them on others. You can stretch your empathy and compassion by learning more about what makes people engage in these behaviors. You can search harder for creative, collaborative solutions, and create circles that draw in those who you have excluded.

You can also choose not to have these people in your life, and go elsewhere. But if you choose to go elsewhere, make sure you do not give up too soon, let yourself off the hook, and lose an opportunity for growth, resolution, and transformation. If you don't take time to understand the behaviors that strike you as difficult and how you may have contributed to them, wherever you go you will find yourself surrounded by people who act exactly like the ones you left behind.

Solve Problems Creatively and Negotiate Collaboratively

> The greatest and most important problems of life
> are all in a certain sense insoluble. They must be so
> because they express the necessary polarity inherent
> in every self-regulating system. They can never be
> solved, but only outgrown. . . . What on a lower
> level, had led to the wildest conflicts and to
> panicky outbursts of emotion, viewed from the
> higher level of personality, now seemed like a storm
> in the valley seen from a high mountain-top. This
> does not rob the thunderstorm of its reality, but
> instead of being in it, one is now above it.
>
> —*Carl Jung*

Problem solving is a crucial element in resolving any conflict. After you have listened actively, responsively, and empathically, acknowledged and processed emotions, reached below the surface to uncover hidden issues, separated people from problems and positions from interests, and learned from difficult behaviors, the search for creative solutions begins. Problem solving is a watershed point, where the entire process shifts from expansion to contraction, from emotion to logic, from large-scale exploration to practical implementation. We begin by opening up our conflicts and seeing what is inside, including underlying issues, emotions, and interests. We end by closing them down, completing what we started, and addressing options, priorities and agreements as part of a negotiation that will end in resolution.

When we are in conflict, we tend to see what *we* want as the only possible solution. Our solutions nearly always emanate from our emotional responses to the conflict, and do not take into account what our opponent wants, the nature of their emotional needs, or what is logically possible or rationally beneficial.

In our mediation practice it is not uncommon to encounter litigants who demand a million dollars in settlement. But that sum says more about the pain they suffered than what a judge or jury would be likely to award if they went to court. It is designed to inflict pain on the person whose evil actions caused their distress.

To resolve disputes without forcing the other side to surrender, but engage in constructive dialogue, and reach consensus on solutions, we need to stop searching for emotional compensation for the wrongs done to us. We need to start calculating logically and practically what we actually need, and what we actually can get. We need to move from redress to restitution, from processing to problem solving, from revenge to release, if we are to find solutions that will be acceptable to each of us.

Conceptual Preparation for Creative Problem Solving

Problem solving is a five-step process. First, we need to become aware of the existence of the problem, and accept it as something that needs to be solved. Second, we need to analyze the elements of the problem so we can understand how to approach it strategically. Third, we need to generate options and assess alternative criteria. Fourth, we need to take specific, concrete, committed action to address the problem. Finally, we need to evaluate our results, and give each other feedback so we can learn from what we did.

There are also three important conceptual or attitudinal shifts to prepare ourselves for engaging in the problem-solving process. To begin with, we need to encourage positive attitudes toward the problem-solving process by opening possibilities for resolution through imagination and creativity, putting aside the assumption that ours is the only solution, or that the other person needs to be punished, or that there has to be a win-lose outcome.

Second, as we release ourselves from the rigidity of assuming that the only possible solution is the one we suggested, we will discover creative possibilities we could not have imagined beforehand. We will see that the problem-solving process works best when it is open, honest, collaborative, and inclusive of everyone involved in the problem. Problem solving need not be a lonely process. Inviting others to join us in solving the problem enriches the solution pool with ideas no single player could envision.

Finally, we need to address the problem of how we will go about solving our problems. If we approach them with a learning, transformational orientation that thrives on the paradoxes, enigmas, riddles, and contradictions that are at the core of most of our problems, we will be far more successful in discovering fresh options. This shift in thinking is perhaps the most powerful of all. The philosopher Ludwig Wittgenstein reveals the nature of this opportunity, and the shift that is required along this path:

> Getting hold of the difficulty "down deep" is what is hard. Because, if it is grasped near the surface, it simply remains the difficulty it was. It has to be pulled out by the roots; and that involves our beginning to think about these things in a new way. The change is as decisive as, for example, that from the alchemical to the chemical way of thinking. The new way of thinking is what is so hard to establish. Once the new way has been established, the old problems vanish; indeed, they become hard to recapture.

Each of these conceptual or attitudinal shifts will help you move into more effective and creative problem solving. Yet each is also an end in itself and an opening to transformation. As you begin the practical work of problem solving, consider the following steps as a way of shifting the way you are approaching the task.

Step One: Adopt a Positive Attitude
Toward Problem Solving

If you can approach problem solving positively, as an adventure or challenge, and not take your problems too personally or seriously, you will be more successful in solving them. One of the purposes of the emotional processing discussed in preceding chapters is to allow you to complete and let go of your emotions so that you can have a conversation that is actually about the problem and not about your emotional baggage.

Your attitude will be the decisive force in determining how you approach the problem and how open you will be to solutions that fall short of total victory. There are a number of personal attitudes you can cultivate to help you become a better, more creative problem solver. As you review this list of attitudes, consider which ones you would like to practice more often.

- *Acceptance* of the existence and full complexity of the problem
- *Calmness* in the face of paradox or contradiction
- *Empathy* with the person you see as the source of the problem
- *Openness* to all possible solutions
- *Optimism* about the chances for success
- *Balance* in approaching the problem
- *Curiosity* about where it originated
- *Awareness* of your own role in creating the problem
- *Courage* about addressing difficult or dangerous issues
- *Relaxation* to allow intuition and subconscious ideas to arise
- *Playfulness* to encourage creative thinking
- *Surrender* to the possibility of resolution

Think about the sort of person you consult when you are at impasse in solving a problem. Do they possess any of these attributes?

What is your attitude when you confront problems? Are you curious, relaxed, and playful? Are you defensive, stubborn, and argumentative? At each moment you have a choice about how to respond to your problems, and the attitude you reveal will play a significant role in your success. As you search for solutions, try to express the attitude you want to experience and reveal to others. The difficulties you encounter will seem less like obstacles or problems and more like hurdles or challenges.

Step Two: See Problem Solving as a Collaborative Process

We observed a vivid example of collaboration and creative problem solving in an organization we helped transition to self-managing work teams. One of the key teams was failing, responsibilities were falling through the cracks, morale was extremely low, and there was no effective team leader. Team members were blaming each other and escalating their conflicts, and the whole process was at impasse.

The head of the organization wanted immediate action. Forgetting the lessons he had learned during the team training about empowering others, he called the team manager into his office and read him the riot act, including a veiled threat that if he didn't solve the problem his job was in jeopardy. The conversation took place at such a pitch that people down the hall could hear every angry word.

The team manager used the same inappropriate style when he met with the team, barking out a series of orders about how to implement his solutions to the problem. As a result, everyone felt more frustrated, disempowered, and upset, and the problem only got worse.

After giving the executive and manager feedback and coaching, we suggested they go to the team, acknowledge their mistakes, and work with team members to assess the problems and what went wrong in trying to fix them. The manager apologized for trying to impose his solutions on the team and conducted an analysis with them of the problems they were having. They worked together to understand the problem, and reached consensus on solutions everyone was able to accept and implement. A win-win outcome was produced through involvement and participation in the problem-solving process.

When you are asked to solve problems you did not participate in defining, or are given solutions you did not help in creating, you might well react with resistance, resentment, cynicism, apathy, or rebellion. When you see your conflicts simply as problems that need to be solved and the search for solutions as a joint responsibility, you remove a significant source of impasse.

Step Three: Solve the Problem of How to Solve Problems

After we decide to address our problems creatively and collaboratively, the next step is to focus attention on the *way* we are trying to solve them because, as Albert Einstein remarked, "Our problems cannot be solved with the same level of thinking that created them."

There are many approaches we can take to solving our problems, but most of us approach them with the attitude that they are adversaries or enemies that need to be defeated or controlled, rather than seeing them as opportunities for learning and improvement. We face problems all our lives, but only rarely do we stop to consider how we can improve the way we go about trying to solve them.

For example, consider the following comment in a report by Michael Maccoby in *Harvard Business Review* on the success of Japanese management techniques, which makes it clear that we can approach our problems more creatively if we see them as opportunities for improvement:

When I visited the Toyota assembly plant at Nagoya [Japan] I was told that there were an average of 47 ideas per worker per year of which 80 percent were adopted. I couldn't believe it; this meant almost an idea from each worker every week. The Toyota manager said, "I think you in the West have a different view of ideas. What you call complaints, we call ideas. You try to get people to stop complaining. We see each complaint as an opportunity for improvement."

This shift in attitude toward problems—redefining a complaint as an opportunity for improvement—is a small change in terminology that can leverage an enormous transformation in the way you think about your problems. It does so by redefining problems as mutual responsibilities, as sources of growth, self-actualization, pride, and learning. It redefines complaining as pointing to what is not working, and change as recognizing that complaints are just ideas.

The traditional approach to problem solving is very different. It starts from a control-oriented methodology that leaves the other person out of the process and sees problems as enemies to be eliminated. As widespread as the traditional approach is, its results are often disastrous, sometimes creating more difficulties than you had before you started.

The most effective problem-solving process is not one in which you seek to control outcomes or immediately rush to solutions, but one in which you seek to learn from what went wrong, step back, analyze the problem, and live with it for a while. When you have reached a full and complete understanding of the issues involved, you easily discover solutions.

Instead of using power to control the people you see as responsible for your problems, it is possible to support each other in finding solutions and adopt a learning-oriented approach, one that allows you to learn from your problems. The following chart describes these fundamentally different problem-solving styles. Take a closer look at the consequences of each, and choose the one you think will produce the most satisfying results.

It is extremely difficult for most of us to overcome our natural desire to control and immediately solve our problems, rather than

Orientation to Problem Solving

	Control Orientation	Learning Orientation
Goals	• To assert sufficient control to ensure that problems as you define them are solved in ways you see fit.	• To maximize my opportunity to create alternatives and test whether they work or not.
Assumptions	• Other people can't be influenced. • Problems can't be solved unless they are solved "my way."	• Other people can be influenced. • I can be influenced. • Constraints can be altered.
Strategies	• Unilaterally impose your solutions and act as though you are not doing so. • Do not request feedback about your own ideas. • Shoot down others and don't share reasons why.	• Identify shared responsibility for problem definitions and for solutions. • Encourage others to react to your plans, and do the same for others. • Experiment off-line with alternatives.
Consequences	• Reflect privately on results. • Low team commitment and responsibility. • Public "group think." • Private politicking and subterfuge. • Polarized group dynamics. • High risk to raise difficult problems.	• Discuss results publicly. • Increased team participation. • Higher team commitment and responsibility. • Increased willingness to raise problems. • More resources to tackle them. • More creativity and better solutions.

Source: Adapted from Diana Smith's "Working Paper"

live with them, learn from them, and only then try to solve them. Yet our problems are often expressions of underlying paradoxes and polarities that cannot be collapsed or resolved, and should not be treated as problems to be solved, but accepted for what they are.

Paradoxical Problem Solving

In our book *Thank God It's Monday!*, we identified paradoxical problem solving as one of fourteen values needed to make workplaces more human and user-friendly. We used an example from our work we want to repeat here because it expresses what we mean by living with paradoxical problem solving:

> One of our most unusual assignments was to facilitate an intensive three-day planning process for a world-renowned science museum that wanted to create a national teacher-education center. It was unusual because they did not want a linear, final plan as an outcome. Rather, they asked that the process capture and preserve the paradoxes, dissimilarities, conflicts and wide variety of contradictory ideas that would be generated by a diverse collection of staff, science teachers, and international representatives of the science, political and education communities whom they wanted to invite to attend the session and critique their ideas.
>
> To solve the problem of how to design a teacher-training center and organize its programs, they wanted to hold on to all their open questions, to list the main paradoxes and dissimilarities, and to keep all the richness and complexity of their uncertainty. The "charette" planning process we facilitated produced several prototypes which they lived with, discussed, and reviewed. They used these models as sources for a final design workshop from which they created an ultimate plan. This plan was also left open so the center could evolve organically at its own pace, shifting between the four models that were generated during the charette. The paradox of moving in four directions at once created a more powerful program than coming to a single path through a linear process.

Paradoxes and polarities are part of nature and human thinking. It is impossible to resolve the "conflict" between up and down, light and dark, plus and minus, inner and outer, without at the same time abolishing both. The same can be said about life and death, pleasure and pain, good and evil, right and wrong, truth and falsehood. It is impossible to eliminate one without eliminating the other. This idea is described by Italian novelist Umberto Eco: "In those halcyon days I believed that the source of enigma was stupidity. Then . . . I decided that the most terrible enigmas are those that mask themselves as madness. But now I have come to believe that the whole world is an enigma, a harmless enigma that is made terrible by our own mad attempt to interpret it as though it had [a single] underlying truth."

For this reason, we need to respect our problems and not simplify their natural complexity but explore them.

Our greatest teacher in learning how to live with paradox is everyday life. We need only accept the challenge of living fully, conscious of the fact that life might end at any moment. The paradox is to know and accept death as a natural part of life, yet not surrender to it; to live fully in the moment with the certainty that it will end.

By accepting our problems, learning from them, wrestling with them and at the same time not immediately solving them, we are able to discover the paradoxes they express. If we become aware of these paradoxes and do not try to reduce them to a single solution, if we are open to learning and allowing the interplay of diverse and contradictory processes, we can enrich our lives immeasurably— and come to resolution and transformation.

Hurdles to Creative Problem Solving

In addition to the dangers of approaching problems with a closed mind, having a control orientation, and engaging in simplistic, nonparadoxical thinking, there are a number of practical hurdles to successful problem solving. Based on work by Bolman and Deal in their book, *Reframing Organizations*, here are some of the most common barriers or obstacles that stand in the way of creative problem solving:

- *We are not sure what the problem is.* Definition of the problem is vague or competing, and many problems are intertwined.

- *We are not sure what is really happening.* Information is incomplete, ambiguous, or unreliable, and people disagree on how to interpret the information that is available.

- *We are not sure what we want.* We have multiple goals that are unclear or conflicting or both. Different people want different things, leading to political, value-based, emotional conflicts.

- *We do not have the resources we need.* Shortages of time, attention, money, and support make difficult situations even more chaotic.

- *We are not sure who is supposed to do what.* Roles are unclear, there is disagreement about who is responsible for what, and roles keep shifting as problems come and go.

- *We are not sure how to get what we want.* Even if we agree on what we want, we are unsure or in opposition about how to get it.

- *We are not sure how to communicate what we want to others.* We hesitate to communicate what we want for fear of offending others.

- *We don't know what is possible.* We have not explored all the options or disagree about which to focus on first.

- *We are not sure how to determine if we have succeeded.* We are not sure what criteria to use to evaluate success. If we know the criteria, we are not sure how to measure them.

- *We are not sure what we did that was responsible for our success.* Once we succeed, we are unsure if our efforts were responsible, and if so, which ones.

Each of these barriers can be overcome, and many quite easily—for example, by asking people to identify the problems they think are most important, brainstorming before arriving at solutions, observing the problem over a period of time to see how it changes, identifying the key elements in a system that need changing, broadening our definition of the problem, and analyzing what worked and why.

We observed a disaster that took place because key players lacked a shared understanding of the issues and selected the wrong problem to solve. The CEO of a small, successful consulting firm was angered by the failure of his leadership team to generate adequate business and produce enough revenue for the company. In his view, the problem was that they were just not doing their work, and were not finding clients or selling business.

His solution was to yell at them and tell them they had to bring in more business or they would no longer be part of the leadership team. They, on the other hand, defined the problem as his hostile, micromanaging behavior. By focusing on whether they were trying hard enough or he was supportive enough, they both took a simplistic view and chose the wrong problem to solve. They tried to control the problem rather than learn from it because they were not sure how to get what they wanted, or how to work together more effectively.

We suggested they stop mid-solution, back up, and meet to better define the problem. They used a brainstorming process to answer the following questions: Where have we been successful and where have we failed to generate or sell business? What do we need to do to be more successful? How can we target our efforts to make our work more successful? What role can each of us play in this process? What are we each willing to contribute to increasing our business?

As they answered these questions, their entire attitude changed and there was a burst of commitment and creativity in developing strategies to solve the problem. They agreed on a new set of initiatives and each team member identified personal contributions they could make. The team created strategies to support one another, delineated a time line, and targeted actions and results, and everyone affirmed their commitment to produce more revenue. The CEO agreed to stop yelling and micromanaging. The solutions were owned by everyone, and they were able to market the company in a more positive fashion so that everyone's numbers went up.

Five Steps in Creative Problem Solving

How do we implement a learning style to solve our problems? How do we come up with creative solutions? In the middle of conflict, how do we invent options or alternatives that meet both sides' interests and open up possibilities of resolution and transformation?

One definition of conflict is simply feeling stuck in a problem you can't figure out how to solve, or have so far been unsuccessful solving. Yet there are a number of highly practical, specific steps you can take to solve your problems. At the very least, these steps will help you understand why your problem can't be solved. The problem-solving process is most successful, we find, when it is broken down into stages or steps, with each step taken separately. The following discussion is based partly on the ideas of mediator Peter Kneedler.

Step 1. Recognize and accept that you
have a problem, and choose to solve it:

- Admit and accept that you have a problem.
- Name the problem with as much precision as you can.
- Identify the causes of the problem, and separate them from the people involved in it.
- Surface the underlying issues or sources of the problem.
- Choose to commit whatever time and energy is necessary to solve the problem.
- Increase the willingness of the other side to face and work through the problem.

Step 2. Define and clarify the problem:

- Gather as much information as you can about the problem.

- Restate the problem clearly and concisely, based on what you have learned about it.
- Identify the barriers or difficulties that need to be overcome in solving it.
- Compare the problem with others, noticing its similarities and differences.
- Determine what information is still needed to reach a solution.
- Identify the questions you need to answer to solve it.
- Return to the problem after completing these steps and re-state it.

Step 3. Analyze the problem:

- Analyze, categorize, and prioritize the elements that make up the problem.
- Examine the way the problem has been affected by the context and relationships that surround it.
- Consider the history of the problem, its evolution over time.
- Identify the perfect state in which the problem no longer exists and work backward from the future.
- Check for factual consistencies and inconsistencies.
- Identify unstated assumptions and expectations.
- Watch for myths, stereotypes, and clichés.
- Notice the value orientations and ideological assumptions in your approach to the problem.
- Separate out any emotional elements that may have distorted the problem.
- Search for structural and systemic causes of the problem.

Step 4. Develop solutions that satisfy the interest of both sides:

- Determine whether the information you have is adequate, and if not, return to analysis.
- Generate options through brainstorming.

- Search for alternatives that satisfy both sides' interests.
- Develop appropriate criteria for determining whether you have been successful in solving it.
- Predict the probable consequences of your actions.
- Test your conclusions and hypotheses in a pilot project.
- Develop a strategy for solving it, and an action plan for carrying out the strategy.

Step 5. Act, evaluate the results, and acknowledge the effort:

- Engage in committed action to solve the problem.
- Give each other feedback on what you are doing that is working and what is not.
- Periodically evaluate interim results.
- Ask opponents of the implemented solution to participate in the feedback and evaluation process.
- Make midcourse corrections where needed.
- Summarize what you learned from the problem and the process of solving it.
- Identify ways of improving the problem-solving process.
- Start all over again.

Negotiating Your Differences

If you cannot arrive at a mutually acceptable solution to your problems you may need to negotiate, and agree to disagree in ways that are not destructive to your relationship. Negotiation is a process by which both parties get some of what they want and put a stop to unnecessary combat. It is a cease-fire based on mutual compromises that leave the fundamental conflict unresolved.

Negotiation can also be seen as a process by which people collaborate on the basis of their disagreements, which helps them identify what is not working in their relationship, come up with solutions, create deeper understandings, and open possibilities for resolution and transformation.

Negotiation is as important a skill as listening, responding to emotions, and problem solving. It requires us to look carefully at what we negotiate, how we negotiate, the assumptions we bring to the negotiation process, and the relationships we create as we interact with each other throughout the negotiation process.

We usually negotiate to secure some *quantity* such as money, time, or space. Yet while doing so, we also indirectly negotiate some *quality*—something invisible, which may be discussed indirectly or not be mentioned at all. While we are negotiating the amount of office space we will be assigned, we may actually be negotiating our status within the organization. As we are negotiating for salary, we may also be negotiating recognition or respect.

In this way, qualities are far more important than quantities, and we can pay a high price in trust for a small victory in dollars. It is important to negotiate for both. If we care about the people on the other side of the conflict, or are in an important ongoing relationship with them, we cannot afford to negotiate only for quantities. We need to alter our negotiating styles to obtain the qualities we want as well.

Aggressive Versus Collaborative Negotiating Styles

There are two fundamentally different negotiating styles from which you can choose. Aggressive negotiators move against their opponents in a competitive struggle for domination. They feel it is acceptable to reduce or destroy trust by being inflexible, intimidating, demoralizing, or threatening. They browbeat their opponents, conceal facts and motivations, and refuse to listen or compromise, attributing blame, defining problems as caused only by their opponent, and manipulating the process to get what they want.

Collaborative negotiators move *toward* their opponents in a mutual effort at improvement, and use listening, establishing common ground, emphasizing shared values, and taking responsibility for problems and solutions. They try to behave in a trustworthy, fair, objective and reasonable way, and refuse to manipulate the process other than to get what both sides want.

Aggressive negotiators make extreme demands and few concessions. If concessions have to be made, they do so grudgingly and make small ones. They create "false issues" to gain advantage elsewhere. Collaborative negotiators work to establish credibility and good faith by making concessions, even unilateral ones. They seek the highest joint outcome in which both sides feel they have won and "false issues" have been minimized.

Because the aggressive approach generates distrust and misunderstanding, agreements take longer to reach and consume more resources. There are more failures and a stronger likelihood of retaliation even when this approach wins. Where there are ongoing relationships, an aggressive style results in smaller gains over the long run than a collaborative one.

Elements of Collaborative Negotiation

In our experience, the collaborative style is more useful than the aggressive style in resolving conflicts inside organizations and in the workplace, where opponents will sit at the same table again and again, and old grievances can complicate each new negotiation. This section will give you some tools to implement a collaborative style. Many of the elements of the preparation and negotiation process we describe are based partly on Roger Fisher and William Ury's classic, *Getting to Yes*.

To prepare for a collaborative negotiation, each side needs to identify and understand each of the following elements for itself, and for the other side as well.

- *Goals:* What are your goals? What do you want? What does the other side want?
- *Issues:* What issues does each side want addressed? In what order?
- *Alternatives:* What will you do if no agreement is reached? What will the other side do?

- *Interests:* What are your interests? What are the other side's interests?
- *BATNA:* What is each side's "best alternative to a negotiated agreement"?
- *WATNA:* What is each side's "worst alternative to a negotiated agreement"?
- *Options:* What creative ideas can you develop to meet each of your interests and those of the other person?
- *Criteria:* Are there criteria or standards that could help you agree on what is fair?
- *Relationships:* What can be done to improve trust and make the next round of negotiations less difficult?
- *Reality testing:* Are the ideas proposed realistic? Will they work for both sides?
- *Satisfaction:* What do both people need in content, process, and psychology to feel satisfied with the outcome?
- *Commitment:* Will both sides try to make it work?

Structuring the Process

Creating collaboration in negotiations is not simply a matter of having the right intent, although collaborative intent is extremely important. It is also a result of using the right process. Just as the procedural steps included in the typical adversarial negotiation process often enhance the probability of stalemate, there are a number of procedural steps that can be introduced into the negotiation process to encourage collaborative results.

The processes listed here can help you move your negotiating process, or one that is taking place between parts of your organization, in a more collaborative direction and improve outcomes, hopefully to the satisfaction of both sides. A number of these steps are best taken before the negotiation begins, while others can occur during the process, and still others may encourage collaboration after the process is formally over.

Before Negotiation Begins:

1. Agree on Common Goals for Your Relationship.   Meet together for a few minutes to agree on four or five goals you each have for your relationship. Alternatively, develop lists of goals separately, then come together and share your lists, marking the goals you have in common or on which you can easily agree. Next, identify the problems or barriers that stand in the way of meeting them. Share your results again, and identify the ones you have in common or on which you can easily agree. Next, brainstorm strategies for overcoming these barriers and achieving your common goals. Reach consensus on all the strategies you can, and leave the goals, barriers, and strategies you were unable to agree on for later discussion.

2. Identify Issues and Interests.   If you are part of two groups in negotiation, call a joint meeting, ask people to sit alternately around a circle rather than on opposite sides of a table, and use a facilitator, flip chart, and someone to record ideas. Start a round robin process in which each person is asked to identify an issue or problem for negotiation, say what is important about the problem, and why it is important to them. Continue around the circle until there are no more issues or problems. Next, group the issues into a single, manageable list. Together, or in small joint teams, analyze, categorize, and prioritize the issues for each topic, and identify any common principles or values you share with respect to how they should be resolved. Brainstorm recommendations for each problem, and list these before beginning actual negotiations. Have the list typed up for everyone to use and revise as ideas change.

3. Develop Shared Vision or Values.   As an alternative, meet together to create a vision of where you would like to go or what you would like to create together. Next, analyze the barriers or hurdles that stand in the way of getting there, and agree to take small steps to overcome them. Or, agree on a set of shared values for your behaviors with each other. List the real behaviors either of you engage in that support or undermine those values, then agree to encourage the supporting behaviors, discourage the undermining ones, and give each other feedback so you know when you are doing either.

4. Discuss Past Negotiation Experiences. Meet informally to discuss in detail what happened during the last round of negotiation. If you are involved in group negotiation experiences, dramatize through a role-play your best and worst negotiation experiences. Then, after the role-play or discussion, brainstorm ideas on how you can improve the process the next time around, and make recommendations for specific improvements.

5. Develop BATNAs, WATNAs, Options, and Positions. Meet separately to identify your own best and worst alternatives to a negotiated agreement for each of your own interests, and those of the other side as well. Next, brainstorm alternative ways of achieving those interests and develop initial, fallback, and bottom-line positions. Share these lists confidentially with each other, or discuss them openly in the group.

6. Meet Informally. Build trusting relationships through socializing, storytelling, and personal sharing. Consider holding a retreat or having potluck dinners, seminars, sports teams, fun days, or other social events to give all sides an opportunity to get to know one another on a personal level.

7. Receive Joint Training in Collaborative Negotiation. Meet together and agree to participate in a joint training session on techniques for effective communication, relationship building, collaborative negotiation, and conflict resolution. Use courses, workshops, and outside consultants to raise issues and improve your skills. Training can add an element of openness to the negotiation process, as both sides share a learning experience together.

8. Use an Outside Facilitator or Mediator. Jointly hire an outside facilitator or mediator to assist you and the other side throughout the negotiating process. An experienced outsider can help you resolve disputes before and as they occur.

9. Agree on Ground Rules for the Negotiation Process. Establish a timetable and agree on a set of ground rules for the negotiation process. Include confidentiality and other ways of improving trust, together with fail-safes and escape clauses in the event that collaboration fails. Ground rules might also include a preamble, or joint statement of the reasons each side has decided to use a collaborative bargaining process, which affirms their intentions for resolution.

10. Form a Joint Process Improvement Team. Form a joint team for process improvement that operates by consensus and sets agendas, suggests and reminds people of ground rules, stops the process if it is not working, and makes certain the negotiation is running smoothly. By agreeing on an agenda, you can help keep your focus on issues that are of primary concern to everyone. The experience of coming to consensus on process improvement gives both sides a sense that their goals are achievable, particularly if collaborative negotiating is new to them.

11. Seek Advice from Allied Third Parties. Form a joint advisory committee or board, consisting of representatives from concerned groups or third parties who may be affected by the success or failure of your negotiations. Report to them periodically on successes and results, and seek their advice or intervention when you get stuck.

12. Hold a Facilitated Public Forum. Consider holding an open public forum, facilitated by a third party, where representatives of all interested groups can discuss the issues being raised in the negotiation. This public venting process may be useful in putting an end to past history. It can be an opportunity for people to be heard before moving on to problem solving. After the group has analyzed the issues, ask them to suggest alternatives or recommendations, and take time to consider their contributions.

13. Jointly Research Alternative Methods of Negotiating. Research might include jointly reading collaborative bargaining classics such as Getting to Yes or Getting Past No, or jointly researching alternative bargaining literature, experiments, and methods. Both sides might agree to visit individuals or organizations that have used collaborative negotiation techniques and interview participants or consultants to learn their ideas about how to improve the process.

14. Choose Negotiating Team Members Jointly. Select people to negotiate who have good interpersonal skills and who are respected and credible in the eyes of people on the other side. You might consider allowing the other side to veto anyone they don't trust, or even select one or more members of your bargaining team.

15. Keep Lines of Communication Open. Allow sufficient time to communicate fully with each other, and plan to meet on a regular basis, with added sessions where needed. Make sure both formal and informal lines of communication are left open, and ask to meet with the other side away from the table if you get stuck or run into problems.

During the Negotiation Process:

1. Meet in Comfortable, Informal Surroundings. Meet, if possible, off-site, and avoid an "our side against your side," across-the-table setting. Sit in an alternating pattern, rather than on opposite sides of the table if you can. Use a round robin speaking order. Dress informally. Bring food and beverages. Help both sides feel they are part of the same team. One manager we met actually refused to start a session until the person on the other side of the table came over and sat next to her.

2. Use Experts.   Designate someone who has subject matter expertise, or a strong interest in particular areas of the negotiation, or an ability to solve problems. Ask them to meet with both sides beforehand and agree on information protocols and procedures, and, if possible, on joint recommendations.

3. Create a Single Version of the Facts.   Both sides should work together to develop agreement on a single set of facts, especially regarding chronology, essential facts, or economic information. This will prevent senseless disagreements over questions that have only one right answer, and ease tension over potentially hot issues.

4. Eliminate Surprises.   Ask the other side to reveal their bargaining agenda in advance, and agree that both sides will avoid surprise demands at the last minute. Joint agenda or process improvement can be used to limit and prioritize topics for discussion. Each side should be open with the other about the maximums they are willing to concede and the minimums they are willing to accept. Keep in mind that there will necessarily be trade-offs and compromises, and that either or both may have to alter their expectations in the interest of improving their relationship.

5. Record Everything.   Pick a mutually acceptable recorder to note the issues, discussions, recommendations, ideas, and actions taken. Minutes of meetings should be available to both sides. At the end of every session, ask each person to give a brief plus-and-minus evaluation of the process used during the session and suggest what could be done to improve it next time. Make sure these ideas are included in the minutes, and that changes are made in future meetings.

6. Negotiate in a Spirit of Problem Solving.   Agree that anything that is a problem for one side is a problem for both. Refocus your attention on the future, recognizing that you are not only in the same boat but likely to remain there, and that it does not matter which end of the boat is leaking, you will all go down together. Therefore, do not adopt strategies that run the risk of jeopardizing long-term relationships. Make a good-faith effort to resolve all issues through the collaborative process, and approach your problems with the idea that is "us versus it" rather than "me versus you."

7. When You Get Stuck, Change the Process. If it's not working, change it. Start by changing the process, or stop cold and start over again. If you get stuck, appoint a facilitator, recorder, time keeper, process observer, or mediator to make the process work. Encourage process interventions, regular discussion of process problems, and elicit ideas for improvement.

8. When You Get Stuck, Open Up the Negotiations. If you get stuck, allow other concerned individuals to attend the negotiations. Allow customers, coworkers, colleagues, community members, or partners to express their sentiments, and ask observers to make suggestions about how they think you might resolve difficult issues or break impasses. Then meet and consider new strategies.

9. When You Get Stuck, Jointly Generate Options. Jointly brainstorm options or alternatives based on the interests each side has expressed. Choose the best alternative, then fine-tune or improve it by incorporating the other side's ideas. You might also identify the barriers that stand in the way of achieving each objective, and create specific, concrete solutions to overcome these barriers. Ask: "What would it take for you to give that up?" Then look for options that satisfy those interests.

10. When You Get Stuck, Work to Resolve the Impasse. Specifically identify and name the issues that need resolution. Reach consensus on terminology or the reasons for overcoming impasse. Have each side state the reasons the other side's proposal is unacceptable and suggest specific ways it might be improved. In groups, form bilateral subteams to discuss the problem, prioritize each set of options, and report back on top choices or consensus recommendations.

11. Extend the Negotiations.   Create year-round negotiations, and build small negotiations into everyday life. Don't wait for a contract to end or problems to develop or conflicts to occur before sitting down together to agree on how you will act to resolve issues with one another in the future.

After Negotiation Ends:

1. Improve the Process.   At the end of the process, ask each person to summarize their own experience, and thank the other side for helping the group work collaboratively. Ask each person to indicate what worked and what didn't, and say one thing that could be done to improve the process the next time around.

2. Publicize Your Accomplishments.   Generate support among nonparticipants for the collaborative process. Focus on what you achieved, but do not hide what you did not. Periodically remind yourself and others of how much worse it could have been if you had used an adversarial approach.

3. Support the Other Side in the Eyes of Its Constituency. Acknowledge the legitimacy and cooperation of the other side, speaking not only to participants personally but their constituencies as well. In group conflicts, beware of praising the other side's negotiators too highly, and recognize that some people are afraid of collaboration and need to feel their particular self-interests have been satisfied. Negotiators always need to strike a balance between cooperating and pressing aggressively for the satisfaction of their needs. Because they are expected to be strong advocates for opposite sides, professional negotiators cannot become too closely aligned with each other. When a settlement proposal is presented, both sides should take steps to alleviate the concerns of constituents who feel they may be sacrificing something because agreement wasn't reached through an adversarial process.

4. Remember the Problems.   Make sure both sides recall the problems and issues that were encountered during the negotiation, and in administering the agreement afterwards. Keep everyone informed and try to solve the problems, if possible, before returning to the negotiation process. Encourage people who are not happy with the process to air their feelings—and hear them out. Take their comments not as criticisms but suggestions about what is not working and might be done better in the future.

5. Honor Your Agreements.   Be committed to fully honoring the agreements you reach. In groups, create a joint evaluation team to follow up and make sure that all agreements are being honored, and to fine-tune any that require adjustment.

6. Continue Solving Problems.   Keep a list of unresolved issues or problems to return to in the future, and continue to search for solutions. Also keep a record of objections or complaints that were expressed about the process or the agreement. If necessary, stop or reopen negotiations to discuss these issues. In groups, establish a joint team to identify problem areas that crop up following negotiations. Put a process in place for defining how these issues will be handled, and make sure everyone is aware that channels are available to resolve these problems. The primary purpose of negotiation is *not* to reach agreements but to solve problems and achieve both sides' long- and short-term goals.

7. Continue Negotiating.   Don't allow issues to accumulate. Negotiate solutions to problems before or while they occur. Identify ongoing issues and create a permanent search for solutions in these areas. Schedule regular problem-solving meetings to deal with issues before they have a chance to get blown out of proportion. Meet regularly even if there are no items on the agenda, to continue trust-building and communication.

8. *Continue Communicating About Collaboration.* New people who enter the process or join the organization will need to be told about the collaborative negotiation process and trained in its methods. While collaborative negotiation is based on common sense and a team approach to problem solving, it should not be taken for granted that everyone will understand it. Make efforts to rotate leadership and include different people in the process to broaden the range of support. Offer opportunities for negotiators to continue improving their skills.

9. *Celebrate Your Successes.* Take time out to celebrate what you have accomplished. Congratulate yourselves and the other side on what you have jointly done.

The Power of Problem Solving

Our greatest problem is not the issue we are trying to solve, but the way we are thinking about and approaching it. Sometimes, if we define something as a problem it becomes one; if we do not define it as a problem, it ceases to command our attention. This means our problems are attractors of attention. We present ourselves with problems so we can work on them, partly because problems and problem-solving processes are more interesting than solutions.

We often do not actually solve our problems so much as we learn from, transcend, and outgrow them. We think of our problems as external, yet for every external problem we face there is an even more critical internal one we may or may not have faced. Every external solution or transformation we find corresponds to an internal one that awaits our attention. Our problems may actually be internal calls for transformation that we have mistakenly assumed came from outside.

Problems are an inseparable part of growth and change, and as you solve them, you make way for other problems to take their place. As Buckminster Fuller reminded us: "Once you solve your problems, what you get is a higher order of problem."

Committed Action

Your ability to overcome resistance, build trust, and successfully solve your problems depends on your willingness to engage in committed action. Committed action is different from going through the motions, taking a stab, or giving it a try. It means taking risks, making a stand, acting before the outcome can be known. As the German writer Johann Wolfgang von Goethe wrote, there is no substitute for committed action:

> Until one is committed there is hesitancy, the chance to draw back, always ineffectiveness. Concerning all acts of initiative (and creation), there is one elementary truth, the ignorance of which kills countless ideas and splendid plans: that the moment one definitely commits oneself, then Providence moves too. All sorts of things occur to help one that would never otherwise have occurred. A whole stream of events issues from the decision, raising in one's favour all manner of unforeseen incidents and meetings and material assistance, which no man could have dreamt would have come his way. Whatever you can do, or dream you can, begin it. Boldness has genius, power, and magic in it.

Having traveled this path of finding and negotiating solutions to your problems, we leave you with a choice: whether to act on them in a committed way or pass the responsibility for making it work off on someone else. If you are committed to deepening your understanding, improving your relationships, transforming your organization and yourself, you will be able to overcome your particular conflicts—and potentially conflicts in general—not by wishing them to go away, but by being committed to working through them, no matter the cost.

Path Eight

Explore Resistance and Mediate Before You Litigate

> Discourage litigation. Persuade your neighbors to
> compromise whenever you can. Point out to them
> how the nominal winner is often a real loser—in
> fees, expenses and waste of time. As a peacemaker
> the lawyer has a superior opportunity of being a
> good man. There will still be business enough.
>
> —*Abraham Lincoln*

Some of your conflicts will be beyond your skill or ability to handle, even if you have tried all the techniques and applied all the suggestions in preceding chapters. You may be too close to the problem to think creatively, or the issues may be too deep for you to engage, or the positions may have become too entrenched, or the other side may be committed to keeping the conflict going for psychological reasons you cannot affect. What do you do then? It may be time to reassess your options, turn your attention to ways of breaking the impasse, and consider using a mediator or professional conflict resolver to help end your dispute.

Success and Failure in Conflict Resolution

To start with, it is important not to feel you have failed if you are at impasse or are unable to reach a resolution. Winston Churchill, in the midst of war, is said to have defined success as "moving from failure to failure with undiminished enthusiasm." A similar definition might be applied to conflict resolution, which begins at impasse and remains there until, often for no definable reason, an opening appears and resolution takes place.

Success and failure are statements not only about what you did but about how you feel about what you did—and about who you think you are. Your ideas of success and failure may be deceptive. After all, the effect of success is to repeat what you successfully did before, which does not lead you to growth or change. But when you fail, you rethink what you did, experiment, take risks, and become more creative, which promotes your learning and growth. So in the long run, which is the success and which the failure?

If our goal is to learn from our conflicts, labeling the result a success or failure does not help us. What matters most is our growth and learning. The questions are: Did you increase your skills? Did you make any discoveries? Were you seduced by your desire for success? Were you willing to experiment and take risks without fearing failure? In answering these questions, consider this reversal: that failure means trying too hard to succeed, while success means being willing to accept the possibility of failure.

As you consider how to overcome resistance and impasse, keep in mind that the reasons for resistance run deep, often pointing to lessons we are unable to hear or refuse to learn. Give yourself permission to take risks and fail—and you will succeed regardless of what happens in your dispute.

For example, Sam had applied for a position as team leader, a job for which he felt qualified because he'd spent six months as coordinator on a successful project. His manager disagreed, favoring a more traditionally qualified candidate. When she told Sam the job was not his, she was abrupt and insensitive. She surprised him, because he thought the job was his. He tried to convince her he was qualified, but she did not take time to listen.

Sam went to the organizational ombudsman in charge of conflict resolution to request a hearing, and to Human Resources for advice. He groused with colleagues and bad-mouthed the manager, who retaliated when she learned of his disloyalty. In mediation, we assisted the manager in listening while Sam presented his case. He felt respected, acknowledged, and heard, and she apologized for not having listened the first time. Sam was able to drop his resistance and apologize for his efforts to undermine her. They agreed Sam would be included in the next leadership training program to earn the credentials he needed for the position he wanted, and the manager would get feedback and coaching from human resources on how to improve her listening skills.

Reasons for Resistance

There are many reasons we get stuck and end in impasse. In fact, we are always at impasse in all our conflicts until the moment when we arrive at a solution that works for both sides. Impasse simply means that whatever we've been doing hasn't worked, and we need to try something different.

People who resist always do so for a reason. Instead of thinking of their refusal as unreasonableness or as difficult behavior, start with the assumption that *all* resistance reflects an unmet need. The resistance can be seen simply as a request by the resistor to understand why their needs have not been met. Consequently, it is important to find out what unmet need caused the stalemate. Then you can discover solutions to move the resolution process forward.

Many reasons for resistance flow from the process used to resolve the dispute. There may be a perception that the process is unfair or one-sided. Your opponent may not have fully agreed to use the process, or may not be committed to following through. You may not have created adequate ground rules to keep it on track, or the ground rules may not have been followed and the violations have been condoned. The process you have been using may be too structured or formal—or too unstructured and informal—to allow for a real exchange of views and the real content of the dispute to emerge. You may have not been honest enough, or tried to manipulate the process.

Resistance may also be caused by unresolved issues in your relationship. Communication may have been so poor between you that the content of your dispute has become twisted or swept under the rug. One of you may be using an adversarial conflict style that is creating a perception of disrespect or prejudgment. One of you may be trying to fix blame or humiliate the other. There may be false expectations of each other that are not being addressed. There may be a need to hear an apology or acknowledgment that has not been spoken.

We were invited into a large urban high school being torn apart by conflict. The parents accused the administration of institutional racism, citing remarks made by teachers in their classrooms and data on achievement by students based on their race and national origin. The administration was willing to mediate, but the parents and teachers refused to meet. There was great distrust, both by parents who felt they had been treated unfairly in the past, and by teachers who were afraid of being personally attacked by parents.

The resistance began to break when an administrative leader spoke to the parent group. He apologized for the mistakes that had been made in the past, and acknowledged that institutional racism existed in the school and in the district as a whole. He reached out to the teachers by offering them practical support in increasing their students' achievement, and to the parents by offering to work with them to eliminate disparate treatment at the school. His acknowledgment and willingness to speak directly to both groups' issues reduced their resistance to joining forces and creating an improved environment for all students.

Techniques for Breaking
Resistance and Impasse

If you feel stuck in resistance or unable to get beyond impasse, here are some of the methods we have used as third-party mediators and conflict resolvers, each of which has helped us discover or create a breakthrough. As you read them, consider how they might apply to your conflict, even though you may not be a third party in the dispute:

- *Break the issue down into smaller parts, isolating the most diffi-cult issues and reserving them for later.* If you are stuck resolving a large issue, break it down into parts and solve each separately. We resolved a dispute involving $500,000 by first reaching sixteen points of agreement on how the parties would talk to each other on the telephone. The rest was easy.

- *Ask the other side why your alternative is unacceptable, then look for narrow solutions tailored to the reasons they give.* If someone rejects your proposed solution because they don't believe it will work, suggest trying it for a month to see. We resolved a sexual harassment dispute by asking the harassee why she refused a generous offer of settlement. It turned out she did not really want the money as much as she wanted the company to train her so she could move into a job she really liked. The company agreed, and both sides were satisfied.

- *Go on to other issues that might be easier to resolve, or take a break and ask the other person to take some time to think about the alternatives you presented.* When people take time out and step away from the conflict, they become more reasonable and realistic about what they need. We often suggest in mediation that both sides think about the problem overnight and come back the next day with three proposals for resolution they think would be acceptable to the other side. We also find that people become more reasonable after bathroom breaks, which we call "restroom revelation."

- *Review the other side's priorities and your common interests.* Go over your priorities and see whether you have any in common. Identify your common interests and see if they match. We worked with two teachers in conflict who agreed their priority was the children. Their shared interest in school safety and improving the language arts curriculum allowed them to create a partnership and overcome their differences.

- *Explore hidden agendas and the willingness to compromise.* Often hidden agendas prevent us from reaching agreement. If you surface and explore these agendas, you can find a compromise—or see that the one you've advanced is impossible. We worked with a manager whose hidden agenda was to look managerial to his boss and enhance his chances of promotion by appearing capable of resolving conflicts. The employee understood his agenda and was able to negotiate ways of making the manager look good to his boss.

• *Split the difference.* Simply dividing a sum in half and splitting the difference is an easy way of resolving a dispute. We mediated a conflict in which the parties agreed on $400,000 worth of claims, and the entire mediation almost fell apart over $35. We suggested they split it, and they each agreed to pay $17.50.

• *Try to reach agreement on your original expectations.* Going back to original conversations and expectations expressed before the dispute began can help you realize you need to stand by your original agreements. We mediated a dispute between two business partners who had worked together for several years. They were in a heated conflict over what would become an unfair division of labor, and were considering dissolution. When they recalled their original agreement, which was to share the work equally, they broke the tasks into two equal groups and flipped a coin to decide who would take which set of tasks.

• *Look for possible trade-offs or exchange of services.* You may find solutions to your conflicts by discovering collateral needs that can be satisfied, bartered, or traded against each other to resolve the dispute. We mediated between a model and photographer over fees for a set of prints. She thought his photos were unflattering and refused to pay for them. He claimed she hadn't looked very good when he took the shots, and that she had refused to take his advice when he suggested how she could look better. She wanted a flattering set of prints, and he wanted to be paid and do his job without interference. They traded, accepted each other's conditions, and reached an agreement that he would take the photos, she would accept his suggestions, and she would pay him for his work, including film costs from the earlier shoot.

• *Recognize and acknowledge the other side's feelings and points of view, and encourage them to acknowledge yours.* A common reason for impasse is inadequate recognition or acknowledgment of others' feelings. It is extremely difficult to overacknowledge someone in a way that is sincere. If your opponent says, *"You don't think I'm a very good [whatever],"* start by praising them for whatever they do well and give them honest feedback. If you can't think of anything, you're not seeing them clearly. We resolved a dispute between a manager and team member in which the employee had told others the manager was incompetent and had given her tasks she thought were beneath her. The manager complained that she was always resisting his ideas and had a "bad attitude." We asked each of them to describe three things they respected or liked about each other, and acknowledge them for something they had done well. It turned out the entire dispute was based on each one thinking the other one didn't like them, and as they began to praise each other, the conflict disappeared.

• *Tell the other person you are stuck and ask for their ideas.* Sometimes telling the other person you need their help encourages them to step forward with creative ideas, or let go of their resistance. We were asked to resolve a dispute in a school in which most of the teachers had requested that the principal be removed. We convened a faculty meeting in which she admitted she was stuck, and asked for their help. In small groups, the faculty came up with a list of the things she was doing that were causing problems, a list of the things they were doing that were not helping, and a list of creative ideas for how they could work together in the future.

• *Ask the other person to indicate what would change or happen after reaching a solution.* One reason for impasse is a perception that what will happen when you reach agreement will be unpleasant. We mediated a dispute in which an employee was taking a very long time to sign a settlement agreement, insisting that commas be changed into semicolons, then back to commas again. We asked him what he thought would happen if he signed the agreement. He dodged the question three times. We told him he was ducking the question, and he finally said he was afraid he would never find a better job than the one he had. We assisted him in accepting the inevitable by strategizing about how to find a better job, so he could complete the past, let go, and move on with his life.

• *Stop the process and consider whether it is helping you to get where you want to go, or if it is preventing open and honest communication.* If your process is not working, stop it and improve the way you are communicating. We mediated a dispute in a federal agency where the director encountered employee resistance to a number of changes she was trying to implement. She ran staff meetings with an iron hand, rarely asking employees what they thought. She did not give them an opportunity to speak before telling them what they were going to do. We stopped the next meeting midstream and asked her publicly if she wanted to hear what employees thought about her plan. She said she did, and we changed the process, breaking the large group into teams of four or five employees, asking them to identify three to five useful elements in her plan, and three to five ways it could be improved. The results shocked her, as she learned that her employees knew how to make the plan work better than she did.

• *Compliment the other person on reaching earlier points of agreement and encourage them to reach a complete agreement so as to put the dispute behind them.* Every conflict resolution process creates a momentum toward resolution. This is increased by periodically recognizing the gains you've made and acknowledging your successes. You can also encourage the other person to resolve the conflict so you can both get on with the rest of your lives. A team in an information systems department was blocked from meeting its commitments to clients as a result of an impasse over a strategy for developing software. We convened the team and asked each person to identify one point of agreement about the strategy and one thing on which they still needed to agree. It turned out they agreed on twelve points and only really disagreed over two. We worked with them to identify the factors that were keeping them from agreement over the two, reminding them of what they would lose if the customer went elsewhere. They were able to come to complete agreement in three hours. This process ties in to the next suggestion as well.

• *Remind the other person what will happen if they do not settle— what each of you stands to lose.* Say what you stand to lose if you are unable to resolve the dispute, then ask the other person what they stand to lose. We mediated a dispute between a manager and an employee where we asked this question, and they both answered that they might lose their jobs and chances for promotion. Once they saw what was at stake they put their animosities aside and negotiated a working relationship that made them both look good.

- *Ask for a minute of silence so you can both think about the conflict and what to do about it.* In conflict, it is easy to get caught up in the dynamics, and lose the forest for the trees. Silence allows you to stop a process that is not working, reassess your position, center yourself, and return to what is really important. We mediated a divorce where a husband made a generous settlement offer to his wife. We asked her how she wanted to respond, and she said, "I don't know." We asked what she thought she needed to be able to respond, and she said, "I don't know that either." We asked for a minute of silence to let her think about it, and before a minute passed, she said, "I'm afraid if I say yes, our relationship will be over." We now knew the true source of her resistance. We supported her in letting go of her marriage and telling her husband that what she really wanted was a friendship. They negotiated a friendship that would not be confused with a marriage, and she accepted his offer of settlement.

- *Ask more questions—about the problem itself, and about feelings, priorities, alternative solutions, flexibility, hidden agendas, compromises, anger—and return to agenda setting and problem solving.* If you are completely stuck, double back to the beginning and ask questions as though you were just starting to resolve the dispute. We mediated a conflict where both sides had attorneys involved. The original reasons for the impasse had gotten lost in the legal issues and advocacy. We asked the parties to meet without their lawyers, and were able to ask questions that cleared the air, returned us to the original issues, and got the process back on track.

- *Generate options by asking the other person to brainstorm with you, without considering the practicality of any of your suggestions.* Ask the other person if they have any ideas about how to resolve the dispute, then add your own. Don't critique or evaluate ideas until you both express them all. Use a flip chart if the conflict is hot. We mediated a dispute between family members operating a family business, in which two brothers were competing to see who would run the operation. We brainstormed options and discovered neither wanted to run it, they just didn't want the other one to do so. They agreed that the present general manager was more capable and motivated than either of them, and that he would be given the job.

• *Go to a third party and ask them to say which alternative they believe is fair and why.* Going to an expert or someone who has a reputation for fairness to request their advice often resolves impasse, as does jointly researching options and discussing the merits of each proposal. In a collective bargaining dispute we settled over the salaries of a group of employees, it was helpful to consult an expert to put a value on their pensions and benefits, and compare their total package with what employees were receiving in similar organizations.

• *Ask the other person if they are willing to mediate the dispute, or if not, go to arbitration rather than litigation to settle the conflict.* If all else fails, bring in a third party to mediate. A mediator will have the permission and hopefully the skills to resolve the dispute, perhaps because they are outside it and are perceived as unbiased. If mediation doesn't work or is unacceptable to one or both sides, consider final and binding arbitration, which is quicker and less expensive than litigation.

What Is Mediation?

If the methods we have described in this book have not been successful in resolving your dispute, your next step may be to use an unbiased third party mediator to create a process that encourages you and your opponent to discuss the issues, communicate your ideas and feelings to one another, and negotiate a solution to the conflict.

So what is mediation? Mediation has its roots in the ancient conflict resolution practices of all preindustrial cultures, and at the same time is a modern, highly sophisticated set of techniques for depolarizing and depersonalizing conflict. Many of these techniques have already been mentioned in this book, but their effectiveness is enhanced in the hands of a skilled practitioner. Mediation is simply an informal problem-solving conversation facilitated by a third person. It is a voluntary, consensus-based method of dispute resolution that uses facilitated communication, problem solving, collaborative negotiation, exploration of options, compromise, and impasse resolution.

Mediation differs from litigation and arbitration in that the mediator is not a judge or arbitrator who decides the issues for the parties. It is a process that encourages participants to be creative, collaborative, and nonadversarial. Mediation is future-oriented, and less concerned with deciding who was right or wrong than with solving problems so they do not occur again. Mediators are not so much neutral as they are omni-partial, and on both parties' sides at the same time. Mediation sessions are generally informal and off the record, so as to encourage direct dialogue.

Mediation has proven highly successful in resolving a wide range of interpersonal, workplace, public policy, environmental, and organizational disputes, and divorce, family, neighborhood, and community disputes as well. It reaches solutions quickly, saving costs and attorney fees, preserving confidentiality, helping people learn better communication skills, and enabling them to avoid a great deal of bitterness and hostility over results. On average, experienced mediators resolve 95 percent of the disputes, and agreements are often reached in a single session. Agreements reached in mediation face fewer enforcement problems because they are reached voluntarily.

Much depends, of course, on the insight, competency, training, and experience of the mediator in assisting parties to come to agreement, on the timing of the request for mediation, and on the willingness of the parties at that moment to engage in the process. But even if you are certain your opponent will not accept mediation, we recommend you try it anyway, since we often convince people to mediate their disputes after they have refused to do so when asked by the other side.

You can contact a mediator by calling a local or national mediation organization, personal friend, court, therapist, lawyer, church, or community agency, or you can contact us at the Center for Dispute Resolution in Santa Monica and we will help you find someone in your area. Make sure the mediator has been trained and is well thought of in the community, and that you and your opponent both agree on the selection.

Why Mediation Works

We have conducted many thousands of mediations over the last twenty years. We have certified hundreds of people to become mediators, and trained tens of thousands of people in mediation and conflict resolution techniques. In the process, we have developed a vision of the real value of mediation and a sense of why and how it works.

Mediation works on many levels. It can stop a fight, initiate a dialogue, facilitate a negotiation, settle a dispute, resolve the underlying issues that gave rise to the dispute, promote forgiveness, and achieve reconciliation. As the resolution process moves to deeper levels, the skills and experience required to overcome obstacles grow geometrically. Yet mediation works at each of these levels—sometimes for the same reasons, even though these reasons require increasing subtlety and artistry on the part of the mediator.

Mediation works because it encourages people to try to understand each other's positions and interests. It works because it promotes authentic communication, minimizes emphasis on people or personalities, structures interactions to discourage escalation, reduces stress, and encourages mutual compromise.

Mediation works because it invites adversaries to become more human with one another. It allows dialogue to take place in the language of metaphor, acknowledges the emotional needs of the parties, and allows both sides to tell their inner, subjective truths along with their objective points of view. It brings individuals together through empathy, rather than dividing them in anticipation of revenge or victory. It draws on compassion and love rather than hatred or dispassionate neutrality. It allows each side to listen to the other and encourages collaboration without defensiveness.

Mediation works because it helps people reestablish lost connections. It emphasizes the wholeness of human experience. It enables people to surrender by permitting them, and the other side, to win in the process. It lays open the secret sources of motivation because it recognizes each human interest as valid. It equally empowers combatants and democratizes their conflict. It looks to the future rather than the past. It gives constructive feedback as opposed to judgment. It helps hostile parties create solutions for themselves and choose to accept them, rather than having them imposed. It acknowledges that no one enjoys being the object of another person's wrath or being trapped by their own, and thereby releases people from their rage and that of others. It creates an expectation, encourages modeling, and sparks an imagining of what it would be like to be at peace.

Mediation works because the motivation of each person becomes the center and object of the process. By separating people from problems and positions from interests, surfacing motivation, and generating options, mediators initiate a joint problem-solving process in which both sides form a partnership to reconcile apparently conflicting self-interests.

Mediation works because it shifts the communication process from accusation and defense to negotiation and problem solving. It respects the person. It creates a process that is open. It encourages responsibility, both for problems and solutions. It accepts people as they are, yet encourages them to change and become better. It does not judge their actions but helps them do what they believe is right. It encourages empathy, hospitality, honesty, friendship, collaboration, and respect, while acknowledging disagreement, anger, disappointment, rejection, denial, and revenge. It accepts human beings as they are while supporting their desire for self-improvement.

Mediation unites reason and intuition, love and self-interest, law and justice. It is unique in each case and the same around the world. It provides each of us with the opportunity to see our enemy as a reflection of ourselves, and to see ourselves as no greater than the least of us, nor worse than the best. It works because the possibility of resolution is already within each of us, trying to emerge.

Reaching Closure

Whether or not you have been successful in resolving your impasse, you still need to find closure. There is a fundamental difference between stopping the conflict and reaching closure, which means coming to completion, and ending it with nothing left over. To reach closure, you need to be willing to say everything that is really bothering you, and communicate whatever will allow you to get the conflict off your chest and allow it to be done.

The paradox is that in order to fully say everything, let go of the conflict, not hold anything back and come to closure, two steps are necessary. Each person has to be willing to acknowledge their own role in the conflict, and each person has to be willing to recognize their opponent as a human being.

You may start the closure process by saying there are some things you need to talk about for the conflict to be over for you. Or you can ask if there is anything the other person needs to say. To do so, you must not get back into the conflict. Instead of saying, "This is what you did to me"—which returns you to accusation and unresolved conflict—say, "This is what I learned from this conflict about what I need to do to protect myself from behaviors that are difficult for me to handle." This is a statement that reflects real resolution and completion.

The second step is easier, and consists of acknowledging the other person. If you can't think of anything positive about them or what they did, you are not ready for closure. It is always possible to acknowledge them for being willing to meet and talk about the problem. You can say, "I know it took some courage to come here today and face our problems and try to work them through with me, and I want to thank you for doing that."

You can also acknowledge them in areas where you would most like to see them grow. You can usually honestly praise your opponents for facing their problems squarely, listening openly, being willing to compromise, sticking with the process even when it became difficult, being honest and forthcoming, giving you good feedback or food for thought, standing up for themselves, reaching a number of agreements, or being willing to engage in a difficult conversation.

You should also identify what *you* need to reach closure. Ask yourself: If you end the conflict and do not reach closure, what issues or feelings will be left unresolved? What may happen as a result? What do you need to say to the other person to reach closure? What positive things could you say about your role in the conflict resolution process? What insights about the conflict or yourself have you gained through your efforts to resolve it?

Small ceremonies are useful in reaching closure, even simply shaking hands or agreeing to let bygones be bygones. Think of creative ways you might ceremonialize the end of your conflict. In one conflict we mediated, two coworkers who had personally insulted each other repeatedly over a period of five years in staff meetings and private conversations agreed to jointly ask to be put on the agenda at the next meeting, tell everyone how they had resolved their conflict, speak about what they had learned from their experience, and hug each other at the end, as a way of showing everyone the dispute was over. When the meeting was held, you could hear a pin drop. After the hug, other staff members said they had problems with people in the group and wanted to resolve them too, and a series of problem-solving sessions were scheduled. But as the meeting ended, some people just went up to their enemies and hugged them, as a way of saying they wanted their conflicts to be over!

We encourage you to search for a way of completing your conflict that has heart and soul in it. We support you in your determination to get there, and ask you to give the resolution process a greater level of energy, insight, courage, perseverance, and commitment than you have given to engaging in your conflicts.

Our Conclusion

We have traveled together over eight paths, which we hope have led you from impasse to transformation in resolving your conflicts. Perhaps you have completely resolved your conflicts or moved them into a space where they are easier to handle. In either case, we hope you have learned that conflict is a rich source of learning, growth, and improvement, in both your organizational and personal life.

Whenever you encounter conflicts, you basically have only two choices. You can either tighten up, pull back, and prepare for battle, or you can relax, move toward your opponent, and prepare for peace. Our question to you is: Instead of preparing for war, isn't it better to prepare for peace? Isn't the person you become when you go to war less happy and fulfilled than the one you become when you are at peace? Which do you prefer to be?

As organizations, as a society, and as individuals, our challenge is to learn better how to resist warfare and its civilized form, litigation. We can do so by consciously, consistently, and proactively improving our capacity to resolve our conflicts. Warfare and litigation are nourished by our antagonistic responses to criticism and differences of opinion, by our refusal to accept the gift of dissent, and by our inability to recognize that our conflicts lead us to learning and improved results. We need, as organizations, as a society, and as individuals, to discover mutual gains *precisely* in our conflicts. We need to reject the win-lose limitations that are supported by our adversarial culture.

The opportunities for learning from conflict are infinite and unbounded. We encourage you to keep your openness and capacity for learning alive as your conflicts swell, dissolve, soar, stall, or suddenly vanish. We encourage you to find resting places, lookouts, safe harbors, and guides to help you along your path. As you do so, reflect on your experiences and search out the knowledge you need to grow and reach genuine closure in your conflicts.

If you *want* to find opportunities in your conflicts to learn and grow, where can you locate them? We suggest one of many answers—by relaxing, and moving toward and through your conflicts. As you do so, you will be able to notice each of your ruts, limitations, weaknesses, and stuck places. Noticing obstacles automatically creates the possibility of learning how to transcend them. And who could be better at highlighting these possibilities for you than someone whose behavior encourages you to think the conflict is about them, and not about you?

We hope we have encouraged and supported you on this path of self-discovery, learning, and transformation. At the turn of the century, William James wrote

> Most people live, whether physically, intellectually or morally, in a very restricted circle of their potential being. They *make use* of a very small portion of their possible consciousness, and of their soul's resources in general, much like a man who, out of his whole bodily organism, should get into a habit of using and moving only his little finger. Great emergencies and crises show us how much greater our vital resources are than we have supposed.

For this reason, we wish you *great* conflicts, with endless opportunities for self-discovery and transformation. Good luck!

Index

A

Accusation, as confession, 94

Acknowledging listening technique, 71, 73

Acknowledgment: in closure, 239–240; of differences, 66; of feelings, in overcoming impasse, 231–232; needing, and resistance, 229; of points of agreement, 233

Action, committed: clearing path to, 135, 136; and creative problem solving, 8, 199; defined, 225; and interconnectedness, 17; as requirement for transformation, 6

Actions: to approach conflict, 15–18; to begin collaborative process, 45–46; required for transformation, 5–6; taking responsibility for, 132–133

Acton, Lord, 142

Advisory committees, forming, 218

Agendas, hidden, exploring, 71, 230–231

Aggression: and demonizing, 33; examining assumptions about, 35; hypnotic power of, 20–21; rewarding, 26; shifting away from, 37–38; and stereotyping, 169; using, to spark communication, 13

Aggression response strategy, 33–36, 39, 40, 41, 42, 43

Agreeing listening technique, 74

Agreements, original, expectations of, 231

Allusion, 24, 25

Anger: defusing, through apology, 109; in demonizing, 31; discovering source of, 99–100; as distorted expression, 102; as emotional mask, 97; exploring reasons for, 100, 103, 107; giving up, reasons for, 106–107; hidden assumptions and beliefs about, 103–105; long-term effect of, 32; and mediation, 238; methods for managing, 107–109; paradox of, 106; releasing, 106; responsibility for, 100, 107; uses of, 101–103; as vulnerability, 95. *See also* Emotions, strong

Anti-Semitism, 169

Apathy, as caring, 95–96

Apologizing: alternative ways of, 109–110; resisting, 4

Apology: defined, 109; need for, as reason for resistance, 229; as sign of responsibility, 109

Arbitration, 235, 236

Assumptions: about aggression, examining, 35; about communication, 48; about emotions, 86–87; in demonizing, 26, 27; listening for, 71; and metaphors, 26, 27–28; in orientations, 205; of outcomes, 28; putting aside, 199–200

Assumptions, hidden: about anger, 103–105; and language use, 22, 23

Attack, as smoke screen, 95

Attitude: and self-fulfilling prophecies, 68, 147; towards problems, 199, 201–202, 203–204

Avoidance response strategy, 39, 40, 42, 43

Awareness of interconnection, 114–115, 123

B

BATNA (best alternative to a negotiated agreement), 215, 217

Behaviors, difficult. *See* Difficult behaviors

Bolman, L. G., 207–208

Boundaries: confusion over, 164, 165; emotional, 124; questions to identify, 165–166; respecting, 185

Brainstorming: analyzing choices from, 162; disadvantage of, 161; to expand range of solutions, 16; to increase cooperation, 46; for options, 160, 221, 234–235; in overcoming obstacles, 209. *See also* Problem solving, creative

Buddenbrooks (Mann), 96

C

Camus, A., 20

Castaneda, C., 196

Center for Dispute Resolution, 237

Centinela Valley Juvenile Victim Offender Reconciliation Program, 133

Ceremonies, in closure, 240

Change: creating, 187; improving process of, 194–195; lasting, 5, 14; readiness for, 13; reality-testing intention to, 64; resistance to, 43–44, 186–187, 194–195, 232; in society, of conflict cultures, 22; supporting, 178–179

Changes, as an invisible, 122

Childhood. *See* Families

Choices, separating options from, 139, 160–162

Churchill, W., 226

Clarifying listening technique, 72–73, 108

Closure: ceremonies in, 240; paradox of, 239; the past as barrier to, 154; reaching, 239–241; reaching for, 17–18, 185

Coaching, 177

Collaboration response strategy, 37–38, 39, 40, 41–44

Collaborative negotiation. *See* Negotiation, collaborative

Collaborative relationships, establishing, 44–46

Collusion, as an obstacle, 118

Commitment, identifying, 215

Commonalties, separating, from differences, 139, 151–152

Communication: accepting responsibility in, 49; anomalies in, 58; assumption about, 48; commitment to, 62, 64; deepening, 119–120; distortions in, 59–60, 61; elements of, 57; gender differences in, 48–49; and ground rules, 50–51; hidden framework in, 58–59; honesty in, 129–130; influence of hierarchies on, 60–62; integrity in, 46; keeping lines open for, 219; and mediation, 237, 238; poor, cost of, 49–50, 51–52; setting the stage for, 15; superficial, 12; using aggression to spark, 13; vulnerability in, 116–117

Communication skills: improving, 76; lack of, 3–4

Communicators: committed, becoming, 63–64; successful, defined, 48

Competition: in hierarchies, 61; as obstacle to change, 187

Completion. *See* Closure

Compromise response strategy, 39, 40, 41, 42, 43

Conflict: avoidability of, 2; avoiding, 20, 187; center of, 13; cost of, 2; dark side of, 3–4; distance and location in, 8; hypnotic effect of, 117–118; as opportunity, 4–5, 14, 31–33, 241–242; sources of, 1–2; suppressing, 11–12

Conflict audit, 51–52

Conflict cultures: changing, 22; and context of opposition, 33–36; and cultural messages, 20–22; defined, 19–20; defined by superficiality, 127; and language, 22–24; and metaphors, 24–31; understanding, 7. *See also* Organizational cultures

Conflict, unresolved: assessing cost of, 51–52; costs of, 10–11, 12, 80–81; paralyzing effect of, 135–136

Consequences: in orientations, 205; reminding of, and resistance, 233–234

Constituents, supporting, 222–223

Content: and difficult behaviors, 184; separating process from, 139, 156–160

Context: of commonalties and differences, 151–152; discovering opportunities through, 31–33; of listeners, 48, 49; in response strategies, 33–44; and shift to collaborative responses, 36–37, 45; understanding, 7

Control orientation, 204, 205

Covert behavior, as obstacle to change, 187

Craziness, as coping strategy, 171–172

Criteria: assessing alternative, 199; identi-

fying, 215; separating, from selection, 139, 162–164
Cultural messages, 20–22
Cultures. *See* Conflict cultures; Organizational cultures

D

De Mello, A., 195–196
Deal, T. E., 207–208
Defensiveness, as egoism, 95
Demonizing: and anger, 31; assumptions in, 26, 27; cost of, 27; as dark side of conflict, 3; in defining the problem, 146, 168, 169; as obstacle to change, 187; resulting in aggression, 33
Desires, as an underlying issue, *114, 115*
Differences, separating commonalties from, 139, 151–152
Difficult behaviors: confronting, 172–173; defining, as the problem, 172, 176; and emotional buttons, 182–183; family origins of, 179–181; handling, techniques for, 17, 183–185; learning from, 7–8, 195–197; and organizational cultures, 186–189; reasons for, 173–174; as resistance to change, 194, 195; responding to, 148, 183; responding to, in meetings, 190–194; rewarding of, 174–175, 176, 177; and separations, 147; strategies for changing, 177–179; suppressing, effect of, 195–196; working with, 167–168
Disney Studios, 26
Distortions, 59–62, 96, 102
Don Juan chronicles, 196
Dreamworks, 26

E

Eco, U., 167, 207
Einstein, A., 203
Elaboration listening technique, 74–75
Emotional buttons, 30, 182–183
Emotional compensation, 199
Emotional masks: looking behind, 94–96; and power plays, 98–99; taking off, 96–98
Emotional needs: and mediation, 237; stating of, 15; supporting, 84
Emotional responses: analyzing origins of,

92–93; and impact of family histories on, 84–85, 86, 87; stages of, 88–90
Emotions, strong: acknowledging, 7; assumptions about expressing, 86–87; benefits of managing, 94; and effect on health, 80–81; and effect on listening, 78; elements of, 87–88; expressing, 90, 97–98; gender differences in expressing, 84; hidden behind masks, 98–99; hypnotic effect of, 3, 118; as an invisible, 121; learning from, 79–80; letting go of, 201; methods to manage, 91–92; negative, costs of, 82–83; responding to, 81–82; separating, from negotiation, 139, 154–156; suppressed, accumulation of, 91; suppressing, 83, 84, 86, 90, 154–155; transcending, 111; as an underlying issue, *114, 115. See also* Anger; Fear
Empathizing listening technique, 73
Empathy: cultivating, 185; and honesty, 126–127; and mediation, 238; power of, in probing underlying issues, 123, 124–125, 127; and role-playing, 124, 125–126; versus sympathy, 123–124; as way to collaboration, 45; as weakness, 3
Empty space, as an invisible, 121
Encouraging listening technique, 72
Enigmas, 207
Eskimo carver, 22–23
Evaluation: in creative problem solving, 199, 212; degree of, 185; of negotiation process, 220; and preventing difficult behaviors, 190
Evaluation teams, 223
Expectations: as an invisible, 121; letting go of, 71; as an underlying issue, *114, 116*
Experts, when to consult, 220, 235
Eye of the storm, 13

F

Facts: agreeing on, 220; describing, 24
Failure, success in, 226–227
Families: and conflict cultures, 20, 22; and distortions in, 102; dysfunctional, strategy in, 172; hypnotic trance and, 118; as origin of difficult behaviors, 179–181; as origin of emotional re-

sponses, 84–85, 86, 87, 92–93; as source of conflict, 1; unresolved conflict in, cost of, 11

Family background, as an invisible, 122–123

Fear: of change, 194, 195; of conflict, 11; of emotions, 83; in exploring underlying issues, 115, 117; of expressing emotions, 81; as an invisible, 121; letting go of, 79; of letting go of control, 97. *See also* Emotions, strong

Feedback: in creative problem solving, 199; in defining the problem, 178; definition of, 189; degree of, 185; honesty in, 46, 133, 188; in improving communication, 51, 64; and mediation, 238; in orientations, *205*; and preventing difficult behaviors, 189–190; in time-outs, 192

Feelings. *See* Emotions, strong

Fight-or-flight reflex, 15, 32, 35, 36

Finger-pointing responses, 175–176

Fishbowl discussion, 192

Fisher, R., 141, 143, 163, 214

Follett, M. P., x, 9

Forgiveness, 30; asking for, 110; and letting go, 17; and mediation, 237

Friedman, H. S., 80

Fuller, B., 225

Future, separating, from past, 16, 139, 152–154, 238

G

Gender differences: in communication, 48–49; in expressing emotions, 84

Genocide, and stereotyping, 169

Getting Past No (Ury), 141, 219

Getting to Yes (Fisher and Ury), 141, 163, 214, 219

Glaser, M., 111

Goals: agreeing on, 148; identifying, before negotiation, 214, 216; in orientations, *205*

Goethe, J. W., 225

Goldsmith, S., 133

Gorbachev, M. S., 68

Gossip, 62

Ground rules: for communication, 50–51, 148; concerning process, 157–160, 218; and managing difficult behavior, 192, 193; negotiating, 16; and resistance, 228

H

Harvard Business Review, 203

Health effects, of negativity, 80–81

Hearing versus listening, 53, 69

Hegi, U., 118

Help, asking for: from mediators, 194, 217–218, 226, 235, 237; from opponent, 232

Heraclitus, 183

Hierarchies, effects of, 60–62, 104

Histories, as an invisible, 122

Hitler, A., 12

Holocaust, the, 132

Homophobia, 169

Honesty: as attack, 3; avoiding, rationalizations for, 129–130; difficulty in achieving, 128–129; in empathy, 126–127; in feedback, 46, 133, 188; and mediation, 238; rationalizations for, 131–132; and responsibility, 132–133; risks associated with, 127

Hui-Wu, 5

Humanizing, 147, 148, 170, 237

Humor, maintaining, 185

I

Iceberg, beneath the. *See* Issues, underlying

Iceberg metaphor, 112, *114*

Iceberg, tip of the. *See* Issues, superficial

Ideas, as an invisible, 121

Illusions, 14, 140

Impasse: identifying reasons for, 221–222; overcoming, 16–17; resistance in, 8, 228–229; techniques for breaking, 229–235; truth of, 2

Inaction, responsibility for, 132–133

Individualism, as obstacle to change, 187

Insults, meaning in, 23, 94–95

Integrity, in communication, 46

Intention: as an invisible, 121; in listening, 69, 72

Interconnection, awareness of, 114–115, 123

Interests: acknowledging, 188; and actions involving, 45; identifying, before negotiation, 215, 216; identifying, during impasse, 230; illusion about, 140; and mediation, 237; and multiple truths, 136–137; satisfying, 211–212; separating positions from, 16, 139, 140,

142–146, 238; as an underlying issue, *114*, 115
Invisibles, 120–123
Isolation, as obstacle to change, 187
Issues, superficial, 4, 113, *114*, 115
Issues, underlying: applying knowledge of, 116–117; awareness of, 4, 32, 117; and awareness of interconnection, 114–115, 123; and breaking into parts, 230; and difficult behaviors, 184; exploring, 15–16, 114–116; focusing on, 46, 234; identifying, before negotiation, 214, 216; listening for, 71; and mediation, 237; probing, using empathy, 123, 124–125, 127; resolving, importance of listening in, 69; revealing, steps to, 119–120; searching for, 7, 112–113; and structural relationship of layers, *114*; unresolved, 93, *114*, 116, 223, 228–229, 240

J

James, W., 242
Japanese approach to problems, 203–204
Journey, metaphors of, 29–31
Judgments, letting go of, 17, 71
Jung, C. G., 198
Juvenile offenders, mediation and, 133

K

Katzenberg, J., 26
King Henry VI (Shakespeare), 135
Kneedler, P., 210

L

Laing, R. D., 172
Language: and context, 33; hidden meanings and assumptions in, 22, 23; and "I" versus "You" statements, 97–98; word choices in, 23, 24. *See also* Metaphors
Learning orientation, 200, 204, *205*
Lincoln, A., 226
Listeners: asking questions of, 66; committed, 54–55, 72; context of, 48, 49; and distortions, 59, 60; effect of hierarchy on, 62; and hidden frameworks, 58; interpretation by, 64; responsibility of, 53; uncommitted, 76

Listening: active and responsive, 69; active and responsive, techniques for, 72–76; committed, 54; effect of strong emotion on, 78; effective, 53, 70–72; with empathy, 7, 15, 32, 76–78; versus hearing, 53, 69; intention in, 69, 72; lack of, 50; and mediation, 238; power of, 47; preparing for, 71; setting the stage for, 55–57
Listening teams, 192
Litigation, 8, 235, 236, 241

M

Maccoby, M., 203–204
Mann, T., 96
Markham, E., 188
Masks, emotional: looking behind, 94–96; and power plays, 98–99; taking off of, 96–98
Meaning, hidden: as an invisible, 121; and language use, 22, 23; of metaphors, 24–25, 28, 31; searching for, 7, 71
Media, conflict messages in, 20–21
Mediation: benefits of, 8, 108; definition of, 235–236; involving juvenile offenders, 133; in overcoming impasse, 16–17; and splitting the difference in, 231; success of, 236; and why it works, 237–239
Mediators: locating, 237; when to use, 194, 217–218, 226, 235
Meeting informally, before negotiation, 217
Meetings: managing difficult behaviors in, 190–194; speaking up in, 188; and taking minutes, 220; as a team process, 188–189
Metaphor, of the iceberg, 112, *114*
Metaphors: assumptions and, 26, 27–28; and context, 33; as a hidden framework, 58–59; hidden meaning of, 24–25, 28, 31; of journey, 29–31; and mediation, 237; of opportunity, 27–29; reframing, 31; and using mirroring, 74; of war, 25–27, 28, 29. *See also* Language
Minutes, 220
Mirroring listening technique, 74
Miscommunication: costs of, 52, 82–83; phrases that lead to, 66–68; in popular culture, 21
Myths. *See* Assumptions

N

Native American view, of opposites, 196
Needs: emotional, 15, 84, 237; as an underlying issue, *114*, 115; unmet, and resistance, 8, 228
Negotiation: defined, 212, 213; separating emotion from, 139, 154–156; styles of, 213–214
Negotiation, collaborative, 215; after process of, 222–224; benefits of, 16; committing to, 8; elements of, 214–215; and mediation, 237; primary purpose of, 223; before process of, 216–219; during process of, 219–222; researching alternatives in, 219; structuring process of, 215
Negotiations: changing process of, 221; discussing previous, 217; interest-based, 141–142; international, process in, 156
Negotiators, 222; types of, 213–214
New Age manipulation, 76
Nietzsche, F. W., 14
Normalizing listening technique, 73

O

Oe, Kenzaburo, 84
Office environment, 55–57
Office, meeting away from, 15, 57, 219
Opponents. *See* Others
Opportunities, as an invisible, 122
Opportunity, metaphors of, 27–29
Options: brainstorming for, 160, 221, 234–235; generating, 160–162, 199, 238; identifying, 215; separating, from choices, 139, 160–162
Organizational cultures: avoiding conflict in, 20, 187; avoiding honesty in, 128, 129–130; definition of, 186; and difficult behaviors, 186–189; impact of hierarchy on, 62; improving, 22; and resistance to change, 186–187; and rewarding aggression, 26, 187; suppressing conflict in, 11–12; suppressing emotions in, 83, 84, 86. *See also* Conflict cultures
Organizational issues, interconnectedness of, 17
Orientations, 200, 204, *205*
Others: as reflection of self, 239; separating self from, 139, 164–166
Ownership, in meetings, 193

P

Paradigms, shifting, 45
Paradox: accepting, 185, 207; of anger, 106; of closure, 239; in conflict, 13, 151; and learning orientation, 200; of paths, 8; of separations, 166
Paradoxical problem solving, 206–207
Passivity: as aggression, 95; as obstacle to change, 187
Past: holding on to the, 154; presence of the, 117–118; separating future from, 16, 139, 152–154, 238; unresolved issues from the, 93, *114*, 116
Past histories, as an invisible, 122
Paths, overview of, 6, 7–8
Peers, childhood, effect of, 85, 180
People: defining, as the problem, 168–170, 172, 237; separating, from problems, 6, 16, 139, 146–149, 238
Personalities: defining, as the problem, 35, 170–172, 176, 237; as an underlying issue, *114*, 115
Political responsibility, 14
Popular culture, conflict messages in, 20–22
Positions: being locked in, 136–138; competition over, 7; and mediation, 237; separating, from interests, 16, 139, 140, 142–146, 238
Power, as basis of resolving disputes, 141, 142
Power plays, and emotional masks, 98–99
Prejudice, 2, 169, 229
Problem solving, creative: and attitude in, 199, 201–202, 203–204; as collaborative process, 44, 202–203; and committing to action, 8, 199; definition of, 199; and focus on the problem, 149–151, 178; importance of, 198; as informal process, 16–17; and mediation, 238; and obstacles in, 207–208; orientation in, 200; overcoming obstacles in, 208–210; in spirit of, 220–221; steps to, 210–212. *See also* Brainstorming
Problem-solving orientations, 200, 204, *205*
Problem solving, paradoxical, 206–207
Problems: analyzing, 149–150, 199, 211; attitude towards, 199, 201–202, 203–204; as attractors of attention, 224; defining, 35, 146, 168–173, 176–179, 209, 210–211, 237; keeping

list of, 223; learning from, 224–225; recalling, during negotiation, 223; separating, from solutions, 139, 149–151; separating people from, 6, 16, 139, 146–149, 238
Process: awareness of, 177–178; changing the, 221; and difficult behaviors, 184; as a hidden framework, 58–59; improving the, 220, 222; as an invisible, 121; and mediation, 238; recording objections to, 223; separating, from content, 139, 156–160; as source of resistance, 228; stopping the, 233
Process agreements, 156–160, 218
Public forums, holding, 218–219

R

Racism, 2, 169, 229
Reactiveness, as obstacle to change, 187
Reality-testing, 64, 215
Reframing: in meetings, 193; of metaphors, 31
Reframing listening technique, 75
Reframing Organizations (Bolman and Deal), 208
Reinventing government, 176
Relationship: as a hidden framework, 58–59; as an invisible, 121
Resistance: to change, 43–44, 186–187, 194–195, 232; exploring reasons for, 6, 8; in exploring underlying issues, 115; to honesty, 127; reasons for, 227, 228–229; techniques for breaking, 229–235
Resolution: versus settlement, 11–12, 127; versus suppression, 127
Responding listening technique, 75
Response strategies, 33–44
Responsibility: absolving, 170; for anger, 100, 107; and interconnectedness, 17; and mediation, 238; in mediation, 133; resolution as expression of, 14; sharing, 45, 178; of speakers, 49, 53; steps to encourage, 133–134; taking, for actions and inactions, 132–133; taking, for behaviors, 149, 184; through apology, 109; willingness to accept, 166
Restroom revelation, 230
Rights, as basis of resolving disputes, 141, 142
Rilke, R. M., 19
Role-playing, 124, 125–126, 193

Round robin, 160–161, 216, 219
Rumi, J., 124
Rumors, 62
Rushdie, S., 79

S

"Sally and Freddy scenario," 143–145
Satir, V., 98
Satisfaction, identifying, 215
Secret ballot, 161
Selection, separating criteria from, 139, 162–164
Self: others as reflection of, 239; separating, from others, 139, 164–166
Self-esteem, as an underlying issue, *114*, 115
Self-fulfilling prophecies, 68, 86, 147
Self-perception, as an underlying issue, *114*, 115
Selfishness, as obstacle to change, 187
Separations, 6, 16, 139–140, 142–166, 238
Settlement versus resolution, 11–12, 127
Sexism, 169
Sexual harassment: cost of, 10; and failure to communicate, 58; and tailoring solutions, 230
Shakespeare, W., 135
Silence: conspiracies of, 127; as an obstacle, 118; use of, 193, 234
Social fragmentation, as obstacle to change, 187
Social issues, interconnectedness of, 17
Social responsibility, 14
Society: and conflict cultures, 19, 22; and conflict messages in popular culture, 20–22; and litigation, 241; as source of conflict, 1–2
Soliciting listening technique, 73–74
Solutions: brainstorming for, 16; one-sided, 199; separating problems from, 139, 149–151; tailoring, 230
Speakers: and context, 48; and distortions, 59, 60; effect of hierarchy on, 62; effective methods for, 64–66; and hidden frameworks, 58; as listeners, 49; and phrases that miscommunicate, 66–68; and questions to make separations, 164–165; responsibility of, 49, 53
Stereotyping, 169
Stones from the River (Hegi), 118
Stress: effects of, 80–81; and mediation, 237; release from, 30

Subconscious suggestion, 161
Success: celebrating, 224; in failure, 226–227
Summarizing listening technique, 75–76
Supplementing listening technique, 74
Suppression versus resolution, 127
Surfacing, to define the problem, 177
Surprises, eliminating, 220
Surrender, loss of opportunity in, 17
Swindoll, C. R., 197
Symbolism: as a hidden framework, 58–59; hidden meaning of, 24, 25; as an invisible, 121
Sympathy versus empathy, 123–124

T

Tannen, D., 48
Teams, 177; choosing members of, 219; evaluation, 223; listening, 192; meeting as, 188–189; process improvement, 218
Terminations, anger in, 101
Thank God It's Monday! (Cloke and Goldsmith), 206
Third voice, internal, 113
Thomas and Kilman research, 39
Time, as an invisible, 122
Time-outs: and breaking resistance, 230; for feedback, 192; and managing anger, 108
Trade-offs, 231
Training, in collaborative negotiation, 217
Transcendence, 4, 111
Transformation: actions required for, 5–6; awareness of, 24; and choosing emotional path, 85; definition of, 5, 6; and the eye of the storm, 13; and honesty, 129; internal call for, 224; and listening as way to, 69; openings to, 200;

opportunities for, 9, 14–18, 44; and shifting metaphors, 28; through conflict, 4–5; truth of, 2
Trust, 215
Truths: about petty concerns, 4; of being right, 153; hidden, of resolution, 136; of impasse, 2; of separation, 140; shifting from single to multiple, 136–138; of transformation, 2
Twain, M., 112

U

Ueland, B., 47
Unmet needs, and resistance, 8, 228
Ury, W., 141, 143, 163, 214

V

Validating listening technique, 76
Values: as an invisible, 122; shared, 16, 148, 187, 216–217
Victimization, as obstacle to change, 187
Vidal, G., 68
Vietnam War, 156
Visions, shared, 148, 216–217
Vulnerability: anger as, 95; in communication, 116–117; and honesty, 128

W

Warlike metaphors, 25–27, 28, 29
WATNA (worst alternative to a negotiated agreement), 215, 217
Withdrawal, as rage, 95
Wittgenstein, L.J.J., 200
World War II, 12, 118

Y

You Just Don't Understand (Tannen), 48
Yourcenar, M., 1

This page constitutes a continuation of the copyright page.

Excerpt from *Memoirs of Hadrian* by Marguerite Yourcenar. Copyright 1954, renewed 1982 by Marguerite Yourcenar. Reprinted by permission of Farrar, Straus and Giroux, LLC.

Excerpt by Brenda Ueland copyright © 1987 by the Estate of Brenda Ueland. Reprinted from *If You Want to Write* with the permission of Graywolf Press, Saint Paul, Minnesota.

Excerpt from *The Moor's Last Sigh* by Salman Rushdie. Copyright © 1995. Reprinted by permission of Pantheon Books.

Excerpt from *The Pinch Runner Memorandum* by Kenzaburo Oe. Copyright © 1994. Reprinted by permission of M.E. Sharpe.

Excerpt from *Stones from the River* by Ursula Hegi. Copyright © 1994 by Ursula Hegi. Reprinted by permission of Simon & Schuster, Inc.

Excerpt from *Foucault's Pendulum* by Umberto Eco © 1988 by Gruppo Editoriale Fabbri Bompiani Sonzogno Etas S.p.A., Milano. English translation copyright © 1989 by Harcourt, Inc., reprinted by permission of Harcourt Inc.

Excerpt from *Heart of the Enlightened* by Anthony De Mello. Copyright © 1989 by The Center for Spiritual Exchange. Used by permission of Doubleday, a division of Random House, Inc.

Excerpt from *Strengthening Your Grip* by Charles R. Swindoll © 1982 Word, Inc., Nashville, TN. Used by permission of Insight for Living, Anaheim, CA 92806.

Excerpt from *The Basic Writings of C. G. Jung* by C. G. Jung. Copyright © 1991. Reprinted by permission of Princeton University Press.